CRITICAL ISSUES IN OFFICE AUTOMATION

CRITICAL ISSUES IN OFFICE AUTOMATION

Walter A. Kleinschrod

McGRAW-HILL BOOK COMPANY

New York St. Louis San Francisco Auckland
Bogotá Hamburg Johannesburg London Madrid
Mexico Montreal New Delhi Panama Paris
São Paulo Singapore Sydney Tokyo Toronto

Library of Congress Cataloging-in-Publication Data

Kleinschrod, Walter A.
Critical issues in office automation.
Bibliography: p.
Includes index.
1. Office practice—Automation. I. Title.
HF5547.5.K53 1986 651.8 85-19837

ISBN 0-07-035034-5

1234567890 DOC/DOC 89321098765

ISBN 0-07-035034-5

The editors for this book were Stephen G. Guty and Georgia Kornbluth, the designer was Mark E. Safran, and the production supervisor was Thomas G. Kowalczyk. It was set in Century Schoolbook by Achorn Graphics.

Printed and bound by R. R. Donnelley & Sons Company.

TO PAT

Contents

Preface

A basic issue in office automation is that so few people even agree on what it is. OA is an arrangement of technology which helps business use and move information more effectively. It is an evolving business phenomenon with origins in data processing and word processing, spreading now into personal computing, networking, and other professional use of electronic systems. It is not evolutionary but revolutionary, as an *idea* replacing management's older understanding of what offices are with new understanding of the competitive tools that offices can become. It is a powerful agent of change, affecting organizational structures and individual ways of working, altering society and the world at large. It is some of the above and all of the above. Office automation, like beauty, is in the eye of the beholder.

Because technology is the most tangible of OA's manifestations, technology gets the most attention in the lectures and literature which have enveloped the field. There can be little argument about the functions or speeds or capacities of hardware and software—they can be demonstrated and described—although the *inability* of these products to perform certain tasks with ease gives rise to a special class of arguments, as discussed in the book. Technology is also where most "news" in the field comes from. Hardly a day goes by without several announcements of new or forthcoming products, new or forthcoming enhancements, new companies, new partnerships, and even new publications in which to find word of the major and minor events of this fast-moving, high-tech industry.

As a journalist who has covered the office scene for more than thirty years, I continue to share the excitement of the new, the fast, and the powerful which can be felt in the beat of technology. But I also continue to feel there are deeper and more meaningful stories to be told about office automation—the clash of ideas which surround it; the effects it has on organizations, workers, and work*places*; the fears it can engender; the turf battles it can spark; the jobs it can threaten. These are OA's emotional negatives to set beside its immediate and longer-range positives: first, the costs it can cut, the productivity it can boost, the time it can save; and second, a payout only now being recognized, the executive and professional *performance* it can enhance, the competitive *edge* it can sharpen, the informational *capital* it can create for corporate strength and success. These negatives and positives are the less told stories. Together with issues of technology, they are what this book examines.

There is no question that managements serious about introducing automated information-handling systems into their offices must have technological expertise on call, and must themselves have some basic understanding of what technology can and cannot do. There is no question that organizations introducing OA must go through a fairly involved planning process if they are to manage the change successfully. Bookshelves and magazine racks brim with the literature and "specs" of OA's intricate, abundant ware; and many so-called cookbooks can guide a reader step by step through the fact-gathering and vendor-assessment process of OA planning.

Though this book also deals with planning strategies and product options, it does so more on a basis of the issues these options raise than on any basis of settled procedure. I have endeavored to present here the views of many of the OA authorities—managers, consultants, vendors, fellow journalists—it has been my privilege to know and sometimes to cover over the years. Their views often clash. At this early stage, we can be grateful that certain OA issues are at least definable; settling them is a matter of sorting out solutions as the issues clarify. How to settle them is ultimately what you, the reader, must determine for your own particular situation.

This book, then, is less a "how-to" manual than a "think-through" examination of a range of issues which affect OA and to which OA itself gives rise. It is a book that covers the OA scene broadly, critically, questioningly, and sometimes, I confess, with a bit of deserved irreverence. But if this book enables the business executive, the business student, and the lay reader to have a better understanding of what office automation is, does, means, and *can be* for us and our world, as well as what yet must be reconciled if OA is to truly fulfill its promise, I will have accomplished my mission.

Acknowledgments

Any author who comes to a given subject as always the journalist-observer of the matters under review, never their actual doer, has more than the usual number of people to thank for the ideas, experiences, and words of advice that have helped to form the book.

And so it is with me. I am grateful to all the many sources I have quoted or paraphrased in the course of this work; their insights and expertise, if not always in agreement one with another, go far toward making the book the "issues" work it is. However, I would be remiss if I did not single out the following for special mention:

John Connell, executive director, Office Technology Research Group, Pasadena, California, and Dr. Raymond R. Panko, associate professor, College of Business Administration, University of Hawaii, Honolulu, both of whom reviewed my manuscript, made valuable corrections, granted me extensive interviews, and shared OA research with me.

Also: Francis X. Dzubeck, president, Communications Networks Architects, Washington, D.C.; Frank K. Griesinger, president, Frank K. Griesinger Associates, Cleveland, Ohio; Belden Menkus, consultant, Middleville, New Jersey; Alan Purchase, consultant, SRI International, Menlo Park, California; and Keith Wharton, Keith Wharton

Consultants Ltd., Richmond-on-Thames, England. All these people responded thoughtfully and at length to my queries about trends and expectations in their respective fields.

Also: John Diebold, chair, and Joseph Ferreira, former vice president, The Diebold Group, New York; John Dykeman, associate publisher and editorial director, *Modern Office Technology,* Cleveland; Marty Gruhn, director, The Sierra Group, Tempe, Arizona; Mel Mandell, editor, *Computer Decisions;* former editor William A. Olcott and the entire editorial staff of *Office Administration and Automation* (now again titled *Administrative Management*); and the management of Geyer-McAllister Publications, Inc., New York. These people have granted me permission to reprint excerpts from their copyrighted works.

Also: The Administrative Management Society and the AMS Foundation, Willow Grove, Pennsylvania; the Association for Information Systems Professionals, Willow Grove; the Office 'Landscape' Users Group, Philadelphia; and N. Dean Meyer of the Society of Office Automation Professionals, Ridgefield, Connecticut.

Also: Stephen G. Guty, my editor, and Georgia Kornbluth, my editing supervisor, at McGraw-Hill Book Company, whose knowledge, counsel, encouragement, and general unflappability helped me—and this book—enormously.

Finally, my dear wife, Pat, whose loving support and patience are what really enabled me to attempt and complete this book.

1

Issues . . . What Issues?

How Management Woke Up to the Office

Big changes are taking place in offices, and I don't mean all that new technology. I mean *big* changes. Attitude changes. People are beginning to see their offices and understand their offices and even get excited about their offices in ways they never did before. These fervent mind openings stir a chain of events we tamely call office automation. What they're actually stirring is a revolution. A business, social, and managerial revolution. Sure, technology plays a part, but it no more causes this revolution than muskets caused the American Revolution. People cause revolutions—when the ideas they get, the conclusions they draw, the feelings of resolve they muster cause them to cause revolutions.

Management begins to realize that in offices it has been focusing on minor targets of opportunity—things like improving departmental productivity and lowering administrative overhead. All well and good, but hardly revolutionary.

Suddenly they see that advanced office technology can help them perform better and compete better—as an *organization*. These are major targets of opportunity; new ideas.

This new technology, properly used, speeds the flow of information and peoples' access to it, and advantages like these give companies extraordinary leverage in today's rambunctious business climate. Business has long used technology to machine its products and increase its profits, but seldom has it employed *information* technology to this extent, and that is a new idea.

Moreover, this technology is office-based technology. And so, suddenly, the office, that taken-for-granted albatross of business, is being seen as a systematized, computerized locus of new opportunity. Its technology puts powerful tools into the hands of knowledge workers and lets information be used in ways that were never possible before. The office becomes a resource for competitive prowess, and perhaps even for survival, at a time when all enterprise stands at the threshold of a postindustrial age. And these are new ideas.

The office is not that different yet, but it is being *seen* as that different, and it is being transformed in many organizations. The vision is revolutionary.

The issue is:

Awareness. Who has it and who doesn't? Many do.

So seek no further for the source of office automation. It lies in this new understanding of offices on the part of countless executives who may have worked in these places all their adult lives, but who never saw offices for what they were, why they were, or what they could become. Technology helps to mold that understanding and to tool up for new levels of business performance, but it is managerial insight and resolve that stir the currents of office change.

HOW IT WAS

Perhaps no institutions of business have been more ossified than offices. They were never *the* business, only unavoidable parts *of* business. Places to send bills out from, collect revenue at, file things in. Places for the boss to sit in. People tended to ignore offices, even though that's where they worked, in order to think about "business." For almost a century, offices hardly changed. Yes, they may have been prettied up from time to time—art going up on the walls, music coming out of the ceiling—but they remained as inefficient and organizationally straightjacketed as the drafty, cluttered workrooms we moderns smile at in old brown photographs. Even when the big computers arrived, back in the 1950s and 1960s, little about offices changed, institutionally.

In late-night movies of Spencer Tracy–Katharine Hepburn vintage, where he is the big tycoon, she the hard-driving executive, we can see the office institution in all its changeless character. The cars look different. The airplanes (or more likely, the trains) look different. But the offices, except for the shape of the phones, not only look the same, but fundamentally are the same, as the majority of offices today.

Bosses and secretaries. Clerks and mail. Phone messages. Meetings. Get me that file. Where's that report? Lots of paper. Organizational strictures. Decisions delayed. Time wasted. Another day shot.

Suddenly executives by the thousand are actually seeing—comprehending—that scene for the very first time. What a mess! Inefficient. Costly. And so long ignored.

To truly see the office, we must look beyond the filing and meetings and all the sending out of bills to what these activities have in common. Information: its management, movement, and use. That's what office work is. Executives and the many other professionals who work in offices are fundamentally knowledge workers, information users. To one degree or another, their support staffs—secretaries, typists, and the like—are their information processors and providers. To an increasing degree, these services are being automated through computers and other electronic devices, linked or "networked" together.

WHAT AUTOMATION DOES

Office automation (OA) has many definitions. It can be:

- The application of electronics to office operations
- A process that improves the flow of and access to information within an organization
- A network-based system of advanced technology which allows workers to perform more effectively
- An organization-wide system which supports the generic needs all office workers have

We shall encounter more definitions as we go along. A common denominator of them all, a generic need, is *work with information*—accessing it, updating it, putting it to use—in two basic types of environments. In the first, increasingly referred to as Type I, work is *processed* and routine, as in data processing or centralized word processing departments. In the second, Type II, work involves *non*-routine informational tasks typically performed by managers, professionals, and other knowledge workers.

Office automation supports the generic needs of both types of workers, and often for different purposes: to improve productivity (best sought in Type I offices) and to improve performance (a Type II rationale).

That managements often seek only productivity *savings* and not performance *improvements* is an issue for later, too. For now let's simply recognize that, for most firms, performance improvement is the second big battle of their OA revolution, the easier objective of productivity through processing having been the first. The goal of aiding the worker, not of processing the work, is a later—and greater—attitude change occurring in offices now.

OA development is and will continue to be as much a series of managerial mind openings as it is of technological breakthroughs.

The issue is:

Understanding information. How workers process it. How workers use it. How OA can best support both activities. And why this is vital to business.

Managers rely on information as a basis for sounder decisions. Financial executives use information to monitor company performance and competitors' performance and other external factors. Office-based professionals such as engineers and marketing executives need information—diagrammatic, tabular, textual—to create and sell new products and services. Sales personnel look up information to handle customer queries. Meanwhile, clerical personnel process the information that others will use. In time, many say, professional and managerial end users will themselves create and process much of the information they use. OA will have made the task easier, or will have changed the task, as OA always changes tasks, so that clerical intervention will not be as needed.

The office has been called "the control system for the business," the "support function" to the business, and an "organism which uses resources to enable better decisions." Those controls and those supports *use resources* which *are* information. The office, in short, is an information center. Soon it may not be possible to distinguish "office" from "business"; the two may blend inseparably.

Today, alert executives grasp the heady idea that offices, as information centers, are not only strong potential profit centers and vital business resources but also, because of management's historic careless attitude toward them, sources for great savings. Through better means and machines for the processing of information—target of easy opportunity though that be—offices are mines of untapped "administrative profits," savings which go right to the bottom line of real profits.

In short, *organizations that process information efficiently and allow workers to use it effectively are organizations that perform well and prosper.* More and more managements now know they must find a way of accomplishing that condition for their own organizations. The way is OA.

OA POWER

So that is the revolutionary call to arms. Power to save. Power to excel. Power to outrun the competition. Power to the worker. Power to the balance sheet.

The weaponry is technology in the form of extraordinary tools, some available and proven, others still more promise than reality. Computers. Word processors. Networks. Printers. Electronic mail. Intelligent copiers. Disk storage. Software. All of them tools to manage, move, and store information.

In many offices today, workers communicate by revolutionary means that threaten to bury the traditional mails and telephone services. Employees send text and drawings almost instantaneously from screen to computer screen. They send messages to the telephonic or computer "mailboxes" of co-workers to avoid the wasteful game of telephone tag—that annoying rigmarole of back-and-forth calling and not getting through because the called party is so often not there. They confer with colleagues in widely separated locations by means of the videoconference—a televised meeting often cheaper to arrange than a face-to-face gathering with its heavy tabs for travel and lodgings.

Office workers process information on machines that resemble typewriters only in that both have keyboards—machines that outperform ordinary typewriters by orders of magnitude. These extraordinary devices—text editors, personal computers, professional workstations, call them what you will—edit text the way older typewriters never could, create charts and graphs the way older computers never could, and direct other devices to print the end products with a speed and artistry that the traditional office duplicator never . . . duplicated.

But have we the manpower and womanpower to shoulder all this weaponry? OA tools are often difficult to use; a worry. They are often very costly. A worry. *Does* OA pay? A big worry. Then there's the strategic planning needed to automate and win—a crucial worry, despite the failure of so many managements to recognize it.

Revolutions are, to say the least, worrisome. They demand sacrifice. They upset tradition. They seldom deliver fully on all they promise. Not all the battles end in victory—sometimes the muskets don't work—and not all dreams of workers' utopia come true even when the computers do perform. These are the kinds of worries—or, to use a less emotional word, issues—this book will attempt to weigh in the trade-off scales of good managerial judgment.

- *Organizational issues.* The effects of OA on work life, work-at-home life, management policy, span of control, worker attitudes, professional competence—effects sometimes dimly perceived among business people, just as the office, until recently, has been dimly understood.
- *Social issues.* The effects of OA on union activity, health and safety rulings, job-bias actions (charges of sex discrimination, and legal or other actions resulting therefrom), privacy laws, security measures.
- *Global issues.* The role of OA in national and international agreements (or disagreements) on equipment standards and information flow across borders; and its contribution to nations' conflicting views on proper uses of information in a world split disproportionately among the highly developed, the developing, and those at subsistence levels.
- *Payout issues.* Can we measure OA's worth? It is possible of course to measure paperwork, but can one ever gauge the productivity of better information and the value of surer knowledge?
- And of course, *technology issues.*

Within a building or campuslike cluster of buildings, machines now talk to other machines over local area networks, or LANs. These loop-shaped and star-shaped arrays of cables could be just the communicational underpinning that office automators are looking for. Or maybe not; they are fraught with controversy. Which shape or "architecture" provides the best system? Which capacity, baseband or broadband? And will new, "intelligent" versions of the good old telephone switch—the PBX (private branch exchange) or PABX (private automated branch exchange)—relegate LANs to a passing footnote in the annals of OA development? Issues of systems design.

Laser printers, laser disks, fiber optics, satellite services, cellular radio, long-distance networks (AT&T's and the others'), and other offerings vie for the chance to move and produce information. If not now, soon. A key issue for management arises from this very abundance. Which OA weapons are the right ones? Which are too limited? Which amount to overkill? Which ones will people actually use? And by the way, with all this rapid advance, shouldn't we wait until something better comes along, as it surely will, and only think about OA then? The obsolescence issue.

OA, depending on whom you ask, is glorious, overrated, liberating, threatening, worth the struggle, too costly, user-friendly, terribly complex, making work easier, straining workers' eyes, creating new jobs, causing unemployment, making information more accessible, bringing on Big Brother. But, whatever the case with any of the above, OA is unstoppable. Today's innovation will be tomorrow's commonplace.

HOW WE GOT TO WHERE WE ARE

Eighty-five percent of the largest U.S. companies said in 1984 that they had, were getting, or were planning for automated offices. A far smaller segment of medium- and small-sized firms were able to say that, but half of them did say they planned to have plans by 1986. What all this means, said the president of Omni Group Ltd., the New York consulting firm which took this survey,[1] is that office automation had "permeated" U.S. corporations. As significant, perhaps, was the thought that ten years earlier, none of the small firms and few of the big ones would have even understood the questions.

Another survey found not mere permeation but outright contagion. After studying sixty-four leading U.S. companies—90 percent of which had OA projects of some kind under way—the Diebold Group reported that OA development was "shifting from the stage of 'initiation' to that of 'contagion.' "[2] OA's initiation stages tend to be limited, a kind of testing of the waters, a source for the New York–based consulting firm explained. But with contagion, a variety of new applications were rapidly being adopted.

The Diebold study further showed that among "contagious" companies, dramatic improvement takes place in the organization's general acceptance of OA. Senior managers become especially enthusiastic, the source said. "They shift from mere awareness to active support."

Whatever happened to rouse all these executives from the torpor of their Tracy-Hepburn offices? How did OA start? I believe, as do other office watchers, that the answers lie in an eye-opening encounter with technology on the part of management and staff in the late 1960s, when word processing arrived on the scene, and in issues raised by that experience throughout the 1970s. In the 1980s came a close encounter of a different kind—with the personal computer.

A machine arrived in 1964 that automated—and subsequently revolutionized—typing. It guaranteed automatic, error-free output; permitted easy text changes without the need to retype everything; and in general sped production. It was a real time and cost saver. If it had never done anything but increase the efficiency of typing, the machine would have been significant: typing was, is, and for a long time will remain one of the most prevalent, most time-consuming, and most costly of all office tasks. But the machine, the IBM Magnetic Tape Selectric Typewriter (MT/ST)—later to be classed generically with other models as a "text editor"—did much more. It ushered in a phenomenal development in office history, known as word processing (WP); and WP in turn ushered in OA. And it did so not through any inexorable advance of technology, but through a series of events, surprises, and even jolts that forced office-based people to confront the office-based issues of inefficiency and purpose as they never had before. Before WP, had you asked a group of office-based executives about office-based issues, they would in all likelihood have asked in return, "Issues? What issues?"

Digressing into that WP experience is worthwhile, because it illustrates what's happening now on a larger scale. Like OA today, WP in its formative years had problems not easily reconciled. Like OA today, the solutions were often not easy on the psyches and egos of the people whose work lives they changed. And somewhat like OA today, and more as promised for tomorrow, the solutions often did lower costs, upgrade output, and boost productivity—impressively. So the struggle seemed to be worth it. The first shots of OA were being heard around the office world.

Ironically, word processing sprang from the MT/ST not because the machine was all that good, but because it had major drawbacks. For one thing, it was hard to learn to operate. For another, it was, by typewriter standards, extremely expensive. Sure, it had marvelous electronic attributes which allowed a typist to capture keystrokes on magnetic tape and to change and reformat whatever text had been recorded there; it allowed canned text to be played out repeatedly and perfectly, in contrast to the slow, error-prone method of manually retyping form letter after form letter. But business wasn't buying that, and IBM had a problem. IBM's marketing solution—the classic original formula for implementing WP—was a stroke of genius, but it was organizationally overwhelming.

IBM adapted some German research which showed that secretaries could be more productive if they stuck to one task, like typing, rather than spending the day doing a lot of assorted tasks, like filing, answering the phone, running errands, and typing. It asked customers to consider such a system of task specialization as a way of upgrading their own secretarial work. Under this scheme, some secretaries would become typing specialists; others would specialize in the rest of the tasks secretaries normally did, collectively called "administrative support" (AS). Use of the MT/ST made sense now, said IBM with reassuring logic, because the typists, being full-time specialists, would learn to operate the machines well. Thus, the complexity issue was reduced to a temporary matter of training. And since all this work would now be concentrated in one place—a word processing center—the machines would be more fully utilized throughout the day. Thus, the costliness issue was mitigated, since a company would get its return on investment much sooner.

But where were these WP specialists and AS specialists to come from? Why, from the ranks of traditional secretaries, who were presently grossly inefficient, as the German studies and later North American research showed. They were idle much of the time, bored much of the time, and—because of the "do this, do that" jumble of tasks they had to handle—interrupted much of the time. How much better it would be if they could specialize and be supervised, not by their present executive bosses, who had never been trained for secretarial supervision (they were there to handle "business"), but by WP or AS professionals who could monitor performance, balance out work loads, and keep everyone busy at something.

It was a powerhouse idea. Marketing gimmick or not, it made sense; it worked and caught on. And it often caught hell. Here were these suave salespeople, and soon a zealous crop of WP consultants, selling top management on productivity gains as high as 400 percent, and then, with management's blessing, tearing down secretarial structures which had been built up and lived in comfortably over decades of office tradition. Bosses heard of plans to cart their private secretaries off to processing centers. "Where will I be without my secretary?" many of them cried. Secretaries themselves were worried. Would those new jobs really be better, as the WP advocates had promised?

The WP advocates patiently explained: The old one-on-one boss-and-secretary setup was demonstrably inefficient. "All of you bosses—or in WP terms, 'principals'—will be better served by the new arrangement," they said. "As for you secretaries, you'll be on professional career paths far more promising than being tied all your working life to some principal, rising or falling only as he or she does. And for all of you, WP is but the beginning of more wonderful things for the office. Already there's talk of communicating typewriters and computer link-ups and. . . ."

The point here is not to rehash all the issues of early WP. They have largely been settled. The point is that for many executives, office issues loomed for the very first time. Executives could not avoid them; they had to consider these issues because they affected the executives so personally. And really, didn't the arguments for WP make sense? Moreover, as WP grew, its impact hit harder and was felt more widely than even the impact of computers, which had shouldered their way into offices some ten or twelve years earlier. It's not hard to see why this happened.

Secretaries. They permeate organizations. They constitute 10 percent of the office work force. As WP changed their jobs, its effects *also* permeated organizations. The work changes WP caused, the all-important attitude changes it caused, reached everywhere. Those first big computers, by contrast, had mainly affected clerical operations—bills out, receipts in, that kind of mass accountancy. Their effects were confined to a few departments. The machines themselves were walled away in mysterious air-conditioned sanctums. Most of the general office population, management included, weren't bothered by them, didn't understand them, and never went near them. Life went on. But these new word processors were right there in the ordinary office where everyone could see them. Sure, they were a bit strange, but they were basically a new kind of typewriter, and typewriters you could understand. The typewriter was and to this day remains the most prevalent office tool beyond the pencil.

These three obvious but potent factors—the visibility of WP, the friendliness of typing even though automated, and the organization-wide impact of WP—helped more to spread an understanding of office work, and of how it might improve, than carloads of mainframes could have done had their tape drives spun for decades.

Computer buffs might argue that the idea of office automation did emanate from the computer, after all. There is no doubt that the computer got there first. By 1960, more than 4000 computers were whirring away for American business. There is no doubt that computer technology made text editors possible. And as a footnote to history, it must be recorded that the term "office automation" did attach itself to these big and costly monsters in the literature of the day. But the usage ebbed, to be revived a decade later in a different context, the context of "real" office work—secretarial, managerial, and professional—as distinct from data processing work. You might ask, "Isn't DP work real office work, too?" And the answer is, "Of course it is." Moreover, links are increasingly being forged today between mainframes and computers used by nontechnical office personnel. When the term "office work" itself becomes an issue, you can see how little attention has been paid over the years to this function which costs so much and employs so many. But you are in the wonderful, foggy world of OA, where odd semantics grow like stubborn weeds.

So, no, it wasn't the distant computer; it was the tangible, pervasive, get-the-work-out qualities of WP, in those thousands of offices where it was installed and managed well, that opened the minds that led to events that launched the real OA.

But yes, it *is* the computer—today's personal computer, or PC—that now impels OA. The powerful PC has everything going for it that WP has, plus greater versatility and generally lower prices. It too performs in the real office, enabling managers and other professionals to work more effectively for business. They represent OA's big target of opportunity. After all, executives and professionals earn so much more than secretaries; they pull down 76 percent of the total white-collar wage bill. Secretaries, for all the automation they've experienced, account for a mere 6 percent of that bill; other clericals make up the rest. Therefore, OA reasoning goes, if PCs and a whole new OA infrastructure can make executives and professionals more effective, the way WP made clerks and secretaries more efficient, what an extraordinary benefit that will be. The payout issue.

And yet again, no, the PC and other OA gear have not ousted WP; they have only subsumed it. WP remains alive and well as one of many interconnected functions possible in a larger OA scheme. Fed the right software, PCs can process words, along with numbers, spreadsheets, graphs, and games. So also can other computers—micro, mini, lap, home, portable (semantics again)—to one degree or another. Meanwhile, the "true" word processors, the dedicated text editors, if fed the right programs, can also crunch numbers, display graphs, play Wump and Aliens, to one degree or another. Functions merge; categories blend. Viewing it all historically, we could say that what the PC is to the 1980s, WP was to the 1970s. The 1980s may yet be known more grandly as the decade of the personalized workstation. For WP, the 1970s were Camelot.

The contrasts between then and now are revealing.

Anyone associated with WP as it burst into corporate consciousness will not likely forget the pioneering excitement, the cascade of products, and the relative simplicity of its issues. Exuberant but far less naive, today's wider OA community confronts weightier issues and a veritable Niagara of new products.

In 1971, the WP field got its first newsletter, in 1972 its first professional association, in 1973 its first magazine[3]—and then came a flood. By now that association has gone through two name changes, currently calling itself the Association of Information Systems Professionals; it is but one of dozens of associations ranging from umbrella groups like SOAP, the Society of Office Automation Professionals, to national and regional user groups devoted to various OA specialties. There are today so many office- and computer-related publications that at least two magazines now track the births, deaths, and hot pursuits of this volatile horde itself.

And then there's the general media. Or perhaps we could say the hype issue. Today it is virtually impossible to turn on the TV and not have some high-tech sponsor conjure magical half-truths about its marvelous green-screened box. (How many times have I seen "Charlie Chaplin" and his Personal Computer find happiness in 60 seconds?) It's almost impossible to open the Sunday newspaper or an in-flight magazine and not find an "advertorial" Guide to Your Own Computer; they look alike, read alike, and always provide a glossary of terms to make things perfectly clear. In the 1970s, as far as major trade shows go, there was little beyond the annual word processing Syntopicans and National Computer Conferences. Today, in addition to these, there are Office Automation Conferences; Federal Office Automation Conferences; Interface shows; Intech shows; Info shows; Comdexes east, west, and wherever; and local and regional expos beyond count. While not all focus explicitly on OA, the products they show and the issues they raise have features in common and potential business relationships.

By 1975, according to one study, some 200,000 of those "complex, expensive" automatic typing devices had been installed in U.S. offices, 80,000 of them being put to use in 9000 formalized WP centers in 5000 user companies.[4] Growth in the burgeoning WP industry was pegged to astonishing rates—20, 40, 80 percent, depending on what you counted and whose study you believed.[5] By one count, fifty-five firms vied in the industry, each scrambling to share in an estimated $500 million of annual revenue. For every firm that fell out, another was planning to enter.

In that same year, 1975, the first personal computer gingerly made its appearance—the Altair 8800, sold as a hobbyist kit. Six years later the IBM Personal Computer powerfully made its appearance. It was some machine. It was surely not the first PC, not even the first office PC—some half-million Apples, Radio Shacks, and lesser kinds had been shipped to U.S. business and professional markets by 1981. The IBM was not even the best PC. But it was the secure PC (look whose name was on it). And soon, it was the PC to which all other PCs were compared—the standard setter. The alacrity with which business now accepted all PCs as a serious class of office tool created an industry sales storm. Compared with this, early WP had produced no more than a cloudburst.

By the mid-1980s, more than 150 PC makers had placed 3.5 million of their machines into business and professional sites, and analysts saw this $14- to $20-billion segment (depending again on what you counted) of the computer industry cruising through the rest of the decade with a 40 to 50 percent growth rate.[6] PC software, meanwhile, a $1 billion industry in its own right, was expanding at a 60 percent clip, filling fat directories with thousands of program titles.[7]

That the entire computer industry was in the doldrums by 1985 was nothing more than a passing case of supplier overindulgence. For the moment, it seemed, everyone who wanted a computer had one, and sales fell. That situation wouldn't last; and both the wary buyer and the surviving vendor could benefit from it in the long run.

But enough statistics. They make the point. More interesting is what's happening in all the offices into which these wares have been placed.

GETTING CLOSER TO THE ACTION

WP at the start had one basic systems design, then some limited options. The original harsh strictures—of having all typing done in one WP center, all other administrative services handled by one AS center—gave way to sensible compromise. New and smaller "clusters," scattered throughout the organization, placed WP/AS personnel closer to the different groups of principals being served. Typing and administrative staffs now had more chance to know the people they worked for. They became familiar with the special languages of law or marketing or whatever department to which they were assigned. This hardly brought back the old private secretary setup, but it may have been a step in that direction.

It did put executives closer to the action, where the text was being automated—often right outside their office doors. Executives could see their correspondence, long reports, price lists, and other documents being keyboarded; and later, as newer generations of text editors came along, they could see the text displayed on screens and spewed from separate printers. They could hear of plans for still more innovation: communication links, for instance, so that what was keyboarded in one place could be printed on similar equipment miles distant. Or what was stored in the main computer could be called out, displayed, and also printed—right in the office or elsewhere; it didn't matter. All in all, it was an insightful learning experience that came with the office day. But except for the fact that WP got out correspondence and other typed work faster and in better-looking shape, it was pretty much a passive learning experience.

In today's wider OA world, a thousand systems options bloom, and the functions they automate are almost as myriad as an office has jobs. Learning may still be passive, but as more and more PCs find they way to executive desks, the learning grows active, hands-on. WP was imposed from above. The PC may be a voluntary buy. (Indeed, the proliferation of PCs purchased outside the bounds of company policies which say that all computer buys must go through the DP department is another of OA's issues, to be dealt with later.)

Also, in a WP environment, while executives may have been abstractly pleased that machines could communicate, they waited until all was hooked up and then took advantage of it through the proper WP/AS channels. With OA and that terminal on the desk, executives impatiently want machines to communicate *now,* despite channels, and become concretely annoyed when they can't. This is the issue of (in)compatibility.

And where executives have acted independently, bringing in different kinds of PCs without regard for larger OA plans, the actions of these executives may more than annoy; they may impede the work of colleagues directly responsible for turning those plans into organization-wide realities. No, the machines don't communicate, simply because everyone has done his or her own thing, not caring about the bigger systems picture; and now much that was done may have to be undone. On the other hand, is management wise to stifle independent experimentation? A lot of learning is going on and a lot of discoveries are being made as PC-using "independents" tinker with spreadsheets, toy with graphs, think about PC linkups between office and home. The experiences have value. Therefore, ought not this tinkering be tolerated for a while and tapped periodically as OA plans mature? These are issues of OA "migration."

THE SHAPE OF OA TODAY

Finally, back to semantics. When WP came along, you might have been hard put to explain what it was, but if you said it automated typing and document production, you covered a lot. With OA, one of its stickier issues consists of trying to get a handle on what—even approximately—it is. In fact, OA is different for different organizations, and even for different departments within a single organization.

Suffice it to say that OA aims to make information easier and less costly to use, move, and keep. It aims at making end users of that technology more effective in the jobs they do and more accountable for *what* they do. In the largest sense, it enables firms to compete more successfully.

OA employs technology (largely electronic), good management (more art than science), creativity (may it arise and be heeded), and people (always people) to accomplish its lofty ends.

By this definition, almost any intelligent use of electronic office gear—a PC, a text editor, even one of those new "smart" copiers—could be construed as office automation. That would be limiting and misleading. As this book defines OA, it has range; it embraces, ties together—integrates—information functions on a scale sufficiently proportional to the size of an organization to have salutary impact on the bottom line and to help significant numbers of people accomplish their work. An underlying characteristic for such integration is telecommunications.

"In simple terms," wrote author John Hermann for *Modern Business Reports*,[8] "office automation is a process by which the activities involving creating, collecting, processing, storing, retrieving, sharing and communicating information are achieved through the use of the computer and other high-technology electronic equipment." Not exactly simple terms, but all right.

As Dr. Raymond Panko wrote for *Office Technology and People,*[9]

> Office automation is the provision of tools for generic needs found in nearly all offices:
>
> - Written communication—creation and distribution.
> - Voice communication.
> - The filing of text at all levels of the corporation.
> - The filing of record-structured information in individual offices.
> - Basic numerical analyses.
> - Scheduling and activity management.

"Office automation," said Roy Ash, industrialist and advisor to presidents, "is not a destination, it's a journey."

"Office automation is a forced march, not a destination," editor Mel Mandell has declared. What "forced" means, he wrote in *Computer Decisions,*[10] is that business has no choice but to operate more efficiently, to lower costs, and to raise productivity.

A march, a journey, a process, an ability. A revolution. Administrative poetry as much as workaday truth.

To summarize:

Changing attitudes, shaped by knowledge of what information technology has accomplished and visions what it yet can do, impel office automation, and OA in turn impels wider change. This mass managerial mind opening is the subtlest, least visible, and yet most powerful agent of change at work in offices everywhere.

Change poses perhaps the most difficult and emotional of all OA issues. As change sweeps through offices, threatening jobs and proffering opportunities, it generates fear, hope, conflict, winners, losers. On a higher plane, change of this magnitude generates genuine professional differences of opinion and conflicting management philosophies. It is to these issues of OA, and not to technology or formularized procedure, that this book is addressed.

As a journalist who has covered the tumultuous office scene for more than a quarter century, I know too well how today's report on technology can be—will be—outdated by some development tomorrow. Books are no place for bulletins on the state of the art; we must look to the media horde for that. But issues endure. They arise from human intellect and feelings and from all the good and bad instincts of people. Breakthroughs in technology create their own excitement, of course, but the human side of OA—the trade-offs facing managers, the reactions of workers—at least for me as a writer, has always been the real story.

2

Issues of "Does It Pay?"

Sloppy Statistics versus Solid Arguments for OA and Its "Worth"

The personal computer looks at first glance like a $2000 to $5000 item. An expense.

Buy additional things like software, printers, and other peripherals, and each desktop computer could end up costing more than $20,000.[1] A big expense.

The more powerful executive workstation computers range from $15,000 to $20,000, for openers. Figure another $15,000 or so for options. Multiply that by the number of executives to equip and, as the late Senator Everett Dirksen liked to say, it can soon add up to real money.

Tie the terminals to a local area network and figure on $300 to $500 per connection, assuming the LAN is one of the baseband kind. Tie into a heavier-duty broadband LAN and figure on $800 to $1200 per connection.[2]

Add translating devices—the so-called black boxes which enable unlike machines to communicate with one another—and there goes another $1000 to $2000 per unit, assuming the boxes employ fairly simple asynchronous or bisynchronous communications methods. Go for multiprogram, multichannel protocol translators and watch the price climb to $6000 to $10,000 per unit.[3]

And if you want to get into satellite transmissions—for example, the way the Alcan Aluminum Corporation has done to send orders and inventory information between sales branches and warehouses—then figure on $500,000 to install the system and another half million a year to run it.[4]

Well, those are the kinds of prices they're charging down at the OA store. Are they worth it?

STATISTICS: USE WITH CAUTION

If you read the literature, attend the seminars, and see the OA-vendor audiovisuals, you cannot avoid an avalanche of statistics carrying you off to a certain conclusion: Yes, all that OA gear is worth it.

- In the United States alone, enough paper is on file to wrap up the planet earth twenty times.
- Each day, for each of our 18 million office workers,* we produce thirty-two pages of computer printout, print four pages of reports and other documents, make eighteen photocopies, file ten of the papers, retrieve five and then refile them, and buy forty-six sheets of fresh new paper to get ready for work tomorrow.
- The office labor to move all that paper costs more each year, about 6 percent more each year lately.
- Electronic means could manage the information on all that paper far more efficiently, and happily, here the costs are dropping. During a recent five-year period, communications costs declined 10 percent per year, electronic parts costs fell 20 percent per year, and electronic memory costs dropped 40 percent.
- To automate offices as fully as industry and agriculture have automated their respective sectors might have cost business some $18,000 to $20,000 per worker back in 1980—and that for hardware alone. Prohibitive. By 1990, with costs dropping the way they are, and holding with 1980 dollars, that figure will fall to $7500 and will include not only hardware but also software and all that powerful 1990s technology. Plausible.

*The term "18 million office workers" was copied verbatim from one of the many white papers on office automation proffered freely by OA vendors and consultants—papers which often seem to copy verbatim from one another. As we shall see, different people mean different things when they use terms like "office," "clerical," and even "white collar." By one calculation, there were in the United States by September 1983, more than 55 million "office" workers.

- Even so, $7500 is three times the $2500 in capital equipment which supported every office worker back in 1980. Industry was then supporting the blue-collar worker with $25,000 in workplace machinery, and down on the farm, the average agricultural worker had $35,000 in equipment supporting him or her. And look at the results! Over the ten previous years, that farmer was reaping a productivity gain of 185 percent. The factory worker gained 90 percent. But the poor underequipped office worker was scratching out a measly 4 percent productivity gain over the same ten years.[5]

"So, come on, all you businesspeople," the argument has run, "get with it. Automate. Give your people the tools to match those big gains of the farm and factory. The office is now where it's at."

The issue is:

The accuracy of OA statistics and assumptions in OA argumentation. Use with caution.

For years, numbers like the above have been passed along, repeated, republished, pressed into corporate automation studies by eager researchers, and generally accepted as tenets of OA faith. I do not say they are false, but I do say they are sloppy and the source of much confusion. I plead guilty of having passed some of them along myself. It's good to see a more sophisticated generation of office researchers take apart these hackneyed arguments and rebuild more solid rationales for OA and its worth.

Maybe it is true that the planet earth can be wrapped up twenty times in existing office paper. If that's what the statistician said, I accept it. But I would ask to what degree all paper must be viewed with alarm. Sure, it's expensive to file and retrieve and transport, for these are essentially people costs which automation could reduce. And sure, there's too much paper around, with more being added to the pile (just check at your local copier). But paper is also an extremely convenient medium for conveying information. You can file it, retrieve it, mail it, stick it in your pocket, write on it, and dispose of it without ever plugging one device into an outlet, without ever keying one command at a terminal. *That's* user-friendly! OA consultant Amy Wohl's wisecrack about the "paperless" office has made the rounds as much as the statistics: "The paperless office," she says, "is about as realistic as the paperless bathroom!"

If anything, OA seems to be increasing, not cutting, the volume of office paper—but that's an issue we'll save for later.

Maybe it is true that farm and factory productivity gains have outpaced the office's, but those figures on growth in the three sectors are myths. I kept hearing them so often that for a variety of reasons I thought I'd trace them to their source. One of my reasons had more to do with issues of farm automation than with issues of office automation. Permit an illustrative digression.

Productivity, by classic definition, is the ratio of output to labor input—for example, the amount of grain a field hand could cut and thresh in a day. Whatever the amount, it's believable that a farmer riding a mechanical combine could cut and thresh a great deal more. The productivity of worker with machine is plainly higher than that of worker alone. Some environmentalists and sociologists, however, have begun to criticize this simple labor-in–product-out formula, with its remarkably high-growth results. What about the high energy costs of mechanized agriculture? What about the social costs, borne not by the farmer but by the public in general when workers displaced by automation end up as the urban unemployed? Are such costs factored into these remarkable scores?

The issues raised by these questions intrigued me. I decided to get to the sources of the productivity data—not just for the farm, of course, but for the factory and the office. The assertions of great growth (the office being the lagging exception) were everywhere. Surely someone would know where they came from.

Wrong. None of the many experts I contacted could cite the source. B had simply borrowed the numbers from A who had heard them from C who copied them from Z. I traced the matter to the very capital of productivity interests, the authoritative and influential American Productivity Center (APC) in Houston. APC's vice president of measurement, Carl Thor, laid my quest to rest. The much ballyhooed office-factory-farm figures, he said, were "a legend and nothing more." What may have happened was that someone "sloppily confused" white-collar workers with service workers, lumping everyone from miners and waiters and professional football players in with managers and administrators and clerks. Under classic productivity formulas, Thor went on, office productivity wasn't even calculable. Using the APC's own methods, however, which take into account the inputs of both labor *and* equipment (as costs), and not just labor (per hour or per day, as an expenditure of time), Thor cited these less extreme, though still dramatic, productivity growth rates covering a twelve-year span:

- Agriculture, up 23 percent
- Industry, up 21 percent
- "All other," up 6 percent

THE "FAMILIAR UNKNOWN"

I put all this into an editorial, and, still searching for the source, asked publicly, "Would the author of those figures please stand up?" No one ever did.

But four years later, what should arrive but an analysis of how the figures were calculated, and a great deal more, sent to me by a professor in Hawaii.

Dr. Raymond R. Panko, an associate professor with the Department of Decision Sciences, College of Business Administration, University of Hawaii at Manoa, is one of the keenest analysts of office data active today and an astute interpreter of the trends to which the numbers point.

In a marvelously lucid paper titled simply "Office Work,"[7] Panko calls office work "the familiar unknown." The phrase comes from marketing, where the familiar unknown is the customer. Everyone knows what a customer is, yet for marketers real knowledge of customers is often sorely lacking. Everyone knows what office work is . . . but what is it? Few people seem to know, and as we saw in Chapter 1, fewer have cared.

If management is going to spend huge sums to automate office work, it had better have a clearer idea of what it's dealing with. Panko's paper goes a long way toward making the unknown known.

One of the professor's conclusions is that you can't rely on federal government data to tell you anything directly about office work, office workers, or office productivity, although you can draw useful inferences if you sort the numbers and work with only the relevant ones. For example, from data on the government's *own* productivity growth, Panko found it possible to isolate operations that are heavily "office" in character—as distinct from operations which are largely industrial, like power generation at Grand Coulee Dam or presswork at the Government Printing Office (which, despite the name, is here not engaged in office work).

A second conclusion states that office work is so difficult to define and to serve because it is so highly segmented from industry to industry, company to company, and even department to department. Even so, a three-level "taxonomy"—or method of classifying—office work can help OA planners to better understand it in relation to organizational needs. The three levels are (1) the organization itself, (2) departments within the organization, and (3) individual workers within the departments. They are separate yet interrelated, much as organs are separate within a body yet together support its overall life.

Let's examine the conclusions more closely.

WHITE-COLLAR VERSUS OFFICE WORK

One of the customary arguments in support of OA is that the white-collar work force has been growing explosively, and unless something is done to contain it, administrative costs will go out of sight. Government data do confirm a growth surge if measured from 1900, but a closer look at recent data shows the surge is petering out.

At the turn of the century, 17.6 percent of the U.S. work force was white-collar. By 1983, 53.7 percent of it was. One recent study by the Bureau of Labor Statistics (BLS), however, projects the white-collar segment for 1990 as diminishing somewhat to 51.2 percent.[8] Still, it's been proper to say that more than half of the work force is, and will continue to be, white-collar.

But on the basis of this information, it is not proper to say that more than half of the work force works in offices. Many of the workers on the official BLS list of white-collar occupations are plainly not office employees—musicians, photographers, and newspaper carriers, for example. Excluding these and other categories, Raymond Panko arrived at the answer that a bit more than one-third—38.5 percent—of the work force works in offices. That figures out to 38.3 million people. But before you write that down, read on.

Classing certain jobs as office work and others as not amounts to a judgment call. Panko classed as office workers such white-collar people as accountants, stock and bond sales agents, and most clerical workers. He included religious workers but excluded teachers, engineers, and technicians. He also excluded "hucksters and peddlers." Actually, many hucksters I've known do work in offices.

And of course, teachers, engineers, and technicians do work in offices, too, part of the time or most of the time. One must thus distinguish between "office work" and "working in offices." A file clerk does office work; architects, lawyers, and physicians do some of their work in offices. In a way, the BLS has also tried to make this distinction, although it uses different terminology. Before 1983, it had lumped all occupations into four broad groupings: white-collar, blue-collar, service, and farm. Since then, it has used this six-group system:

- Managerial and professional specialty
- Technical, sales, and administrative support
- Service
- Precision production, craft, and repair
- Operators, fabricators, and laborers
- Farming, forestry, and fishing

Panko argues that the first two groupings can serve as a useful enough substitute for "office work" as well as "work in offices." Work force nomenclature provides no official name for this pair; Panko proposes they be known as simply "information work."

Applying subjective judgment again to job categories within the two broad groupings presumptively joined as one, Panko figured information workers as constituting 54.2 percent of the work force. Here, engineers, teachers, lawyers, and other professionals are included. The figure comes close to the 53.7 white-collar percentage cited earlier and also makes it possible to say that, yes, more than half of the work force does work in offices, after all. This whole exercise may seem, thus, not to have mattered. But it does matter. In seeking answers to "Does OA pay?", knowing exactly what you're talking about matters very much.

In seeking answers to "Automate how?", the distinctions can matter even more. The kinds of OA tools assigned to a file job to make a clerk more efficient can differ widely from those given to an architect or physician to make each of them more effective as professionals.

If nothing else, the exercise should make two things clear: that enormous varieties exists in office-based jobs, and that great care should be taken with any generalizations about them.

TARGETS OF OPPORTUNITY

In general (take care!), greater variety exists among managerial, professional, and technical office-based jobs than among the more routine support jobs like clerk and secretary. It follows that the routine jobs, because they are routine, make good candidates for automation. In general, this is true. The mass of routine clerical work—payroll, billing, receivables, customer accounts, and the like—was what computers first targeted. Further, the single biggest and most routine aspect of secretarial work—typing—was what word processing targeted.

It also follows that *non*clerical work is so diverse that automating it, or supporting it, becomes more difficult. Again, this is generally true. But here, let us take special care. Some professionals spend surprisingly large amounts of time processing fairly recurrent information. Pharmacists, for example, spend up to 40 percent of their time on paperwork, much of it routine, as more and more state governments in the United States and provincial governments in Canada pass laws requiring them to cross-check prescriptions against the other medication a patient may be taking.[9] This type of work thus becomes a good candidate for at least two types of automation—the routine, production-enhancing kind and the professional, performance-enhancing kind.

Managers represent so diverse a group that, at first glance, little about their work appears sufficiently routine to stand out as an automation target. Yet despite their differing responsibilities and many specialties as sales managers, marketing managers, city managers, administrative managers, and dozens of varieties more, managers do have traits in common. Study after study has shown that two-thirds of a manager's day is spent communicating. On the phone, in face-to-face meetings, in the act of writing to others, in reading what others have written to them, managers, like so many of their professional office-based colleagues, exchange and exchange and exchange—information.

Clearly, this overriding *generic need* of the manager and the professional to communicate presents a fat target of opportunity for the tools of personal automation. And so do their specific needs: automation provides computer-aided design (CAD) tools for the engineer, financial modeling software for the accountant, and so on. And so do the other needs of these workers in that third of the day when they are not communicating.

What might they be doing then? A 1980 study by Booz, Allen & Hamilton, the worldwide, New York–based consulting firm, found managers and professionals engaged in a mixture of tasks, some useful, others not, but nearly all having a basic "getting ready" quality about them. The managers and professionals were, among other things:

- Trying to locate information
- Doing clerical tasks (many of which might better have been assigned to others)
- Scheduling and organizing future work
- Traveling, or waiting idly prior to travel
- And, as all good managers must, following up on previously assigned work and urging the staff to expedite it

Almost every task on the list could be automated with systems support of some kind—database systems for efficient information retrieval, calendar-management software to expedite scheduling and the coordination of meetings among groups of people, tele- and videoconferencing to allow groups to "meet" without need of travel, even preprogrammed alarm clocks to remind principals to check up on previously assigned projects and find out how they're coming along. Where a project lagged badly, a principal could even send a good chewing out via voicemail to everyone on the project team. Whether such remote-control discipline would be effective is another story.

THE THREE-LEVEL OFFICE

We can only go so far with targets of general opportunity. They may help define broad objectives, but to win the OA revolution we must home in on the individual needs of individual workers. In the case of managers and professionals, with their highly diverse jobs and job needs, that's a lot of expensive homing in to do. But remember what was said in Chapter 1: Managers' and professionals' workplaces are the turf on which most of the rest of the OA revolution will be fought. This is where the big payoffs are. Managers and professionals pull down, in payroll costs, three times as much as secretaries and clerks, whose work has been amply automated already, thanks to WP and DP.

Indeed, there are plenty of these routine clerical operations yet to target; they're eminently worth going after and easier to hit. The *non*routine executive workplace, though, is the big one. Despite generalities that it requires good communications support and good administrative backup and that it may have some routine information processing needs as well, the executive workplace is much harder to target. It may be necessary, as Panko and others believe, to build an individualized system for each executive workplace. That sounds terribly expensive, but new approaches to OA, and new organizational structures being considered, might ease that burden and resolve a couple of other OA issues in the bargain.

Right now, in the organization-department-individual taxonomy of office work, the department is where most automation has taken place. And most of this has taken place in what Panko calls Type I departments—the highly structured, routine, information processing kind of place. Customer billing exemplifies a Type I department. Type II departments deal in complex, nonroutine processes; these include departments like engineering, legal, corporate planning, even Executive Row.[10] As we've seen, relatively little automation has occurred here yet. But it will.*

Type I departments are weighted heavily with secretarial and clerical workers. Type IIs are weighted with managers, professionals, and technicians. Type Is also have a historic tie to traditional DP operations, with which they are often lumped in office literature. Type IIs are linked to end users and to present and future OA. All this rein-

*Semantics: What one person may call Type I and Type II, another may call something else. IBM, for example, favored the terms "custom" and "production" to distinguish two basically different kinds of office work. Then, finding these terms too value-oriented ("Many offices are more 'production' than they'd like to admit," an IBMer told me), the company reverted to a more neutral nomenclature: "standard" and "nonstandard." Many OA consultants prefer these or similar terms.

forces the much too artificial split in some minds between DP and real office work, as though those mainframes were not really in the office and had no role in OA. As end users seek to draw upon central files and processing power, and for technical reasons, DP has an expanding role in—though not necessarily an expanding control of—OA integration.

WP, with a foot in both Type I and Type II departments, long ago began a process of blurring the lines which separated traditional office departments. OA may finish this job. When text editors linked up with laser printers, for example, enabling a WP operator to control high-quality print runs, the system also performed a quiet end run around traditional "repro" operations. Where were these operations truly centered now? In the traditional reproductions department down in sub-basement B, or in WP on floors 2, 4, and 9? When text editors exchanged data with the big computers of DP, where was information processing centered? In DP? WP? Both places? Some other place?

The *functions* of in-office printing, computing, record keeping, communications, and more will remain and, indeed, will strengthen. But the departments which traditionally governed them may not, especially as more and more executives and WP workers at their automated workstations govern more of these functions themselves.

What may happen is a melding of office functions across the three office levels, with greater stress on individual needs and greater cohesion among departments as organs of a tighter organ*ization*—a "seamless environment," to quote Panko.

Panko and others, like Ralph H. Sprague, an authority on computer-based decision support systems, see companies moving to a new regrouping of functions and resources, not along the old Type I–Type II lines but more along lines of an organization-wide technical foundation onto which can be set a host of individual work applications.[11]

Sprague, in the decision support area, and in a paper jointly written with Panko, speaks of systems tools tailored easily, quickly, and relatively inexpensively for individuals by means of underlying, commonly shared system "generators."[12] Panko speaks of a "technostructure" built to provide basic communications, computing, and other technical support throughout the seamless environment, and, above this, an individual "applistructure" built for specific services. He writes,

> Office automation has traditionally foreseen its products being delivered through workstations built for OA, over OA networks, with OA servers providing OA services. We now see, however, that the ideas of workstations, networks, and servers form a general picture of how *all* services will be provided in the future, whether these services fall into the traditional domains of office automation, data processing, engineering computation, or any other area.

OA authority John Connell echoes the same ideas in broader terms. Connell, who runs a membership organization for OA users and planners, the Office Technology Research Group, says what's needed are two new functions: "A service function to provide central support, a facilitating function to move technology out."[13] He sees data centers continuing to handle mass processing operations but serving less as a computing resource for "clients" in other departments; they, the end users, will do more of this information work and local processing themselves. One underlying architecture must support both needs. It will be maintained by technicians probably resident in the centers and managed by executives who understand the differing environments and the need to keep them functionally separate yet organizationally and systemically whole.

The issue is:

Defining OA terms; defining the generic and specific work needs of differing office workers; and defining the differing OA solutions for supporting those needs. Optimally, the issue involves defining these terms within as large an organizational context as feasible, all as a prelude to answering the question "Does OA pay?" with some surety.

We have taken this long discourse through office data and the familiar unknown of the office itself to illustrate how hard it is to answer the question directly.

- The data, if available at all, don't always mean what they seem to mean.
- Office work is so extremely varied that to ask about automating "it" is almost to ask the impossible.
- Productivity half-truths persist, confusing the issue.
- The office itself, so long unchanged, is beginning to transform radically. In assessing OA investment, one must not only glean the scraps of past experience but also try to fathom how OA might pay off in a future office environment.

HARD DOLLAR, SOFT DOLLAR

"Paying off" implies objective measurement, but by what yardstick can anything as subjective as executive work be measured? In a routinized, high-production WP center, lines per day, documents per day—quantities of some kind—can be measured and costed, and, indeed, in many departments they are. But the output of managers, professionals, and myriad other knowledge workers? What do you count? Decisions per day? Phone calls made? Chewings out administered? About the best you can do, many office watchers say, is to measure overall effectiveness—bottom-line results—over an extended span of time. It's soft measurement.

Not good enough, say others. You've *got* to come up with hard-dollar benefits. Business realism demands it. Too much is at stake. Even assuming a worst-case situation—only $2500 in equipment supporting each office worker, as the literature says, for the 55 million information workers Panko counts—that's a $138 billion investment right there. Add all that new equipment which market studies predict—PC growth of 40 to 50 percent annually, software growth of 60 percent (see Chapter 1); add an estimated $36 billion being spent annually on office telephone systems and $26 billion on WP, paper, traditional mail, electronic mail, and other text-moving items;[14] and that soon builds up to *really* real money. Business can't expend sums like that and not know what it's getting beyond encouraging words on soft returns.

"The tricky question of defining costs and justifying costs for OA equipment has troubled business for years," says Randy Goldfield, president of Omni Group Ltd. "While it is difficult to put price tags on many intangibles, such as better, faster decision making . . . it is necessary."

"It's absolutely irresponsible not to build a financial case for any installation," emphasizes Vincent Pica of E. F. Hutton.[15] "Without justifying the cost, how can top management make an informed decision about moving ahead with OA?"

Advocates of management by objectives (MBO) say this technique can effectively gauge executive performance, including *automated* executive performance, and yield concrete results. Using MBO, executives and their superiors agree on objectives of performance the executives will accomplish. Then after a period of time—a year, say—that performance is assessed. Did it meet, exceed, or fall short of agreed-upon goals? Because executives equipped with OA tools might be given larger objectives than those without them, OA payoffs might later be separated out. Business makes soft non-OA investments all the time, MBOers point out. Every time it adds a person to the staff, it invests in a human asset, and yet it would be hard pressed to calculate the return in hard dollars.

Michael J. Hammer of the Laboratory of Computer Science at the Massachusetts Institute of Technology rejects the notion that anything less than direct financial measurement is also less than reliable. Speaking at the 1982 Office Automation Conference in San Francisco, Hammer said,

> Hard-dollar savings are no more reliable a basis for justifying office automation than any others. . . . Nor are they more meaningful. The measures that the management of the unit feels are most indicative of its performance are usually the most appropriate ones to use. On the other hand, we also reject the opposing concept that the benefits of office automation are inherently nonmeasurable and nonquantifiable. If benefits cannot be measured, then it is relatively safe to assume they do not exist.

This approach, the well-known writer-consultant conceded, "allows us to finesse" the thorny issue of cost-benefit analysis. What cost-benefit analysis ultimately must rest upon, he added, is management decision.

> The essence of management is making decisions in the context of incomplete information. The [manager] must examine the anticipated costs and returns, evaluate the accuracy of this information, and make a judgment call on whether the anticipated benefits are sufficiently likely to justify the expected costs.

The issue is:

Somewhat unresolved. There is not much to go on in the area of hard-dollar executive productivity measurement, but OA authorities keep trying to gather up more.

EXECUTIVE PRODUCTIVITY STUDIES

One of the most notable attempts to measure executive productivity, the pioneering, incomplete, but much quoted 1980 Booz Allen Study of Managerial/Professional Productivity, took 90,000 separate time samples of the activities of 299 office-based executives. Like most other research into managerial and professional work, the study found that these executives spent the bulk of their time communicating—67 percent of their time, it turned out. The report's author, Harvey Poppel, stated that if these same executives had been equipped with proper OA tools, they would soon have been able to accomplish the same tasks with a 15 percent savings in time.

That's significant. It's more than an hour a day. We might ask what these executives might have done with that hour. They might have addressed new work they didn't have time for before. They might have done their present work more thoroughly and achieved better results. These are what the OA crowd calls "value-added" results. More and better.

On the other hand, as one acerbic critic remarked, these executives might have sat around in that saved time and shot the breeze with their colleagues. Even had they not, the company for which eight of these executives worked might have pooled their spare hours and eliminated one executive. That's a "cost-displacement" result. Not better, just cheaper. Obviously, this raises contentious OA issues which may prove costly in other ways.

Nevertheless, added value and displaced costs are both worthy goals of OA, and which of them to go for is another management decision. In the opportunity to add value or save money, as shown by the Booz Allen study, OA appears to pay.

We could search long and hard for similar broad-gauged rules of thumb which might state, "For every dollar invested in OA, *x* dollars are returned." Such guidelines just don't exist. There is, at best, a grab bag of statistics, some already cited, which may or may not fit into any specific OA study. A sampling:

- Cost trends:

Computer memories	Dropping	40 percent per year
Computer logic	Dropping	25 percent per year
Communications	Dropping	10 percent per year
People	Rising	15 percent per year
Administration	Rising	6 percent per year

- Secretaries' time: 40 percent typing, 60 percent administration (useful perhaps for a WP assessment).
- Managers' time: about 40 percent spent in formal or informal meetings, 28 percent on the phone, 23 percent reading.
- Average number of interruptions in a manager's day: 15 (an argument for electronic mail or voicemail).
- Average number of phone calls needed to schedule a meeting for ten people: 35 (calendar management software).
- Percentage of business phone calls that don't get through to the intended party the first time: 50 (voicemail or electronic mail, again).
- Cost of a dictated business letter, including principal's and secretary's time: $8.10 as of 1984 (definitely a WP argument).

Like all OA numbers, use with care. The bag I happened to grab them from held such valuables as notes taken at an IBM customer-education seminar in Dallas; the outline of an OA report by a former executive at the Continental Group, New York; and a press release from the Dartnell Corp., Chicago. Given the paucity of OA data, such scraps have value. You will run across them from time to time, and you may want to start your own collection.

Sometimes we can cull the best idea of OA's worth from real-life examples of what happens when a company—or more likely a department or even some system within a department—is automated; then we can draw conclusions from any pattern which shows up in the manifold outcomes.

Example. A computerized filing system at AT&T Technologies has eliminated 500 square feet of file space, allowed a 20 percent reduction of accounts payable clerks, reduced filing backlog by 95 percent, and virtually eliminated misfiles. Bottom line for the Kearney, New Jersey, facility: savings of $62,000 a year.

Example. A manual index-card system that was costing Abbott Laboratories $49,500 a year to maintain was replaced by two computer-aided retrieval (CAR) systems, which together cost $35,000. Under the old system, preparing, sorting, and filing the cards alone had cost this Chicago health products firm $26,670 per year; the new DBMS, or database management system, handles these tasks for $11,570. One of the CARs locates records produced through COM (computer output microfilm), in which computer data are written directly onto microfiche—compact 4- by 6-inch film records—bypassing bulky paper printout. Each fiche holds about 160 pages (with 55 lines to a page) and represents a savings, says micrographics analyst Mary Louise Schramm, of $48.50. In time terms, manual updates of records once took six hours to process; now they take two, eliminating the need for one operator.

Example. At Sun Co., the big oil concern based in Radnor, Pennsylvania, a teleconferencing system has saved more than $100,000 per year in travel costs alone. The system, part of an evolving OA structure which includes WP, electronic mail, and a computerized library, has won management's nod as a successful, permanent company feature. "Our grand plan," says advanced-systems manager Thomas Kelly, "is ultimately to enable anyone to perform data processing, text editing, graphics, and communications functions at his or her own workstation."

Example. At the Health Care Financing Administration (HCFA), the agency which handles Medicare and Medicaid, a freeze-frame videoconferencing system not only pays for itself in reduced travel expenses but, in a year and a half, has returned more than $2.50 for every $1 spent on it. The freeze-frame system, less animated than full-motion TV, can link HCFA's Baltimore and Washington headquarters to ten regional offices. In an eighteen-month period, the system was used for some 1000 teleconferences involving 9000 attendees. This cost $141,824, the agency said, while travel savings and productivity gains totaled $379,852.

Example. Savings of $2 million in annual document production costs are but the first results of a major OA project at New York City's Human Resources Administration (HRA). Working with the Office of Management Design, the city's internal OA consulting group, HRA converted a largely manual operation involving 1400 clerical workers and costing close to $23 million per year into a computerized workstation system needing only 400 operators. The next step, officials say, is development of workstation applications to support managers and professionals.

Example. A computer-based financial modeling system called TIMS enables financial executives at Tenneco Inc. to prepare income and cash flow statements; to play "what if" games using various estimates; and, interactively, to shape analyses as complex and strategic as divisional five-year plans. TIMS, which stands for Tenneco Interactive Model System, is more than a time saver, says Arnold Panella, manager of planning models for the Houston-based conglomerate. It's a quality enhancer: *better* planning occurs. All soft benefits, true, yet TIMS usage continues to grow at a compound yearly rate of 65 percent.

Example. Turnaround time for the production of training manuals was cut in half at Combustion Engineering's C-E Power Systems in Windsor Locks, Connecticut, after that division brought in seven professional workstations which electronically set and delete type, cut and paste text, add graphics, and perform other page-makeup tasks. Linked by local area network to an electronic file capable of holding 35,000 made-up pages, the machines are credited with a 30 percent cut in production costs six months after being installed.

Example. Order processing costs lowered to $5 as against an industry average of $12 to $15; back orders reduced from 50 percent to less than 5 percent; delivery cycles cut from forty-eight to twenty-four hours; keypunch staff reduced; plans to hire additional staff scrapped—these are some of the paybacks of a wide-ranging OA system at the Bayvet Division of Miles Laboratories. The system has grown steadily since 1977, when this animal health and veterinary products firm replaced an outmoded order processing operation with a powerful mainframe. Surrounding this core today are thirty-two minicomputer terminals, thirty-six major peripherals, and a variety of dial-up and dedicated lines linking Bayvet headquarters in Shawnee, Kansas to sites in eighteen cities of the United States, Canada, and West Germany. Still a DP-based order processor at heart, the system also tracks inventory, handles payroll, generates government reports, maintains personnel records, updates mailing lists, and word-processes myriad documents. An electronic mail capability lets executives in widely separated locations keep in touch effectively. Statistical software helps R&D scientists to quickly resolve questions and provide proofs necessary for government approval so that products can move to market. What all this has cost over the years is now beyond calculation; the minicomputer alone costs $30,000 per year. "What it has given us is a quantum leap to areas where we'd never scratched the surface before," sums up systems manager James Amend. "Tremendous, tremendous productivity!"

See also the examples at the beginning of Chapter 3.

WP'S LONGER TRACK RECORD

If there's any pattern in these examples, it's one we've noticed before: the *variety* of office work.

None of the OA systems, with perhaps the exception of Bayvet's, is "total," and even there development goes on. The efforts are piecemeal, departmental, at best interdepartmental. Even so, managers speak of plans and goals. The systems will grow, some in the direction of savings, others in the direction of fostering quality work.

In the more focused, routinized realm of WP, with its longer track record, we might expect to see cost and benefit guidelines. And yes, there are a few. Bruce Payne & Associates, New York management consultants who pioneered WP work measurement, state that WP techniques can usually result in savings of from 15 to 30 percent of clerical costs at workstations placed under such programs. SRI Augmentation Laboratory of Menlo Park, California estimates that users who replace standard electric typewriters with text editors can save from $1 to $2 per final printed page.[16] But the situation is essentially the same as OA's—a file of individual cases.

Example. At Alaskan Air Command headquarters, Elmendorf Air Force Base, Anchorage, six text editors and an ink-jet printer saved the organization $45,968 over five years.

EXAMPLE. Ten WP operators were able to handle work which previously required the services of forty-two employees at Lever Brothers Co., New York.

EXAMPLE. In New Orleans, South Central Bell increased document productivity between 50 and 100 percent during WP's first year there. In one case, six operators prepared 500 original three-page letters in nine hours. Using traditional methods, the same job would have taken seven days.

EXAMPLE. At the Department of Labor's Employee Standards Administration, analyst William Holmes compared the time and cost of preparing nine assorted documents using conventional methods as against WP. Applying norms of $7 per hour for clerical labor, $15 per hour for professionals, and $138 per month for renting each text editor, Holmes calculated conventional costs to be $3290 using liberal assumptions, $1645 using conservative assumptions, and $800 as the actual cost with WP. Savings thus ranged between $2490 and $845. In time terms, WP saved between sixty-four and ninety-one worker hours.[17]

THE GOVERNMENT EXAMPLE

Another pattern that emerges from these cases is the prevalence of government examples. No accident. Government, especially the federal government, has been in the vanguard of OA/WP development. The popular image of government offices as a tangle of bureaucracies through which paper moves at a snail's pace is another of those half-truths in need of full correction.

Again, the astute Dr. Panko may help set the record straight. In his analyses of government data on information workers, he also measured the populations of these workers in various industries. Some industries, naturally, have more information workers than others. In the construction industry, for example, 13 percent of the workers are managers or professionals; another 8 percent are in the second of BLS's broad groupings—administrative, technical, and sales workers—for an information worker total in the construction industry of 21 percent. In transportation and utilities, on the other hand, 50 percent of employees are information workers. One of the heaviest concentrations of such workers (68 percent) is in public administration—the government "industry."

Now, in addition to these data, the U.S. government also publishes productivity data. Some is useful, as with manufacturing, where output is relatively easy to measure. Much is useless, as for service industries, which, like managerial and professional work, are often impossible to measure. In some service sectors, in fact, the government abandons all effort to measure, but that doesn't stop it from issuing data. It arbitrarily sets output equal to input, making productivity growth come out to zero, when it actually could be increasing!

Of course, not all federal workers are office workers, but more than two-thirds of them are. Availing himself of relatively useful data on federal productivity, and confining himself to office-intensive sectors for which data exist going back to 1967, the indefatigable Dr. Panko concluded that federal office productivity rose 25.5 percent from 1967 to 1981, or *at an average rate of 1.7 percent per year.* The economy as a whole during that time had a productivity gain of only 1.5 percent per year. All this is even more startling when set against the oft-quoted figure for office productivity of only 4 percent over *ten* years, a mere 0.4 percent per year.

Data obtained from Panko as this book went to press disclose these annual gains in productivity:

	Office		
Year	*Federal*	*Private*	*Manufacturing*
1967–1981	1.7%	1.4%	2.7%
1967–1972	1.6	2.3	4.0
1972–1977	1.0	1.3	2.2
1977–1981	3.0	0.1	1.1

"Note the extremely strong performance of federal office productivity in recent years," Professor Panko says. "Obviously, a conscious effort was being made to control costs."

Panko tells me that he has also found the source of the 4-percent-in-ten-years myth: "It comes from dividing the gross national product by the number of white-collar workers," a calculation that for reasons cited earlier (page 22) makes a number of assumptions which "cannot produce valid productivity information." The "finding" was the result of some back-of-an-envelope calculations made at Stanford Research Institute in the 1960s, which were no more than a first cut at trying to calculate for the office the kinds of productivity data BLS regularly published for industry. "The annoying thing," Panko says, "is that those tentative calculations for the 1960s are still being quoted today."

THE ART OF MANAGEMENT

As Michael Hammer suggests, management is not just a science of measurements and scores; it is an intuitive art as well. A good manager often *knows* what he or she cannot prove. The good manager knows that the cost of proving something may exceed the quiet, unmeasured enjoyment of the benefit itself.

I once discussed this with John Diebold, the internationally known consultant whose prophetic 1952 book, *Automation,* put the word in the dictionary. *Automation* still makes remarkable reading. You could spend a lifetime, Diebold said, trying to quantify OA's benefits among managers and professionals, "but I'm not sure that's a good use of resources." If a financial analyst can spend an afternoon in solving a problem with OA tools, versus a week and a half without them, he went on, "you know you've got a big yield in productivity." If a machine designer can come up with an optimum manufacturing combination in a day or two versus a month and a half, he reiterated, "you know you've got a big yield in productivity."[18]

OA is both an investment in costly tools and tasks, made in hopes of gain, and a creative act done out of need to inform better, think better, *be* better. It holds forth bottom-line profit to take to the bank, top-of-the-line power for workers to become more than they already are.

How do we manage this investment to extract its optimum good? This question involves issues of OA approach, which we turn to in Chapter 3.

3

Issues of "Automate How?"

OA Czars, OA Camels, and Topsy

Before a single piece of automated office equipment ever arrived at the loading dock, managers of Rubbermaid Inc. could look five years into the future and know with fair precision how far along on their OA journey they would be at any time.

The executives knew not only where they were going, but more important, *why* they were going. They were going, they had said, in order to avoid business costs, not to reduce costs. OA wouldn't be a way of cutting overhead—getting rid of people, for example. But it definitely would be a way of helping everyone accomplish more without adding to costs. The goal was cost *avoidance*.

The journey was well mapped for this major housewares and business supply firm based in Wooster, Ohio, and the schedules, at least for the first and second years of the five-year plan, were well set. From Wooster to plants in Texas and Virginia, the OA system would grow in range and complexity, step by deliberate step. At journey's end—not the end for all time, surely, but the end for this first cycle—a network of integrated information systems would be operational company-wide. The beginning, like so many OA beginnings, involved basic word processing and the space planning needed to house it.

OA manager Sue Lyons-Gunn often used the metaphor of a pyramid to explain essentials of the plan to company personnel. At the base, in addition to WP, are its related functions, dictation and facsimile. The next-higher layer involves advanced communications for optical character recognition (OCR)—the automatic reading of documents into computer memory by machines called "scanners"—and photocomposition. Then come electronic files and the sharing of databases. And still later . . .

From top to bottom, the tiers of Lyons-Gunn's OA pyramid look like this:

8. Integrated information networks and systems
7. Multifunctional executive workstations
6. Multifunctional administrative support workstations
5. Intelligent copiers and laser printers
4. An electronic mail network
3. Electronic files and shared databases
2. Advanced communications for OCR and photocomposition
1. Word processing, dictation, facsimile, and the requisite space planning

What all the buzzwords mean and how this gear would fit together need not concern us here. The important point is that Rubbermaid set clear corporate goals for its OA efforts; it looked ahead five years; and, while giving itself leeway for unexpected circumstances in the farther-out years, the company mapped its way carefully from stage to stage over reasonable periods of time.

At this writing, Rubbermaid is halfway up the pyramid, and climbing.

ANOTHER OA JOURNEY

Slow and deliberate is not the only way to win the OA race. Sometimes, for pressing business reasons, racing may be the only sound approach. Consider the case of the Kentucky revenue collectors.

The state's tax department, or Revenue Cabinet as it is officially known, was burdened with such archaic systems as recently as 1982 that the old commonwealth was losing an estimated $100 million in uncollected taxes each year. The cabinet spilled further revenue in the form of constant overtime. John Y. Brown, Jr., then governor, issued a not-impossible order: "Automate." He then added a near-impossible condition: "In three months."

Well, it took four. But what Cabinet Secretary Ronald G. Geary, OA section supervisor Scott Bartelt, and others accomplished in that time gives support to a different view of OA journeys: the view of getting on with it. "The know-how is there, the technology is there," say proponents of this view, "so move!" All that "need to plan carefully" is often nothing but a cover for procrastination.

The Revenue Cabinet's OA team got on with it.

Phase 1. The team found out where in the cabinet OA technology could best be applied. Everyone from secretaries on up was contacted in a swift, intensive study.

Phase 2. With needs determined, the team selected equipment. Here, two criteria stood out. Because of the relentless deadline, the equipment had to be sufficiently user-friendly for operators to learn quickly. And the vendor had to be well enough set up locally to assure a high degree of support. Wang bested competitors and got the contract.

In little more than a hundred days after the governor gave his order, five compatible yet different Wang systems were wheeled into five Revenue Cabinet buildings in Frankfort, the state capital. Phone lines then connected four of the systems to each other; the fifth stood alone. Other links tied the four to remote sites for dictation and to the state's IBM mainframe, which in turn reached county offices for property value data. With all that reach and power, the integrated cabinet system was able to handle WP, legal searches, and statistics, in addition to the original goal of speeding the collection of taxes.

A year after the system went "on-line," Bartelt could report improvements in worker productivity of 75 to 100 percent; overtime was practically eliminated; and that costly backlog of paperwork was reduced to almost zero. The people of Kentucky paid $500,000 for the system, but the tax evaders among them, whose arrears were twenty times that outlay, now more readily pay what they owe.

THE "NO-APPROACH" APPROACH

There's yet another approach to an OA journey—no approach. It might be likened to traveling without a map, at a pace that suits you, and going wherever the need of the moment takes you. It sounds careless, but a lot of organizations take that approach. It would be wrong to say they don't plan, because each short-range move is thought through well enough, and most results pay off well enough, too. But the growth is haphazard, Topsy-like. It follows no grand design, no master strategy.

Still, there are things to be said for the no-approach approach. There's movement (if spasmodic) and OA growth (if uncoordinated) and payoff (more immediate than thorough planners get). Indeed, the payoff is better than you get if your organization just "thinks about" OA and then decides to wait. It waits for the picture to clear, the technology to improve, the price to drop—something. That's not a no-approach approach, but simply no approach: nothing ventured, nothing gained.

The issue is:

OA planning stategy: how thorough should it be?

A 1985 study by the Administrative Management Society (AMS) Foundation among veteran OA executives found wide-ranging answers to that question, based on the subjects' experiences. It also found many agreeing that they would allot more time to the effort were they to begin planning anew, especially in the areas of cost, training, and systems architecture.[1]

Their actual experiences ran a gamut from "We strategized long-range about our industry or field [before addressing] our organization and its needs" to statements like "We recognized we had specific problems and went for quick remedies." The former were more numerous than the latter, however.

While the short answer to the question is to plan thoroughly and carefully in as wide an organizational framework as possible, there is plainly no shortage of ways to automate, and there is no lack of opinions on what these alternatives are worth. There's more than one way of costing out OA, the hard-dollar way, the soft-dollar way, as we saw in Chapter 2. There's more than one goal to pursue: the elimination of cost, the adding of value to work. More than one "issue of approach."

- The issue of OA planners. How many should there be? And "planees," what of them? How much can you involve in the planning the people whose work lives will be affected by OA?
- The issue of who's in charge, Part I. Should it be a planning committee or a single "OA czar"? Can one person know all there is to know and decide all there is to decide about anything as complex as OA? On the other hand, do committees only bring forth camels? (You know: "A camel is a horse designed by a committee.") *Or* does a committee representing many disciplines produce real synergy?

- The issue of who's in charge, Part II. Assuming you set up an interdisciplinary committee, who among the equal disciplinarians are most equal? The "techies" in Data Processing, the bean counters in Finance, the generalists from Administrative Services who understand "facilities" and are often happiest among cleaning and maintenance contracts? The question may sound cynical, but it suggests the variation in perspectives that different leaders can bring to an OA mission. And yet someone has to chair the thing.
- The issue of where to start. WP gets many votes. "A great foundation on which to build your bigger OA systems," some people say. "Maybe," say others, "but it's too production-oriented to ever migrate naturally to the nonroutine work of managers and professionals. To get them started," these others suggest, "pick some likely knowledge-work department for a pilot study, and let it become the model for advancement of OA throughout the organization."
- The issue of when to start. Is it better to commit now or to wait for the big technological breakthroughs that are just around the corner? More and more people have begun to see offices for what they are; they ask, "Can we afford *not* to commit now?"
- The issue of timing and pace. Should we be on the fast track or should we move slowly and cautiously? Some office watchers say OA is so big and complex that not only must *it* be planned for and managed, but the very planning *process* must also be planned for and managed. You have to plan *to plan*.
- The issue of equipment selection, Part I. Many would call this the issue of where to end. Only after organizational goals have been set and systems which might attain the goals have been sketched in should vendors be called in to see how well their products match the sketches. Too often events proceed in reverse. Executives dash out to buy computers, then belatedly figure out what to use them for.
- The issue of equipment selection, Part II. Should you stick to one vendor, or at best a few? Many companies now have limited-vendor policies, believing that if things go wrong, they know whom to call. None of that multivendor entrapment for them—you know, the hardware rep saying "The problem's in the software," the software rep saying "Get them to replace the disk drive." On the other hand, limited is limited. Holding to a few vendors keeps you from the price breaks and systems innovations proffered by others not on the limited list. "Besides," say those not put off by multivendor problems, "there should *be* no problem if you insist that vendors prove that brands X, Y, and Z *do* work well together, before you commit to any of them."

In any case, the technological issues that systems and equipment present are discussed in Chapters 5 and 6. People issues are covered in Chapter 7. This chapter looks at the whos, hows, and how longs of planning for OA. Such planning inevitably must take systems, equipment, and people into account, so a certain amount of repetition can't be helped. In writing about OA, it is often difficult to examine separately the parts of what, in Panko's phrase, is a seamless environment. In such holistic* circumstances, pulling out any one topic for discussion tangles us in all its connections with other topics, and some of these are also covered in another context.

THE GOAL-AND-STRATEGY JUNGLE

A cartoon in my files (from the Yankee Group, Cambridge, Mass., artist unknown) shows a jungle scene. A group of bewildered explorers, wearing labels such as "DP," "WP," "Telecommunications," and "Administrative Services," grope toward a distant monument called "Office Automation." A snake labeled "Competition" waits to pounce. Spear-carrying natives labeled "Inadequate Information" and "WP-PC Problems" wait to pounce. Signposts labeled "IBM," "DEC," "Prime," "Wang," "AT&T," and "Data General" point in every direction. One of the explorers is saying, "They never told us about this in business school!"

The cartoon captures well the anxieties felt by more than one OA planner. Why are we here? What *are* we looking for? As we've seen, the goal is manifold treasure: cutting costs, adding value, improving productivity, freeing up managers' time, keeping ahead of competition . . . surviving. OA must ultimately lead to *better performance and financial well-being* or it lacks basic justification.

The office and its automation are but means to business ends. "Nobody wants computers," says Michael Hammer. "They want better business."

Such goals might seem too obvious to mention. They're what everyone uses as a guide as they steer the OA course. Or are they?

Of the four basic OA strategies identified by Karen Orton in her professional contacts with over 300 large companies, the "laissez faire" model—the *absence* of strategy, called the "no-approach" approach earlier in this chapter—is probably most common, she says. Orton, vice president for microcomputer education at National Training Sys-

---

*"Holistic" is an odd word but an important one. Despite its spelling, it has nothing to do with holes; it has to do with wholes and with seeing things whole. OA is holistic.

tems in Santa Monica, California, says that since most companies don't know how to go about automating, they don't plan. "Individuals then use discretionary funds from department or division budgets to buy hardware and software that seem useful to them."

In other words, something less than better business motivates these moves. Something rather like "It looks good here and now." Strung together, these unrelated good ideas amount to Topsy-like growth, and Topsy has her fans, remember. The no-approach approach does pay off, Orton concedes, in its own limited way. It does provide fast start-up. Also, top management, typically busy with other problems, doesn't have to bother about OA. Such lack of control, however, leads to a lack of standards, which leads to problems later. In addition, no one knows how much equipment is being acquired, because no one watches. According to Orton, United Technologies at one time guessed it had a dozen or so personal computers on-site. A count revealed 312 in actual use.[2]

Next-higher in Orton's strategies hierarchy is the "approved-sources-and-vendors" approach. "Some companies," she observes, "simply sanction a brand of computer—or a source—and let people make their own decisions as to what and when to automate." Hughes Aircraft plans to do this through an in-house computer store where employees may select equipment for their work. Du Pont lets employees "automate at will" providing they use specified products. The strategy requires little planning or coordination, yet it lets eager beavers automate at their own pace. Its drawbacks are the same as those of the laissez faire approach: a lack of standards and a payout limited to small personal jobs.[3]

"Task-driven" strategy *is* well-planned but limited, addressing one particular function or department. Next to laissez faire, it's probably the most prevalent OA approach. Task-driven strategy is relatively easy to justify because the task involved is usually discrete enough for planners to calculate some benefit. But unless carried out as part of a larger OA scheme, the limited scope of task-driven change could obstruct moves for departmental integration later.

"Top-down" implementation stands, logically, at the top of Orton's strategies hierarchy. Here, top management *mandates* OA as an organizational undertaking. This approach drives technology through the organization quickly, she notes, blending strategy well overall. Unfortunately, it's slow. Managers grow impatient at the long delays between the commencement of planning and the delivery of equipment. "In the long run, though," Orton concludes, "this strategy is likely to get the best results of them all."[4]

At Atlantic Richfield, Los Angeles, Allen Smith began planning in the late 1970s for the OA systems this major energy company would likely have within five years. Five years later, the corporate information systems manager acknowledged that "no great solution" to Richfield's OA needs had yet been put in place. Still, Smith defends his planning effort and goes right on developing an "OA vision" for the future. Planning gave management "an idea of where we were heading, even if we couldn't reach our destination right away," he says. "The more we learn, the quicker we can take advantage of solutions when they do arrive."[5]

THE WAIT-AND-SEE DILEMMA

Writer-editor Stewart Alter, who has studied the Richfield experience closely, believes the pilot projects Smith set up as part of the planning effort have given Richfield a leg up on competitors. "Many of them are still sitting back cautiously, waiting for the highly touted 'total solution' to link all their office systems together," Alter has written.[6] Allen Smith, who disapproves of such wait-and-see attitudes, says that if nothing else, the pilots exposed employees to OA concepts. OA takes time, and corporations which have held back may find themselves putting workers through a traumatic education when suddenly they do decide to automate.

Other believers in automating now say that waiting deprives companies of more than educational experience; it deprives them of OA's direct payoffs every day. "Sure, there'll be better systems tomorrow. So what? Reap the available harvest today. Then, in five or seven years' time, put in those better systems. You'll not only be better educated," this argument runs; "you'll be ahead in competitive advantage, too."

The temptation to wait is understandably strong, all the same. Almost daily, the computer and OA media report price drops and technological breakthroughs. Rumors circulate about the big announcement that IBM or AT&T (it's usually IBM or AT&T) soon plans to make. Here is a sampling of announcements which lately crossed my desk:

- "Optical recording technology," Creative Strategies International (CSI) is saying, "has progressed to the point where it will present a serious challenge to magnetic media within five or ten years. . . ." And here we were thinking about hard-disk storage.
- "New approaches to input devices will emerge every year," Dataquest, the A. C. Neilsen subsidiary, makes known. "Light pens,

touch-panel CRTs, graphics tablets, digitizers, mouse devices, track-balls, joysticks. . . ." And we were just getting comfortable with our cursor keyboards and ordinary cathode-ray tubes (CRTs).

- "Changing Technology Sparks New Trends in Booming Communications Processor Industry," headlines another CSI release. "Network controllers, remote concentrators, statistical multiplexers, gateways. . . ." And here we are still trying to figure out what the AT&T breakup did for us—or *to* us.

Xerox president and chief executive officer David T. Kearns, as keynote speaker of the fifth annual Office Automation Conference in 1984 in Los Angeles, reeled off the incredible statistics of his industry: 1600 companies in the OA business, another 4000 in software support, 16,000 product offerings from which to choose. "Every six months," said Kearns, "something big occurs in office automation to change one's mind." How can a company choose wisely and plan with confidence in an environment like that?

Kearns' answer: By means of a top-down strategy with clear objectives.

Many planners concur. Again, this is undoubtedly the slowest and most thorough of strategies, but in the long run it is the most effective. Besides, while no one can "freeze the technology," to use the voguish phrase, there are ways to coolly appraise it and approximate its flow.

One way to gauge upcoming technology is to ask vendors if they have made public commitments on their future courses of action. No, they're not likely to discuss specific products before they're released. But many major vendors, sensitive to customer anxieties on this score, have issued position statements which more or less clearly state future intentions.

IBM, for example, has gone on record with its view that automated offices comprise at least four major components: a family of competitive workstations; departmentalization of host systems for DP, document filing, and other applications; architecture for information interchange; and software packages that allow customization for office tasks. Read into that what you will. Said a company spokesman, "IBM's direction is to integrate data, text, voice, image, and graphics, building on our customer's current investments in hardware, software, and communications."[7]

Northern Telecom, which styles itself as North America's second-biggest telecommunications equipment manufacturer, has publicly committed to an "Open World" of fully integrated products and services and to a planning framework involving what is calls the "Five

C's": Continuity, to avoid obsolescence; Compatibility for interconnection; Congeniality, or user-friendliness; Control for user management (with less intervention by technicians); and Cost-effectiveness.

That's about as clear as position statements get—which may be a good thing. Trying to build precise plans on something as uncontrollable as future technology is risky business, notwithstanding the pledges of constancy by those who control technical developments best. It is tantamount to building a strategy on someone else's strategy, says Montclair, New Jersey, consultant Robert Becker—"almost impossible to do."

Another way of gauging technology's course, albeit imprecisely, is to track current trends. N. Dean Meyer, an OA consultant from Ridgefield, Connecticut, and founder of SOAP, the Society of Office Automation Professionals, believes that what you see now is what you're likely to see in the future: continued price reductions and desktop machines with increased processing power. And machines still addressing the same office tasks, the need for which won't disappear.

SHORT TERM, LONG TERM

SOAP founder Meyer also takes issue with top-down strategy if it means trying to implement an organization-wide system all at once. Planners who do that don't help users, he says. They merely create "ideal dream machines" in their heads. It is better to treat each local implementation uniquely, because each user's mission is unique, and integrate them later. "Keep your head in the clouds," Meyer says, "but your feet on the ground."

Robert Dickinson, former Exxon Office Systems manager, sees long-term and short-term planning not as being at odds but as complementary. "A broad view of where you're going to be in five years is absolutely essential to the development of a one-year, short-term plan," he says. "A one-year plan is no good without the perspective [of] a long-term outlook."[8]

Dickinson, now with the New York–based consulting firm Performance Strategies, acknowledges that changes in technology and within the company almost certainly will force changes in any long-term plan. That's why the best plans are general. But without such plans, a company hasn't much basis for judging how new developments might suit the overall scheme. "I don't know of an organization that has suffered from planning far in advance," he says.

Alexia Martin, consultant with SRI International, Menlo Park, California, likens the planks in a long-range platform to "straw men" which planners and users can shape to their liking—or toss out if need be. A long-range plan, for example, might make the following statements:

- All office workers will have terminals through which to access information and will receive whatever other information services they need to effectively perform their jobs.
- To avoid problems of incompatibility, the company will standardize on certain specific personal computers, text editors, software packages, and the like.
- For economy, some resources, such as high-speed printers and graphics plotters, will be shared.
- To facilitate resource sharing and the connection of device to device, a communications network will be developed. Systems tied to it must conform to certain protocols, to be developed from a long-range perspective.

If a statement makes sense, if it furthers corporate goals even though locally inconvenient, it should be adhered to, Martin believes. If it doesn't make sense, it should be dropped. The statements, at least, are *bases* for considered decisions. "Short-term implementations," Martin writes, "only enable an organization to combat immediate problems; implementations carried out under the umbrella of a long-term perspective will ensure continued business success."[9]

GRAND STRATEGY

"If it furthers corporate goals. . . ." If long-term plans are the preferred plans and if the best of them pursue high corporate goals, then it follows that such goals are most useful when they also take a long-range view of things.

Here's where so many OA plans fall short. A certain *systems* vision may have formed in the minds of the planners, but a vision of *corporate goals* has not formed. Top management has the responsibility to determine and express corporate goals. The goals are organizational grand strategy, grander even than OA strategy.

Strategy is the big picture, as every military man and woman knows. British strategy in the American Revolution was to control the Hudson Valley and split the colonies. Tactics involve the particulars of battles fought to carry out the strategy—the ways of attacking hill positions around West Point, for example. "A good strategy with poor tactics has some chance of success," said Admiral Alfred Thayer Mahan of Spanish-American War fame, "but the greatest tactics with poor strategy has no chance of success."

Grand strategy, projecting a bigger picture than even the grandest of OA strategy, is top management's vital contribution to planning—a rare injection of "know-why" to harness the abundant and ever-popular "know-hows" of operational improvement. Corporate know-why transcends the question of whether we add value to work or cut the cost of work with OA—important as that question is. It asks the overriding question of what we're out to accomplish *as an organization.*

Britain's grand know-why in the Revolution was to keep the colonies British—not to grab the Hudson Valley. The modern organization's grand know-why is whatever high goals it sets for itself. Only top management can articulate that purpose, set the pace, and sound the urgency of the company's identity, direction, and goals.

- We're a retail chain. We import steel. We're a major processor of packaged foods. We're a school.
- This is what the economic climate looks like. This is what our market looks like. This is what our competitors are up to.
- Here's an area of uncertainty. Here are strengths we can maximize. Here's the kind of organization that we can be in five years' time, if we work at it.

It's a very big picture, very general. But at least the OA planners, whoever they may be—one person or a thirty-member committee—along with other specialized planners, whoever they may be, have a map and some bearings and can move the project forward because they now perceive where forward *is.*

Still in big-scale terms, planners can address follow-up questions. What kind of services do the company's staffs and managers need? What kind of information do they need? How urgent is the need to communicate among them? *Do* planners try to free up time or is the goal really major cuts in overhead?

Only now, with these guidelines set—or if not set, penciled in—can OA planners get on with the goal setting and tactics of their mission. Only now should planners look at the office as it is and the systems it can have, for now they have some basis for doing so. Now they can approach each department (each hill in the Hudson Valley) and deal with its special character, yet still deal with it as part of a unified purpose.

- Is there urgency to the work here (a deadline environment), or is time not a critical factor?

- Can workers wait an hour or a day for the information they need, or must they have it immediately? Even if they can wait, should they?
- Are there practical constraints on these ideal designs, be they social (meaning organizational unwillingness) or physical (the size and shape of the office) or legal?
- Are there financial constraints? Despite expected benefits, would it cost too much?

From lofty corporate strategy, we've plunged deeply into specifics. In organizations of any size, these soon add up to more specifics than even a committee can deal with effectively. Time for another OA consideration: time itself.

MAKING HASTE SLOWLY

Word processing in its short but eventful life has given new luster to old maxims. "Take it one step at a time." "Look before you leap." (Sample tasks. Analyze needs. Identify opportunities. Set priorities. Draw up timetables.) "*Make haste slowly.*" With OA the maxims apply tenfold.

In managing a process of change so extensive it can go on forever, companies have what appears to bė limitless time. But as a practical matter, they must get on with OA planning within reasonable frames of time. Planning costs money like anything else, and while open-ended time frames sound great, they can lead to procrastination and needless expense. According to Robert Kalthoff, president of Access Corp., a Cincinnati-based systems integration firm, it costs an average of $15,000 per month for a company just to plan for and agree upon an office system in the quarter-million-dollar range. Obviously, you don't want the planning effort to last any longer than it has to. Kalthoff and others advise drawing up a planning timetable and sticking to its deadlines. This involves more guesstimating, figuring out how long planning should take. OA planning may sometimes seem like nothing but guesstimating, but that's part of what office watchers mean when they say you must plan to plan.

The issue is:

OA planning. How long should it take? It can't be rushed, and only the individual management, understanding the scope and urgency of the mission, can answer for each case. However, half the veteran planners polled in the AMS Foundation study said more than a year had elapsed between the onset of OA planning and the onset of implementation. One-third of these said it took two years or more. On the other hand, 20 percent of the study group said the time between planning and implementation lasted six months or less. Again, that didn't mean all were pleased with this fact. In hindsight, many said they wished they had allowed more time.

Atlantic Richfield plans in five-year spans. In 1979, the Continental Group, which many remember as Continental Can, drew up a ten-year plan. Neither firms' plans later followed the course their creators first foresaw. The Kentucky tax collectors, on the other hand, not only planned for but implemented a creditable OA system within four months.

How much time is "enough"? The amount needed to do the job right. Let us back up and recall where we are. We have examined issues of OA approach from the laissez faire to top-down methods, concentrating on top-down as the best and most thorough, if also the slowest, of approaches. We have looked at its grand-strategy dimensions. Let's consider Continental's original *ten-year* top-down plan as we deal with this question of time, knowing the top-down approach to be slow, but knowing also that we can trim for speed, as for anything else, if need be.

The Continental plan remains an instructive example of coordinated planning across organizational, departmental, and individual user boundaries. Its principal creator, Gad Selig, outlined its four successive stages, running to the then-distant year 1989, at an Office Technology Research Group conference in 1979.

Stage 1, lasting about a year, would involve the get-ready activities of "initiation and exploration," Selig explained. The corporate know-whys launching this stage would include calls to improve administrative productivity, decentralize operating structures, and reduce information delays.

Stage 2, "migration and expansion," would see individuals progressing from their original hands-off attitude toward OA, becoming technically dependent participants of sorts. Departmentally, "uncoordinated proliferation" would prevail among WP, electronic mail, electronic filing, and other automated functions. Organizationally, unclear jurisdictions and power struggles would befuddle management control. It would be a rough three years.

Stage 3, "consolidation and formalization," would see a new planning- and control-oriented style of management replacing what Selig termed the "lax" style of the first two stages. Departmentally, new systems involving management workstations, digital networks, and voice and touch entry methods would coincide with the start of integration among applications. Among individuals, "eager participation" would focus more on what could be done, less now on how it would be done.

Stage 4, commencing around 1986, would be "maturity." Involved individuals would fully back OA. Functionally integrated departments would make major use of administrative aids for decision support. A profit-oriented management would create new information resource policies and redirect investments to capitalize on the company's "intelligent" assets.

"While it may require a whole management generation to get the full benefits [of OA], the time to build a foundation is now," Selig said at the close of his talk. "Utilize both a top-down and a bottom-up approach. And, most important, focus on human engineering."

That this plan was never carried out as written is less important here than that it was grounded in long-term strategy. It set a broad basis for later decisions and forewarned of likely problems and trends. And that is far better than having no planning basis at all.

WHO PLANS?

The story is told of a major government agency which put responsibility for OA planning not into the hands of its DP people (too technocratic) or even its top administrators (too preoccupied with other things), but into the hands of its facilities manager. That was the employee's high-sounding title; he actually functioned as a building superintendent. The man blithely went out and purchased equipment without first determining user needs or providing for training and support. The results, as you may guess, were disastrous.

A big eastern corporation, seeing wisdom in a bottom-up approach, asked its secretaries to form an OA study group. A typing pool supervisor became group leader. Unfortunately neither the leader nor anyone in the group knew enough about the company's business needs or even its principals' working needs to effectively automate operations. The group, left to its own devices and doing what it knew best, decided that OA meant centralized word processing, so that's the kind of system it implemented. WP is often the best way to get OA started, but in this case it wasn't. Certainly centralized WP was not the best choice. Support to principals suffered and they were being overcharged for services. "The group never considered end-user efficiency," said a consultant critiquing the chaos. "And when the demand for word processing *was* high, the resources just weren't there." After a difficult year, the corporation replaced the system with more responsive decentralized WP and began looking at other forms of OA technology. "But the whole experience," said an observer, "has left managers with a bad taste in their mouths concerning OA."

What's the point in these stories—that OA planning should not be entrusted to secretaries or facilities managers? No; with WP so efficient for secretarial work and so central to OA, secretaries can contribute importantly to OA development. As for the government case, it wasn't the man's title that was wrong; it was the man himself.

The point is that no individual, whoever he or she is, or even a group of similar individuals, whoever they are, is likely to come up with OA solutions as good as the solutions of a group in which all facets of an organization are represented. "No one of us," goes the maxim, "is as smart as all of us."

Despite the notion that committees beget camels, there is very little overt support in the OA community for the one-person approach to OA planning. That a lot of it goes on anyway is another issue. A "Profile of OA Policymakers" drawn from an Omni Group survey (see Chapter 1, note 1) found that in one-third of the Fortune 500 companies polled, OA authority lodged in interdepartmental committees. In another 23 percent, it rested with single departments having "OA responsibility." In only 8 percent of the firms, OA authority was placed in the hands of an office manager; in another 6 percent, OA responsibility was assumed by the president; while in another 6 percent, the user departments "did their own thing."

In small and medium-sized firms, however, proportions shift. Here, almost 30 percent of the presidents are in charge of OA policy. In one-fifth of the small firms, office managers are responsible for OA; in the same number of small firms, interdepartmental committees are in charge of it. Few small and medium-sized firms have specific OA planning departments, and even fewer allow user departments to develop OA by themselves.

Whatever really goes on, the professional manifesto of the office revolution disowns OA czars. The collective, the multidisciplined soviet, rules.

The issue is:

Who *should* plan?

- Jean Green Dorsey, deputy director of management information systems (MIS) for the city of New York: "Effective OA systems require a team approach."

- Gad Selig: "No one person or function should plan for the automated office."
- Eugene Manno, Office Management Systems Division, Honeywell, Inc.: ". . . the need [in OA] to better understand people and organizations on a holistic basis requires a multidisciplinary approach."

Dorsey believes OA committees must represent a wide range of skills and interests. The skills are by now obvious: DP, WP, database management, communications. The interests to be heard from are not always so obvious; indeed they're often overlooked:

- First- and second-line managers and supervisors whose departments will be OA targets
- Human resource personnel, labor union representatives, trainers, and other "people people"
- Upper-management administrative generalists
- Clerical and secretarial representatives
- And anyone else who deserves to be heard from

Clearly, DP people must be on the OA committee; their technical smarts are vital to anything computerized. WP managers must be on board; their office smarts and service orientation are vital to OA and are neat complements to DP's production-oriented technocracy. Administrative generalists must be on board; their organizational point of view is needed. The "people people" must be there for all the obvious human factors of OA training and reorganization. And the *people* themselves must be there—the departmental managers, supervisors, secretaries, and anyone else whom OA will directly affect—"plan*ees*" as much as plann*ers*.

Except for rare appearances, top management ideally should not be on the OA committees. Top management must give the committee its basic charter, its corporate purpose, and support, but beyond that, the personal involvement of a big boss could actually inhibit committee work.

"Is there a pattern?" Jean Dorsey asks rhetorically, answering in the negative. "The team is necessary, [but] the specifics depend on the scope of the project, the nature of the organization, and the resources available." Sometimes a core group, a kind of executive committee for the whole committee, may be necessary to monitor and evaluate the work and generally see the project through.

WHO LEADS?

It's one thing to name people to a planning committee; it's another to determine who should be in charge. A technician? A high-level executive? An in-house systems consultant? There *is* some pattern to OA thinking on this point. It holds that the *type* of person the leader is matters more than his or her *title*. What type? An all-around type. A leader—an up-front, positive-thinking, can-do type. This person will probably go on to implement whatever changes the committee decides are worth making, so he or she must also be chosen with that dicey job in mind.

Says John Connell, executive director of the Office Technology Research Group,

> No particular preparations make a candidate better or worse for the job. The leader's most important role is that of facilitator [who must] realize that the whole objective of automation is to put technology in the hands of users. His or her mission is to educate employees in the use and capabilities of the equipment.
>
> The reaction of human to machine determines an implementer's success.

Paul Oyer, president of Office Automation Society International, Washington, D.C., calls the successful implementer a jack-of-all-trades. He or she must be "an innovative manager, a technologist, an economist, a cost accountant, an organization specialist, a catalyst, a doer, a planner, an educator, and an ergonomics specialist. In addition, he or she must like people."[10] Any volunteers?

Few leaders, or course, come ready-made as such jacks-of-all-trades; Oyer suggests they make up for whatever skills they lack by hiring the people who have those skills. Two sources of expertise they might tap are OA user groups and outside consultants. Like everything else in OA, using these outsiders raises conflicting issues.

USER GROUPS

If no one of us is as smart as all of us, it follows that the more of us there are, the better. Because of such reasoning, and because in-house OA committees have practical size limits, to say nothing of experience limits, a large league of little cross-industry OA societies has grown up. Commonly called "user groups," some of them are open and publicized, while others prefer low-profile if not downright secretive stances. Whatever their social outlook, the user groups' gatherings amount to colleague-to-colleague "brain-picks" of high order.

Perhaps best known is the oft-mentioned Office Technology Research Group led by former Atlantic Richfield executive John Connell. Based in Pasadena, this group holds frequent seminars and publishes proceedings and summaries. However, dues are stiff: $2400 per quarter at this writing.

Some groups operate under the aegis of consulting firms. The Diebold Group sponsors the Diebold Automation Group. Booz, Allen operates a broad-based multiclient program. Several firms also sponsor limited, deep-probing groups of a dozen members or so. Ad hoc user groups operate informally and quietly among companies with kindred interests in many cities. They seek no publicity, avoid the media, and often don't seem interested in soliciting new members.

While it's natural to play it low-key when confidences are being traded, and while it's understandable that managers don't want OA plans announced publicly before their own staffs learn of them, some of the clandestine groups I've run into as a journalist seemed positively aghast at being discovered, as though planning for OA were some kind of disgrace.

Local chapter meetings of national associations often prove excellent sources of user experience, better sometimes than the big annual powwows of the parent bodies. Prominent among OA's chapter-based organizations are the Association of Information Systems Professionals (AISP) and the Administrative Management Society, both headquartered in Willow Grove, Pennsylvania; the Data Processing Management Association, Park Ridge, Illinois; and the Society of Office Automation Professionals, Ridgefield, Connecticut.

Newer groups with few (or no) chapters include the Office Automation Management Association, Arlington, Virginia; the Office Automation Society International, Vienna, Virginia; the International Teleconferencing Association, McLean, Virginia; and the Network Users Association, Lanham, Maryland.[11]

Anyone who is interested can attend OA briefings, seminars, and courses galore, sponsored by these and other organizations and by institutes, schools, and consultants.

CONSULTANTS

There are now so many OA consultants that they've also formed a council which meets regularly during AISP Syntopicans. Easily half of all OA newsletters are consultant promotions rather than viable products of profit-oriented publishing. Among business types that "you can't live with and can't live without," consultants figure strongly. They can be saviors; they can be charlatans.

One reformed charlatan tells of working for a boss whose rule at one of the "big eight" consulting firms was, "Always act as though you know what you're talking about." If the subject at an initial client meeting was to be industrial engineering, this source would buy a book on industrial engineering, "and next day I was an industrial engineer." If the next session was on operations research, "I'd become an overnight expert on operations research." Another consultant tells of the bait-and-switch game—baiting the client in an initial conversation by dropping the names of nationally known stars in the consulting firm and then, having landed the business, sending in junior people. "Find out where the stars live," this consultant warned. "If they must fly in by jet, you can bet their involvement will be limited."

All the same, OA consultants, by virtue of their ongoing work for numerous clients, have gathered up as much OA knowledge and experience as you're likely to come across anywhere. With OA so new, *any* experience has value: "In the land of the blind the one-eyed man is king."

Moreover, by virtue of their outside status, almost all consultants have value simply because they see things from a detached perspective. "Consultants," as one of their number put it, "can ask the dumb questions that no one else dares ask." The story is told of a government agency whose contract renewal process every four years caused a six-month workload crisis. "Why go through that," a consultant asked, "when you could stagger the workload, renewing one-fourth of the contracts each year?" "It can't be done," he was told; "there's a rule against it." The consultant checked and found that no such rule existed. The agency thereupon adopted the suggestion and saved millions of dollars—all because the consultant asked a dumb question.

OA planners tell of other instances, however, where top management becomes so beguiled by a consultant's early triumphs that they refuse to sever the connection when the projects have long been completed. "The consultants hang on like leeches," a middle manager told me, "constantly finding 'study areas' to justify their presence." Consultants sometimes do admit to selling more services than their clients need—actually being graded on that ability by their own managements. "When you hire a consultant, you're renting," one pointed out. That's fine for the short term, but if a project is long-term, you're probably better off "buying"—that is, hiring someone on a permanent basis.

It can happen that the person hired permanently is the very person first assigned temporarily. Many a young consultant brings the "hidden agenda" of a better job to the assignment, hoping to land one right there in the client's shop. Of course, top management, in hiring the consultant, might also be playing a hidden-agenda game. Management may know in advance which functions or people it wants to ax, using the consultant to build a case for these actions.

So should consultants be part of an OA planning effort? They probably should be, but with a limited contract and open agendas, and with the client alert for other agendas which may be hidden.

ISSUES OF WHERE TO START

With all this getting ready, all this planning to plan, you might wonder if real plans ever result. They do, and therein lie new issues; not again the fundamentals of goals, strategy, and timing, but the action details of turning plans into realities.

- Where to start? What to automate first? To WP or not WP, that is the question. WP makes a strong foundation, but some OA planners say other functions do as well, if not better.
- Should pilot projects be used? You get both viewpoints. If yes, where? If no, why not?

WP, as should now be clear, provides a well-traveled path, but not the only path to states of greater OA. WP's prime target, the traditional secretarial setup, is not very efficient, as we remember from Chapter 1; but neither are many other traditional office functions, such as filing, which can also make good OA foundations.

Typically, WP and automated records management both involve high start-up costs; however, both are now established commodities. Their methodologies are well worked out and early payouts can be fairly well assured. Both also aim more at cost displacement, at least initially, than at value enhancement—in WP through more efficient document production, in records automation through faster, less costly methods of filing and finding information. Ballpark estimates of WP's value are given in Chapter 2; some rules of thumb for automated files include physical compression ratios of 300 to 1 when paper documents are converted to digital form and 1500 to 1 when converted to microform. With office space costing from $8 to $25 per square foot (and even more in some places), savings on occupancy alone can be impressive, to say nothing of the savings in time because of the speed of using automated systems as compared with paper files.

For some organizations, professional time savings, better contact with colleagues, and closer collaboration on projects may be more important, initially, than cutting administative overhead. For them, any of several electronic mail or voicemail systems or another type of computer-based message system (CBMS) may be a logical starting point. Or perhaps a management information system (MIS) or a decision support system (DSS) could serve as a base.

None of these are as easy to measure, to sell, or even to understand as a more straightforward WP or file management beginning might be. But in a communication-rich environment, a CBMS has distinct advantages. Compared to other OA pathways, a CBMS is relatively inexpensive; its tools are increasingly available; and, unlike certain other executive tools, it is fairly easy to use.

An MIS which enables executives to cut through a mass of computerized data for reports tailored for them, and which plumbs external databases for useful information, can generate one of OA's highest payouts if it leads to faster, better decisions. Despite this high leverage, an MIS can require training in such things as database search strategies, either for the direct user or for an intermediary. Because the typical data service charges on the basis of connect time between user and computer, it is important to conduct a search logically and efficiently. This takes skill. The costs mount quickly if a search is done clumsily.

The DSS goes the MIS two or three steps better. Combining databases with mathematical models, statistical formatting, graphics, and various command-response routines, the DSS holds the promise of high leverage in analytical areas such as planning and finance. Depending on the system, users can play fairly powerful what-if games, see several blocks of information displayed simultaneously as "windows" on a screen, and combine or otherwise manipulate the data with relative ease. Because the system is so tailored to individual need, the decision to use a DSS almost without exception must involve the user in the planning process—a boost to its ultimate acceptance. Yet for all its sophistication, the DSS need not be overly expensive. Though this approach is heavily dependent on high-end software, the increasing ease of using this ware can ease the cost of training.

And yet for many firms, "plain-vanilla" WP still offers the safest, most pragmatic, and most credible of all OA foundations. As OA experience spreads, however, more first-time automators, especially in highly professionalized places, will confidently choose other ways to begin. And in large corporations, planners could well choose to initiate several different approaches at the same time in different parts of the organization, tying them together later.

Theoretically, of course, all OA builders can eventually integrate everything. Whatever the starting point, it has the electronic potential of reaching out to all other systems, all other peripherals. File to file, function to function, user to user, the automated office evolves.

PILOT PROJECTS

Pilot projects were once the recommended way of testing OA waters without getting all wet. You know: set up a test area, call it only a test, and find out what you're doing wrong, as well as what you're doing right, before committing to OA for real. Lately, this approach has taken some heat.

Critics say that people make too big a deal of OA, at least certain aspects of OA. For example, hasn't the viability of WP been proved by now? Do you really need another pilot study to see if it will work? "Just another consultant's make-work project," I heard one administrator grumble.

Another charge is that pilot project leaders play with stacked decks. They choose test areas, it is said, where AO success is virtually guaranteed—some computer-literate department where the people are practically begging for executive workstations. "What's that going to tell you," critics ask, "about the use of computers among the rank and file?"

An office systems vice president for a New York investment house says in one of those OA supplements, "Find out what users are rated on . . . what part of their job their pay is based on, and give them a system to help perform those duties. The application *you bring up first* sets the tone for everything else to come" (emphasis added).[11] What's this, more pilot sleight of hand, more guaranteed success? Or is it practical wisdom? Only a goal-oriented management in a particular organization can know for sure.

There's no question that a degree of success, a contagious sense of user enthusiasm, is worth going for, especially if management already knows it will automate and wants to sell OA happily to the rest of the organization. But if a pilot is to have more than surface value, it must validate OA's worth in typical work situations. Ideally, the test group should be emotionally neutral toward OA but willing to try it, and it should represent the kind of department that planners consider a good *organizational* starting point for OA.

Perhaps the most serious criticism leveled against pilot projects is that their role as *tests* is quickly forgotten. They become *models* instead—their good features as well as their bad becoming ingrained in future systems. Proponents of this view say that the limited-function nature of a pilot, if also carried forward, could actually inhibit the growth of the more comprehensive, organization-wide OA systems which newer, more versatile technology now allows.

Pilot projects are to OA what R&D is to product development. Research and development is today an accepted business practice in the prelaunch phase of any major product. In some industries, as much as 10 percent of estimated sales will be budgeted for R&D, to test and refine prototypes, gauge buyer reactions, engineer for production.

OA veteran Edward White, now a consultant based in Santa Clara, California, and a firm believer in office R&D, says pilot projects should not only be pursued; they should be well funded. Below, somewhat modified, is his budgeting formula.

Assume a $100 million company. Assume office overhead eats away 7 percent of that income—a low estimate, but let's be conservative. Assume, too (not unreasonably, White believes), that OA, at least on the cost-displacement side, can cut overhead by some 20 to 30 percent. Let's split the difference and say 25 percent. Thus, $100 million × 0.07 × 0.25 = $1,750,000, a saved amount which can be added to the bottom line of profit before taxes each year. Again to be conservative, take 5 percent of that (or $87,500), not the 10 percent of estimated sales as might be the case with a product. Consider that while the product may have a market life of five or six years, an office improvement can go on forever; however, let's hold to only a five-year "savings life" for the improvement. We thus allocate $437,000 ($87,000 × 5) as our office R&D investment.

Naturally, the above is hypothetical, and organizations may wish to test less thoroughly or, if really serious about OA, invest much more.

QUALITIES OF A GOOD PLAN

No one can prescribe the ingredients of an OA plan for a company better than the people involved. The office products industry can't, though its components and systems and aid—*some* of the ingredients—are essential. OA's traveling gurus can't, though their broader vision, their feedback from the world, can guide and encourage the real planners to stay the course.

Recently, the Diebold Group, with unconsultantlike brevity, listed the "six essential characteristics of good OA design"—utility, flexibility, economy, integration, compatibility, and manageability.

In line with that, some questions to ask are: Is the system truly useful to the user? Does it allow for future growth? Is it worth the cost? Is it comprehensive, foreseeing *office* automation in contrast to some isolated application? Are the components compatible—if not now, eventually? Is the whole thing within bounds and not overdesigned in complexity or bulk?

That's what it takes, Diebold said: a yes answer to all six questions.

Beyond that, make haste slowly, but get on with it. Get everyone's input and put a people-loving jack-of-all-trades (with czarist tendencies) in charge. Go for the long range, but don't bar the door to Topsy. Be flexible and expect surprises. *Virtus in medio stat.*

4

Issues of Workplace Impact

What the Planners Didn't Think of and What the Sales Agent Didn't Say

Sales agent: "We have thousands of satisfied users."
Translation: "This line is at the end of its product life."

Sales agent: "Our computers are upward-compatible."
Translation: "We'll be happy to sell you a bigger one as soon as you discover how limited this bargain model is."

Gotcha! Office automation is full of gotchas. Not to mention fears, fancies, and surprises.

A recent study by Booz, Allen & Hamilton ranked impediments to smooth OA operations at major user sites.[1] Biggest obstacle: complicated, unfriendly software. Second-biggest: another product problem, incompatibility—that common barrier to systems integration.

Beyond these, the obstacles were all internal: lack of top management's support, inadequate training, divided responsibilities, more planning than action. And ominously, "labor uneasiness . . . even at managerial levels."

The AMS Foundation study cited in Chapter 3 also measured the severity of problems encountered during OA planning and implementation. Here, turf battles among departments and executives led the list, with one-third of the respondents mentioning it. Next most severe was lack of equipment standards, followed by user anxieties toward OA.

In a field so volatile and competitive, it's no wonder buyers get baffled. Work-life changes are so enormous, it's no wonder workers feel threatened. Even with the most perfect planning, the sheer force of OA rattles the office china. "It's like cosmetic surgery," a manager told me. "You may know what to expect and you come out of it looking better, but it's still a shock to the system."

- For all the cases of people who love their terminals once they get used to them, initial fears of the machines are real and must be dealt with.
- For all the advanced wonders built into these systems, a greater wonder is how backward some of their training guides are. Manufacturers can pack tons of logic into a tiny chip but often seem incapable of writing a clear English sentence.
- For all the talk of compatibility, now especially IBM compatibility, it's remarkable how *in*compatible some machines' abilities are with the sales agent's representations.
- For all the focus on machines and people, it's ironic that planners so often forget *places*—the physical workplaces into which all the terminals and cables and manuals must fit. These bulky things eat space the way kids eat candy, and the results too often are the opposite of what buyers intended. They wind up with cramped, messy, *in*efficient places to work.
- For all the value of pilot projects, they often ingrain their weaknesses as well as strengths into the companywide systems which grow from them. Some office watchers consider this generally ignored issue a key obstacle to next-generation OA development.
- And for all the well-laid plans, count on the unforeseen. Perhaps the biggest surprise in OA's short life has been the upstart PC. Few early planners figured on personal computers; today many planners still don't know what to make of them. Can the freewheeling use of PCs among executives and staffs be controlled? Should it be controlled?

HIGH ANXIETY

Executive secretary Vicki Churchward was said to have almost panicked when told she would have to use a PC for updating production forecasts at Essex Group, a manufacturer of wire and cable. But a year later, according to *Business Week,* she said she'd "fight" to keep her computer.[2]

Churchward is but one of many workers affected by OA at this United Technologies subsidiary based in Fort Wayne, Indiana. What turned anxiety into enthusiasm for her and others was a separate OA resource, a company-run information center, where employees get hands-on computer training under the tutelage of nontechnical consultants. The concept isn't unique; many firms operate similar information-consultation-training facilities. It cost Essex $300,000 to equip this center and train its staff of five—"relatively inexpensive," according to the company's MIS director, F. Richard Lennon.

Not all OA users would agree. Some view the DP- or MIS-run information center as a costly and temporary solution for introducing end users to the ways of OA technology. They see the emergence of a self-sufficient *user-department*–run facility for training, problem solving, and even programming local work applications. But all that belongs to the future.

Meanwhile and more immediately, another school of OA thought takes a "throw-'em-in-the-pool-and-teach-'em-to-swim" approach, reasoning that most computer novices will overcome their fears once they reach out and touch the thing and find they *can* make it work.

The issue is:

Learning to use OA tools. How best to do it? In the earliest stages, neither heavy-handed training exercises nor throw-'em-in-the-pool techniques seem best. What smooths the way is an approach that allows people to practice with the equipment without immediately having to produce anything—familiarization without obligation. Then, early fears dispelled, you can follow up with more formalized training, actual work situations, and reviews.

A publishing company well known to me, which for years had sent editorial copy to outside typesetters, converted to an in-house typesetting system costing more than $300,000. Editors got terminals on their desks, one or two hours of instruction from the vendor's visiting trainer, and a user's manual. Mostly they were told, "Read the manual and practice. For starters, put into the system whatever you want—personal files, lists of good restaurants, girlfriends' or boyfriends' phone numbers, anything. Get used to it." Beyond that, management provided no formalized training. Behold, the system went on-line with no big fuss.

Management privately did fear that some old-timers would balk at the system, the way crusty writers are supposed to do when asked to yield their ancient Underwoods for electric Smith-Coronas. None of that happened.

The approach had drawbacks, nonetheless. Not everyone did the homework equally well. Workers would interrupt colleagues for help with some routine. The lack of supervised training led also, I think, to underuse of the system. You buy a lot of power for a third of a million dollars, yet many of the system's less obvious but no less worthwhile features remained unmentioned, unlearned, and unused.

Happily, staffers eventually took matters into their own hands. They set up a voluntary user group in which they share ideas, techniques, and recently discovered secrets of the system. They confer as needed with the system manager, who never actually fought the idea of more formalized training but seldom had time for it.

On balance, this staff was fairly lucky. The user manuals they were told to read *were* readable. Most OA-product guides start out friendly enough ("Hi! I'm the Gizmo 9; you'll find I'm fun to work with and easy to learn"), but many murk up from there. How would you like to get acquainted with a widely used operating system, CP/M, and find this on its manual's opening page.[3]

> CP/M is a monitor control program for microcomputer system development that uses floppy disks or Winchester hard disks for backup storage. Using a computer system based upon Intel's 8080 microcomputer, CP/M provides a general environment for program construction, storage, and editing, along with assembly and program checkout facilities. . . .

That's easy reading for computer literati but rather heavy for a novice. On the other hand, manuals which are too cutesy or simple get awfully boring as a learner progresses, and they're downright maddening to experienced users who want to quickly look up an instruction. A major challenge before the industry, if it truly intends to be friendly to the new students as well as the seniors, is to provide them both with instructional ware that is brief, well organized, accurate, and above all, clear.

A similar kind of cutesy-versus-klutzy annoyance needs to be straightened out in the computer systems themselves. Software that puts you through a rigmarole of keystrokes to perform a simple function is definitely klutzy. Screens that literally smile at you—like Apple's Macintosh with its smiling disk "icon" telling you everything's all right—strike many as being too cute. Such gimmicks may go over big in a dealer's showroom, as does the idea of discarding old work by dumping it into a "trash can" displayed on the screen, but won't they grow wearisome after a while? It's surprising how quickly even first-time users of almost any computer get the hang of things.

I sometimes think too much is made of the computer jitters—not that people don't get them, but that fears *can* be eased. Any big experience might cause jitters *before* the experience. And sometimes the postexperience reaction is, "Is that all there is?" That first day with a computer may never transport you to ecstasy or agony, but it could well produce the reaction "Is that all there is?"

In my work among office systems users, I've seen that reaction many times. People will sit down at a keyboard, tentatively. They'll poke at a few keys, ask what the keys are for, learn a function, and then, to their everlasting enlightenment, perform the function.

A neighbor of mine, believing I was a computer expert, told me nervously that the small local company she works for was getting a micro. They were asking her to take a computer course at a nearby community college. She was truly distressed. I asked if she'd like to see my computer. She would. I sat her in front of the dark gray box on which this book was written, a transportable Kaypro 4 (something of a klutz, but the price was right). I put on a WP program, virtually the only program I use. Magically, the top of the screen filled with an Opening Menu of commands, P, D, and others. P, the menu explained, meant print a file. D meant open a file. "Let's open a file," I suggested. "That is, let's start a new document." She typed "D". Quickly, more commands filled the upper screen, plus a question: "Name of file to edit?" "You have to give files names," I explained. She typed "Gloria" and hit the Return key. Now a Main Menu with more commands for moving the cursor, scrolling text, and deleting words and characters lit the top of the screen. The file "Gloria" was ready.

My neighbor Gloria typed several "quick-brown-fox" sentences just to have something to work with. "Let's change a 'brown' to 'silver'," I moved along. "There are several ways to do this, but the easiest is to delete the word 'brown,' then insert the word 'silver.' Notice in the delete commands of the menu this prompt: '∧T word right.' That little ∧ means 'Control.' Don't ask why; it just does. See the Control key at the left of the keyboard? Okay, with the cursor on the 'b' of 'brown,' press the Control and T keys at the same time. Why a T? I don't know, it's something you learn. But as the prompt in the menu is trying to tell you, Control-T deletes the word to the right of the cursor." Gloria did as instructed. Zap—"brown" disappeared from the screen. "Now, right there, type 'silver'." Gloria typed. All the following text moved over to accommodate the new word.

Well, we went on that way for half an hour, deleting, adding, moving, copying. Had Gloria learned to run a computer? Not really, but she had overcome her fear of the experience. She didn't say, "Is that all there is?" What she said was, "This is kind of fun."

Quite often, the best computer fear breaker is simply to let the new user play with a machine under guidance. I mean play—not practice. Practice is somewhat formal and comes later; you're *expected* to show progress. But how did all those kids get to know so much about computers, as in the film *WarGames*? By playing video games with computers at home. If they had been told to practice with them, it would have been like piano lessons. A pain!

Now, none of this means there's nothing for workers to worry about when computers, or the other aspects of OA, move in; it simply means that learning to run the machines ought not be one of them. Eyestrain from staring at that screen all day could be a worry. Sharing executive power with others because of OA integration could be a worry. Losing a job outright to automation is definitely a worry.

The reasons behind any fears may or may not be valid, but that the fears exist can't be denied. Those who would automate offices successfully must be prepared to quell and dispel emotions when they try to sell the technology. There are as many ways of approaching this as there are styles of management, from formal styles to casual. None are surefire. On the formal side, Craig Brod, psychotherapist and author of the best-selling if somewhat alarmist *Technostress,* suggests a three-phase, multistep program that companies might follow to avoid—well, technostress.[4]

Phase 1, orientation, should begin three months prior to OA operations start-up, Brod writes. Management should:

- Release bulletins or hold meetings to explain the future system and its impact
- See that users have accurate expectations of the system, and correct any unduly negative or positive notions
- Address unresolved employee issues—tension, morale, and the like

Phase 2, operation, begins as employees go on-line and extends through their learning experience. Management should:

- Promote a buddy system in which more advanced employees can aid neophytes
- Reduce workloads while users learn the system
- Make sure employees understand how the system fits into the office as a whole

- Establish channels of communication to deal with frustrations the system may cause (for example, by holding periodic user meetings)
- Provide frequent positive feedback as the workers progress

Phase 3, mastery, arrives when workers can run the machines expertly and have a sufficient base of knowledge to expand the application. At this stage, management should:

- Set up a suggestion system for new ways to apply OA
- Encourage workers to further upgrade their skills, possibly by establishing a reward system

SPACE EATERS

What technostress may do to workers, technocrowding can do to work*places.* All too often, the physical space that computers and supporting equipment will occupy in an office comes as an OA planning afterthought. Wheeling high-tech machines into a vintage facility and then wondering "Where will this stuff fit?" is hardly the best way of automating.

The issue is:

Workplace design. It involves the "living room" for systems design, the physical "envelope" in which workers and OA tools interact. Handled poorly, it can prevent the best-planned of systems from attaining productive potential.

"LANDSCAPERS"

"Wires, wires, wires!" exclaimed George Hemming, managing space planner for Eastman Kodak Co., Rochester, New York, at a symposium of the Office 'Landscape' Users Group* (OLUG) in Toronto. "We had

---

*Office landscape is a highly refined form of open office layout featuring freestanding workstations, screens, and green plants, with few or no private offices. Developed in Germany and introduced to North America around 1968, landscape permits fast and economical changes in layout. In the purest form of office landscape, offices are arranged along the main lines of work flow and communication, not by organizational rank or other artificial stricture. This fostering of communication, practitioners say, is landscape's greatest benefit, surpassing even the flexibility that allows fast, low-cost change. OLUG, the Office 'Landscape' Users Group, is based in Philadelphia.

been using 'quickie' poles to bring telephone and electric power from the ceiling down to the workstations. Then this [OA] revolution hit. Now we sometimes have to triplex the poles to manage all the cable these computers demand. That means a lot of labor when you need to move a workstation."

The space planners, facilities managers, and others to whom Hemming spoke had a tendency to see computers differently than most: not as electronic composites of memory and circuitry but as physical *objects* whose bulk could actually impede work, not enhance it.

Big boxy objects, plopped on desktops. Odd-shaped objects—modems and auxiliary disk drives, for instance—eating more space. Glass-screened objects, glowing green and throwing off reflections through which workers are expected to read. Then lesser objects by the shelfful: user manuals, diskette cases, inescapable piles of paper. And finally cables, snaking under, over, and around these things and the furniture that tries to support them.

But "things" are what OA requires. The stuff needs room. Trying to shoehorn it into conventional space, even well-planned, flexible space, causes crowding and cable-cramps and wrings out whatever flexibility there had been. OA planners too often forget that. They delve deeply into the hardware and software and see visions of people communicating. What they overlook is the environment and office envelope into which it all must fit.

Robert Sorensen, former controller at Purdue University, West Lafayette, Indiana, and another OLUG speaker, told the story of a university department which wanted to automate. To be located in Purdue's administrative services building—the first U.S. office, incidentally, designed for landscape from inception—the new system required so much electronic gear and cabling that planners were compelled to switch from freestanding partitions to so-called systems furniture, which holds cables *within* the panels.

With systems furniture, which isn't so easy to move, the cost of any later change loomed astronomically. To get what they wanted, people in the Purdue unit had to agree to "never" rearrange that section. It will "stand forever," Sorenson vowed. So Purdue said hello to OA but goodbye to flexibility, goodbye to landscape's economies of change.

Speakers agreed that systems furniture represents a trade-off: it's good on wire management but costly to rearrange. Even so, they said, it still costs less to move a heavily wired power panel than it does to knock down and rebuild a fixed wall. Fixed walls, once anathema to true-believing landscapes, are making a comeback, however, in open-plan environments. They are returning not just because a certain amount of private space has always been needed for private dealings—

confidential chats, reprimands, that kind of thing. They are being asked for, designers say, by OA end users who simply need a conference room or a spare office for nonconfidential matters like discussing a project, solving a problem, or engaging in a voice teleconference. Speakerphones, amplifying sound as they do, can easily distract colleagues a mere partition away who are not part of the conversation and are trying to do their own work.

I dwell on the OLUG symposium because of its revealing insights into OA's impact on the physical workplace. From one reporter's notebook come these additional examples:[5]

- *Greater space needs.* At Kodak headquarters, average space per worker has escalated from 140 to 160 to 175 square feet, George Hemming said, all due to computers and the stuff that goes with them. Computers may be getting smaller, he noted, but the number of accessories they require only increases.*
- *Bigger computer rooms.* Traditional computer rooms will grow larger, too, said OA developer Peter Turk, vice president of Legalware Inc., Toronto, due to so many PCs seeking to interface with mainframes.
- *Greater furniture needs.* Computers need printers, printers need tables, and so it goes. Aggravating the problem is the fact that these devices do not adapt well to building in, as the units of a stereo system at home might do. The on-off switch of the typical computer terminal is in the back, so in addition to the space it takes up on a stand or desktop, the computer must have adequate "reach-around" room as well.
- *"Plena jam."* "I don't want to unthread all those miles and miles of cable," wailed a facilities manager contemplating a remodeling of his much-computerized office. So, typically, this manager won't extricate all the useless cable from among the useful. It will simply remain in the plenum—the space between the raised flooring and the true floor of the office—and soon more cable will be added. And therein lies the problem: capacity. Automated offices run out of it fast. Even flat cable isn't always the solution it's purported to be. Facility planner Jordan Berman of Boston cited instances of flat-wire buildup under carpeting as more and more strands of it crisscross a workplace. Nor is it easily removed when it's no longer needed. It tends to inter-

*Space per office worker now costs between $3000 and $5000 annually. Thus the 14 to 25 percent increase in space cited in the Hemming example could conceivably cost an additional $420 to $1250 per worker per year.

weave like the webbing in a beach chair, so again the solution is to leave it there.

- *Lost aesthetics.* These wire-management solutions deal only with unseen cable, another OLUG speaker observed. But what about all that ugly cable you do see? Echoing the view that aesthetics may not count for everything in an office, but it does count for something ("or else why would manufacturers put all those gorgeous pictures in their brochures"), the speaker postscripted tartly: "And there's a rose in those pictures—unreal!"

THE GOOD NEWS

It would be unfair to paint a uniformly bleak picture of OA's impact on the physical office. Quite apart from its work-aiding benefits, OA in some ways has been kind to the office environment. OLUG symposium speakers reported good news such as this:

- *Lower lighting levels.* To counter the effects of glare upon terminal screens, many companies have simply turned down the levels of light in their offices. To cite again the case of much-studied Eastman Kodak, with its ratio of one terminal to every three workers, lighting is down to an average level of 70 to 80 footcandles, in contrast to the 140 to 160 footcandles of recent memory. "The place was so bright," George Hemming wisecracked, "we had to issue sun lotion." As to ceiling fixtures, the familiar 2- by 4-foot troffer, the kind spread so abundantly across office ceilings, is bad news. It not only throws fat patches of white reflection onto screens, but it also bounces more sound than proper for acoustic privacy. Certain other fixture types reduce glare well but may not be efficient as lighting systems. J. Marshall Hemphill, a manager with Armstrong World Industries, Lancaster, Pennsylvania, said work is under way to perfect a system for rating the lighting of CRT areas.
- *Lower sound levels.* Computer terminals are quiet—again the good news. The bad news is that their printers make a deafening racket. There are basically only two ways to control office noise, said acoustics consultant R. Kring Herbert of Ostergaard Associates, Caldwell, New Jersey. You can *confine* it by sequestering all noisy machines to a remote area or, if that's not convenient, by equipping them with acoustic covers. Or you can *mask* the sounds, submerging them into the background hum of a so-called white-noise system, whose speakers hang in the ceiling plenum.

- *Better furniture design.* In the wake of the space-eating computer has come the influx of space-eating furniture, but happily some of that furniture has been extremely well designed to accommodate an influx of computer-using humans. Adjustable seating, adjustable machine stands, and dozens of features like palm rests and document holders make work life easier for the person who must deal with keyboard and screen for hours. Unfortunately, many of these adjustable features go unused. The original occupant of a workstation may have had a run-through of the controls and may have set chair heights and table angles to personal liking. As newcomers inherit the space, however, nothing further is said, and thus many mismatches occur between workers and workplace, to the detriment of a management which should have been alert to the problem.
- *Ergonomic understanding.* Defining "ergonomics" as the scientific study of people and their work, M. Franz Schneider, senior principal with the New York– and Toronto-based consulting firm Humantech, urged managers to be more aware of the common bodily causes of human tiredness at work. The spine, for example, supports the human frame with less effort when curved forward, as in standing. The backward-curving shape it takes in a sitting position brings on fatigue more quickly. Thus, the lumbar support, or backrest, of a chair should push forward to induce an erect, forward-curving spinal posture. The seat pan, too, should tilt forward slightly, to aid in leaning toward the screen. The head being a fairly heavy object to support, steady head movements also cause fatigue. It's easier to move the head from side to side—to look from a screen, say, to documents on the left or right—than to move it constantly up and down. For this reason, said Schneider, U- and L-shaped workstations, fitting more naturally under the sweep of a worker's arms and suiting horizontal head movements, are gaining acceptance. Optimum eye-to-screen distance, he added, should range between 16 and 22 inches. The foremost comfort factor at a screen-and-keyboard workstation, however, according to Schneider, is adjustability of the keyboard tray. Ranking second is the height and tilt adjustment of the screen itself.
- But for buyers of workstation equipment, the overriding criterion is one question: Are people going to use it? If you're in doubt that they will, Schneider said, don't buy it.

The comfort factors of the workplace can hardly be overestimated. When office workers were asked what would it take to increase their productivity, 48 percent said a raise. But as a major Lou Harris study for Steelcase disclosed, nearly as many workers—45 percent—answered increased comfort.

"GLOBAL" ECOLOGY

In considering the office as a physical envelope, we see ecology—the interaction of different influences which, when balanced, produce a healthy environment. One facility, one office, one organic workplace; a global system.

As OA races on, opening minds and integrating functions, a similar global view of its potential tantalizes managers who have the vision to see it. And so "the global systems concept" finds a place in OA literature. And leading-edge organizations begin to move from limited OA applications to OA systems on a company-wide scale.

"Global systems are not just a matter of ergonomics for individuals," says a confidential client report of the Diebold Group,[6] "they are not just a set of unrelated tools; they are not just a series of localized cost-benefit analyses. Rather, they are a blending of these and other elements at the systems level to support the comprehensive needs of the entire organization."

What is required, globalists say, even before all OA issues are settled or the impacts are understood, is a new and larger view: one company, one system, one organic workplace, global—and planned that way from the start. Plainly, globalists are the Woodrow Wilsons, Wendell Wilkies, and Marshall McLuhans of the OA revolution.

THE PC FACTOR

Wild cards of the OA deck, personal computers are as much impacts *on* OA as *of* OA. They've been called dangerous to give to executives, a threat to old-line computer departments, a primitive product whose biggest value lies in setting the stage for what's to come. What's to come, in the view of consultant and former Diebold Group vice president Joseph Ferreira, is the true electronic workstation.

Many early OA strategies never foresaw the sudden wave of PC buying which put an estimated 3.5 million units in U.S. business and professional hands by the mid-1980s. Many current strategies, shaped with knowledge of this powerful, primitive horde of computers, do not appear to control it well, either. "We can't pretend that we know enough to control [the personal computer in business] or define how it can be used efficiently," says Ferreira.

Unlike other computers and other office systems, the PC is a discretionary tool—and therein lies its wildness. An inventory control system, for a contrasting example, is nondiscretionary. It operates under a tight set of rules which no one can change without permission. The PC, however, is employed very differently by different users. The rules depend on personal work styles.

The issue is:

PC policy. What forms should it take? For reasons of end-user productivity and corporate experience in using PCs, policies probably should lean toward permissiveness rather than toward restriction. But for equally strong reasons of governance and technological compatibility, especially as PC users demand tie-ins to company mainframes, certain bounds have to be put in place to define what is permitted.

Ferreira and others liken PC usage to telephone usage. "When we put a phone in an executive's office, we don't tell him what time to make a call or how long to stay on the phone," the veteran consultant says. "The same thing applies to personal computers."

On the other hand, few executives would use the phone if they had to pull out an instruction book every time they wanted to make a call. That is why some OA planners say it is dangerous to equip every executive with a PC: not all are ready for it. According to Ferreira, companies which do install PCs on a mass basis find only one in five executives really making use of the new machines. That one person, of course, gains valuable experience for the day when true workstations arrive.

Currently, a generalized and more liberal policy toward PCs does seem to guide OA users. Recognizing the discretionary nature of PCs, companies are willing to let employees exercise discretion in buying them—within bounds. Mindful of the need to network, soon or someday, companies confine PC choice to selected brands. Mindful of cost, they try to limit buying to a certain dollar amount, beyond which management, or perhaps the DP department, must also approve the purchase. Among major companies, 44 percent allow discretionary spending for OA equipment, according to the Omni Group study (Chapter 1, note 1). Among small companies, only 21 percent give potential users this leeway. No statistics exist to tell how many odd-fitting PCs are smuggled into companies anyway by users who want what they want when they want it, despite brand restrictions or policies which say that only DP can order computers. But the instances are legion.

There is no doubt that DP and MIS* departments suffered a loss of clout, and perhaps also mystique, once PCs entered the office. DP de-

*Another semantic situation: What some companies call their data processing (DP) department, other firms will refer to as management information systems (MIS), while still other organizations maintain both DP and MIS departments—the one handling basic mass processing of accounts and the like, the other supporting executive groups with specialized business information. For brevity in the text, the term "DP" alone is often used, but should be understood to stand for, or include, MIS where the context allows such interpretation.

partments still govern the number-crunching operations of mass administration, but their role as resources for the special data projects of others seems likely to dwindle. That role, never performed well in the eyes of typical seekers of computer services ("Oh, we can't get to that for another eighteen months," DP always seemed to tell them), will shift to the seekers themselves, who will use their own PCs. DP, if willing, able, and alert to opportunity, could become a new kind of resource, not actually doing the special-project work but providing guidance to those who do. In time, too, DP could build the new and powerful technostructure discussed in Chapter 2, into which users plug "applistructure"—PCs, software, and whatever else they need—for their own information work.

BUYING AND SELLING GAMES

Further evidence that companies have begun setting clear PC policy lies in Omni Group data on how—and where—they buy. Companies small, medium, and large prefer buying directly from the manufacturer, not from a local dealer. They value service above all else. Less than one-fourth of the surveyed firms go the dealer route.

"I deal directly with the manufacturer," said one survey subject, George Caneda of BEA Associates, a New York investment management firm. "I know that if I have trouble, I'll get help." Said another, Wiley Given, a Bank of America vice president: "When you're buying for a number of locations, you need the discount, the training, and the troubleshooting help that only the manufacturer can provide. There is no synergy among retail computer stores."

On the other hand, Jean Chastain, information center manager for Economics Laboratory, St. Paul, Minnesota, does buy PCs from retail dealers because she values having easy access to the products.

What all this suggests is corporate wising up to the ways and weaknesses of computer dealers—attributes at retail that often resemble those of fast-talking car dealers. Sure it's nice to shop, compare, kick the tires, and be free to walk out of the showroom. But it's also nice to negotiate major purchases away from the hurried atmosphere of a dealership, not having to wait your turn at a particular PC to which some brainy teenager seems always to be glued.

Manufacturers' sales reps, no less than dealer reps, have been known to stretch the truth and even sometimes to fib a little, but dealer reps, working in a diversified consumer market, probably have the greater repertoire of stratagems for "peddling that iron" to the gullible walk-in.

At least one rep admitted as much in print. Greg Gianas, responsible for corporate sales at a major retail chain, said candidly that a rep who claims some PC is "a piece of cake to use" probably doesn't actually use it and doesn't know how it works.

Gianas wrote in *Office Administration and Automation:*[7]

> Salespeople know how to compare one program or one machine to another and how to run through a cursory demonstration of some impressive capabilities on certain programs, but that's it. They are, for the most part, like used-car dealers who know how many cylinders the engine has and how to turn the ignition key, but nothing about how an internal combustion engine actually works. Put them on a quota and straight commission, and you're in for problems.

Based in Washington state, Gianas distinguishes today's business PC shopper from the average buyer of a few years ago. Then, "programmer types" prevailed—patient tinkerers who loved to work out problems into the night. Today's "master types" are upper middle class and college-educated, have lots of intellectual pride, and are anxious to get on with business; they don't want to spend a frustrating month doping out confusing manuals. They do want help, get too little of it, take home that "piece of cake" anyway, can't make it work, and fall victim to what Gianas calls the monkey's pride syndrome. "They're too embarrassed to admit that they can't use this new wonder. Like the proverbial monkeys, they keep silent and pretend everything's great. You'd be surprised," he adds, "how many PCs are bought and never used."

Gianas goes on to criticize user manuals, software demonstrations ("magic tricks"), and delays in delivery, but directs his strongest blast against that much-touted claim, compatibility. Many vendors do advertise compatibility, especially IBM compatibility.

Explaining that the question centers on how a computer formats, or magnetizes, a disk, and where on the disk it records information, our tell-all sales agent declares:

> Few "IBM compatibles" format disks like an IBM PC; thus *the disks that many IBM compatibles use will not work on an IBM PC*. Just because an 'IBM compatible' computer has the same 16-bit chip, the same operating system, and the same program availability as the IBM PC, does not mean that the disks of both machines are interchangeable . . . and many salespeople are unwilling to clear up this misunderstanding.

Some OA authorities say this makes too much of what may once have been a problem but is not so prevalent now. Moreover, with the exception of operating system compatibility, they consider media compatibility the lowest level of compatibility there is. Says consultant Malcolm Rubel of Performance Dynamics Associates, New York:

> The real issue is data interchange among different software programs. Can a specific word processing program take the output of a specific spreadsheet program and incorporate it in a document? Can a specific spreadsheet program work with financial information from the company's general ledger without having to completely re-enter the data? . . . Compatibility among IBM machines and their "clones" is really very high.

Although these authorities put it on a low level, media-converting systems to overcome the compatibility problem continue to appear, and companies are willing to pay a price for it. Firms like Fox & Geller, Integrated Technologies, Network Applications, and Software Research Corp. have created their own industry niche by offering such document interchange software. New products like the Altertext, codeveloped by Altertext, Inc. and Data General, have also begun crossing the operating systems barrier, reading disks from a MS-DOS–operated IBM PC, for example, and translating them for use on other PCs using CP/M.

One MIS vice president at ease with PCs just as they are is Vincent T. Pica of E. F. Hutton, the big Wall Street financial services firm. PCs don't *have* to connect to a mainframe or pose a security threat or challenge DP authority, he reasons. The real business of these small computers is not full-fledged computing but work of more limited scope: to be a user's personal tool for "the handling and massaging of data in an organized and accurate manner." Pica believes the PC's most cost-effective application is "bedrock word processing," but even when used not for WP but for executive support or other tasks, the machines are cost-effective. "As long as you buy from major producers you'll have no compatibility problems," he says. "The front-end software that provides the windows to other systems and the mainframe is either here or on the way."

Along with others, Pica maintains the PCs can form the backbone of an automated office. But this takes planning; monitoring; and tolerance for conditions that are new, experimental, and apt always to spring surprise.

ONGOING CHANGE

OA's fundamental impact on the workplace is change—most importantly the intended change of greater productivity, but also the side-effect change of new relationships, new ways of working, new things to learn. There's physical change: people must make adjustments to new types of ceilings, floors, lights, furniture. There's cultural change: more people will have the opportunity to work at home, "telecommuting" via terminal. All the while, there's the need for a steadying hand: management must keep the business running, keep the operations under control, keep the goals in view.

Whatever the sum of the effects—the good, the bad, personal emotions, office politics, resistance, readiness, and the rest—one sure salutary benefit accrues for the long term. Seldom recognized, it is *experience with change itself.* OA begets not change in the singular but multiple changes, a series of ongoing upsets for the rest of a worker's career. The quiet, unchanging office of Tracy-Hepburn vintage (and even, in some of its practices, nineteenth-century vintage) lingers, but it is in for shock and reform, not once but again and again.

By using PCs, office workers gain experience for the day when change will put information tools of extraordinary power in their hands. This experience prepares office workers for the new constant in their lives—more OA impact on the workplace, more technology, more new things to learn.

5

Issues within the Technology

Stars, Rings, Buses, Tokens, and Wizzy-Wigs

It's a numbing experience to walk the aisles of an office automation trade show. The mind can boggle before the feet get sore. On the left, software; on the right, hardware; up ahead, communications. Machines whir; screens fill with charts, graphs, and columns of figures. Glib pitchmen and fluent pitchwomen deliver their hourly spiels. Signs harangue in arcane tongue: "DBMS," "RS-232," "X.25," "SNA," "LAN," "CP/M," "MS-DOS," "SDLC."

Out of these many components, and with the help of many parties, comes OA. And given a reasonable arrangement of the parts and a reasonable break-in period, the resulting system will work productively. *But that's hardly the paramount issue.* Most equipment on that exhibit floor works. The issue is whether it's the proper solution for an organization's needs, the most viable combination of equipment for today's purposes and for tomorrow's growth.

This book is not offered as a manual of technology or a guide to systems design. It is an overview of the major issues managements are likely to face and the conflicts they are likely to reconcile as they begin planning for and implementing OA. Many of these issues have little to do with technology, but other issues arise from it directly. Chapters 5 and 6 examine these technical issues as nontechnically as possible, for general understanding:

- Technological issues that delimit hardware and software interaction and thus user support; that commit the user to one kind of OA architecture or another, that involve the SNAs and SDLCs and other alphabetic concepts of systems performance
- Specific issues that leave the OA planner with more choices to make beyond the strategy choices of Chapter 3: selecting this or that option in electronic mail, this or that type of network cable, and ultimately this or that vendor
- Issues that block the path to OA's ultimate dream, total systems integration—issues often more political than technical, but concerned with standards, protocols, and basically with getting machines to "talk" to other machines

At times, technology must be taken for what it is. It does what it does and can't—yet—do what is beyond the state of its art, no matter who the vendor is. But at other times, vendors stir the competitive pot, offering products based on good-if-limited technology that *they* have developed in contrast to similar products based on differing good-but-limited technology that others have developed.

For example, in computer operating systems—software that controls a computer's basic functions so it can handle application software (two of the most popular application programs being word processing and accounting)—Digital Research has CP/M, which accommodates scads of application programs; Microsoft has MS-DOS, which the IBM Personal Computer makes a virtual standard now; and AT&T has Unix, maybe the big one tomorrow.

In local area networks, Xerox has its Ethernet, Digital Equipment Co. its DECnet, Wang its WangNet, and so on through more than a hundred LANs at this writing. IBM has Systems Network Architecture (SNA), not a LAN but a powerful alternative for transmitting information within an organization.

How a planner chooses among such options *can* make a difference. These are not groups of nearly alike products with separate brand names. An Ethernet LAN differs markedly in design and technology from a so-called PABX-type LAN and even more from SNA. They are as distinctive as 33-rpm records are from laser disks, as different as videotape recorders are from videodisks. (The first pair both play music and the second pair give you rerun TV, but the technology that does the job is not the same in each pair.) LANs allow office machines to communicate with each other within a building or a cluster of nearby buildings and to reach out to more distant systems over telephone lines and other links. But the technology that does the job is not the same in each LAN.

Who cares, as long as it works? Management and OA planners have to care, because they're betting that a technology will carry them into the future—but it may not. This is a sizable bet. Automating a 1000-employee organization or even an office of 50 costs far more than setting up an entertainment nook for a family, and if OA planners bet on a fading technology, they can wind up with loads of expensive gear that can't evolve with the state of the art.

None of this means that, despite technological differences, OA systems don't also freight many "me-too" features. The OA show-goer sees scores of computers with the same Winchester-type disk drives, the same Intel or Texas Instruments microchips, the same operating systems (but remember Greg Gianas's warnings on *in*compatible compatibility).

Nor do the technological differences within a product group necessarily mean that the user is boxed in for all time by the limits of the product selected. The OA industry may get you into a technical box, but then it finds ways to get you out. Products like Integrated Technologies' Soft Switch, for example, enable different LANs to communicate by converting their signals into a common language and retranslating back. Besides, the industry for years has offered conversion software to make the tapes and disks of older, limited systems usable on newer, more powerful systems.

Nothing will—and nothing ever should—stop the industry from bringing out new and better systems that make the old obsolete. And nothing ever should stop management from at least considering the phaseout of a system even as it decides to bring the system in.

THE BIG PICTURE

Despite the seeming confusion on the trade-show floor, we can impose a certain order upon it by likening the entire OA marketplace to a neighborhood with four main product districts: hardware, software, supplies, and communications.

We can further classify the families within each district. In the hardware district are newcomer families like computers, text editors, and printers alongside old-timers like copiers, keypunches, and micrographics equipment. In the software district we find operating and applications programs alongside training aids and user manuals (these manuals are human-readable, not machine-readable, but they're "software" nonetheless). In supplies are disks, tapes, cards, and other media alongside ribbons, print wheels, toner, and other consumables. And in telecommunications are telephones and other workstation equipment; local-area, wide-area, and value-added networks; PBX and PABX* switches; cables; interface devices; and—a contentious family group since the AT&T breakup—local and long-distance telephone services.

But there's another way to get a big picture of the OA marketplace: by seeing family resemblances not so much in the products as in their purposes. Dr. Lee R. Talbert, director of Advanced Business Systems at Bell Northern Research, Ottawa, discerns two basic purposes in all OA technology: to transport information in *space* and to transport information in *time*.

Information exists in three basic forms: as *writing* (that is, text and data); as *graphics* (charts, pictures, maps, and the like); and as *spoken communication*. For each of the two basic purposes, Talbert says, equipment exists to deal with information in each of its three basic forms.

The optimum means by today's OA technology for transporting speech in space—for enabling physically separate parties to converse—is clearly the telephone. For transporting speech in time, when one of the parties can't come to the phone, some form of voicemail—even a telephone answering service—can fill the need. For transporting text and data in space, we have data links and networks—local area networks, long-distance telephone networks, whatever. For transporting the written in time, we can use electronic mail, dispatched out of one terminal now to be read on another terminal later. (Of course, for this purpose, there's always conventional mail: letters and parcels dispatched out of a mailbox now for receipt in another one later. But we're talking OA here, which implies immediacy.) For sending graphics through space, we have facsimile, communicating copiers, and communicating computers capable of running graphics software. For transporting graphics in time, Dr. Talbert reminds us of one other alternative in addition to the methods above: the durable, familiar, low-tech filing cabinet.[1]

Useful as these abstract overviews may be, the only patterns of OA technology that really matter are those that put it to work. It might seem logical to build an OA system like a house—first the foundation, then the upper structure, then the detailing. We would first set up the

---

*PBX stands for *p*rivate *b*ranch e*x*change, which many still know best as a "switchboard" even though those manual plug-in, plug-out models have all but vanished. More computerized is the PABX, or *p*rivate *a*utomated *b*ranch e*x*change.

underlying network, then add the computers and other topside devices, into which the details of software go. But that's not the way viable OA systems are built. Says an oft-heard OA dictum: "Software first, hardware later." After determining what your needs are (see Chapter 3), find the programs that can fulfill them and build everything around these all-but-intangible "details."

In Chapter 5 we follow that advice, not only because it's a sound approach but also because software is so universal. Anyone interested in OA, if only to the point of tinkering with a lap computer, deals with software. We'll cover LAN issues, too, though not everyone involved in OA will necessarily deal with a network. We'll deal with subjects on the basis of the broad OA issues they raise, letting each reader make the necessary adjustments for his or her own case.

THE SOFTWARE SURFEIT

There are now so many software products on the market that software has been developed to keep track of all the software. Sofsearch International, compiler of the Sofsearch Software Database, identified more than 32,000 packaged programs as of late 1983 and reported that software for the IBM Personal Computer alone was adding 250 titles per month. The firm's data show that application packages account for 80 percent of all software products. Nearly half address accounting, financial analysis, and financial management needs, while another quarter handle various operational and support applications—WP, for instance. By contrast, operating systems and other "utility" programs account for only 16 percent of software products.[2] But they're fundamental to the rest.

Operating systems, again, control a computer's basic functions. They ready the system to run any of the many application programs written for it. They direct data and instructions from place to place in the system. They have been likened to waiters in a restaurant: the waiter "operates" the system by placing orders with the chef, serving the diners, clearing the dishes. The *items* served—the specific entrées and wines and desserts—are, in this analogy, the various applications.

The issue is:

Which operating system should be used? In an office where individuals run their own PCs with no systems interaction among them, choice can be left to individual preference. But where OA devices are or will be linked, commonality among their operating systems matters a great deal.

Many operating systems crowd the OA marketplace, but three names stand out—CP/M, MS-DOS, and Unix. They have established themselves as virtual industry standards.

CP/M, which stands for Control Program/Microprocessor, is a veteran among such systems; it blankets the WP and PC marketplace. Literally thousands of off-the-shelf application packages have been written to work with CP/M, and plenty of equipment was built to work with it, too. Therein lies its strength.

MS-DOS, which stands for Microsoft Disk Operating System, hit the jackpot when IBM chose it for the PC and PC-XT models, two of the most popular computers ever. IBM sets de facto standards in almost everything it does, and its choice of MS-DOS was no exception. "Runs on MS-DOS" has become almost synonymous with "IBM compatible," and vast and lucrative is the IBM compatible market. It's no wonder, then, that software developers bring out MS-DOS versions of their application products first, only later going on to CP/M and other versions.

Unix is the most sophisticated system of the three. Developed by Bell Laboratories for AT&T but available through other vendors, it may be *the* operating software of the future. At least, many OA watchers think so. While CP/M and MS-DOS generally function in one-user, one-task situations, Unix aims at multitasking among many users. New "hardware-independent" versions, like Unix System V, work well with combinations of machines from different vendors and different generations. Employed in some relatively powerful minicomputers and in multifeatured executive workstations, Unix is clearly designed for high-end OA and not for just PCs or basic text editing.

So which operating system is best? Happily, rather than only falling back on "it depends," some OA analysts reply that it really may not matter. "Many vendors are planning to offer all three operating systems in their product line," reports a newsletter of the Sierra Group, a Tempe, Arizona, consulting firm.[3] Some vendors say they'll offer utilities which will allow CP/M files to be converted for MS-DOS systems and vice versa. Others, developing Unix systems, say they'll design them to run CP/M and MS-DOS as single-user subroutines under Unix, or that they will again provide conversion abilities.[4]

"IN-AND-OUT" ARCHITECTURE

Another way of classifying software is by what some call "performance architecture"—the basic way the product works. One analyst I know contrasts the "in-and-out" performance of some programs through a menu, as in the Hewlett-Packard line, with the "one-big-program" architecture of, say, an Apple Lisa.

Ins and outs can be cumbersome. To shift from spreadsheet work to, say, text editing could entail the following string of operations: close the spreadsheet program (by whatever steps the system requires); remove the spreadsheet disks from the computer; "re-boot" the system (a bit of DP jargon which simply means clearing the computer's memory for new work—and the push of one button may do it); insert a WP application disk, then another to hold the text; and run through a few preliminary routines to get set up. Returning later to the spreadsheet could mean much the same sequence in reverse—not very productive "automation."

The one-big-program structure, know also as "software integration," permits the user to switch from application to application with relative ease. A bit of spreadsheet analysis, for example, could be called up while you are processing text; indeed, the analysis may occupy its own boxed window over part of the screen and could be incorporated later with the text into a final document.

A program called Lotus 1-2-3, while mainly a spreadsheet package, pioneered integrated software. Introduced in 1982 by Lotus Development Corp., it one-upped previous spreadsheet products by being multifunctional. First-generation spreadsheet packages—heralded by VisiCorp's 1979 product, VisiCalc—were strictly one-application programs. They enabled users to enter numerical data in ledger-sheet format. They efficiently recalculated totals if the user changed any of the entered values in the array of numerical columns. But these early programs were limited, not only by a screen which failed to display at one time all of a VisiCalc's 64 columns and 254 rows, but also by menu restraints. Menus are always limited: In a Greek restaurant, you don't expect French food. That's where Lotus 1-2-3 went further. In a spreadsheet establishment, it could also serve graphics, database management, and rudimentary word processing. Later editions, like Symphony, offered much-improved WP.

Both integrated software in general and spreadsheets in particular have advanced significantly. So also has the DBMS, or database management system, a type of application designed to organize information for rapid filing and retrieval. For example, a Fox & Geller package called OZ, so named for no reason beyond catchiness, integrates data analyses, graphics, and text processing in a way that gives financial executives quick access to data from different points of view—a time-span view (of months or quarters); a line-item view (of travel expenses, for example); or an organizational-segment view (of departments or profit centers). OZ quickly slices through the hypothetical "data cube" formed by these three-view "dimensions" to extract, say, travel expenses for a particular quarter from as many as fifty departments. Moreover, the program eases the task of spreadsheet setup. Early spreadsheets were notably klutzy in their methods of placing and spacing the cells of a data array. The new ware works much faster.

A DBMS advance called Freestyle, a product of On-Line Software International, frees users from many of the constraints associated with earlier database management systems. It bypasses the need to know where data items are stored or how records are structured. Moreover, the power behind Freestyle, a proprietary technology called "Content Address Method" (CAM), allows users to "CAM" an existing file, or upgrade it for Freestyle, in a matter of minutes, with no other conversion steps needed. For arcane reasons rooted deep in the algorithmic nature of CAM, the more complex the criteria of a search, the faster Freestyle works.

All this versatility, however, takes up space in computer memory. When I first saw demonstrated some integrated software from a now-defunct company, Ovation, its presenters touched rather lightly on its size—"under 256K." It occupied something less than 256,000 bit-sized storage spaces in memory, meaning it could fit in a 256K IBM Personal Computer—but barely. There wasn't much room left to store the working data of a particular application. You would need a PC with two disk drives, and you'd have to do plenty of floppy swapping. The software might have come into its own, but never did, in the PC-XT, IBM's extended PC with a high-capacity hard disk.

Apple's first crop of Macintoshes had similar limitations. Of course, here was hardware as well as software, and the hardware had appeal: the compact size, the rollaround mouse for pointing on the screen, the high-resolution screen. And the software also had appeal: all those graphics, the typefaces, and the opportunity to "draw" right on the screen and to tone and texture the art. But all those features took up internal memory space, and there wasn't much left over, at least in early models, for storing many pages of text or graphics. To get around the problem, you had to buy an auxiliary disk drive. (Six months after the Mac's debut, versions with four times more capacity were announced.)

The lesson in all this? Software first, hardware later. Know what you want to accomplish, shop for the kind of software that will comfortably do the job, and only then fit the software to the kind of hardware that will comfortably run the software. If the hardware and software come as a package, judge them as though they were separate. Find out what other software can be run on the system. If a vendor can't *demon-*

strate that the goods meet your needs and can't prove capacity for growth, keep shopping.

MINIS AND MAINFRAMES

PCs get so much attention that a newcomer to OA might think they're the only types of computers that matter. Far from it. As PC users who've pushed these devices know, they have limits. Wouldn't it be nice, many ask, if PCs had the power of those larger systems, the minis, or those really big ones, the mainframes?

That's where much latter-day PC attention has focused: on somehow tying into and using resources of larger computers, *at* the PC keyboard. Meanwhile, in their own right, with or without such links, minis and mainframes remain impressive OA performers.

The minicomputer, no longer so mini in power and growing despite reports of its death, could be the heart of OA for a small firm; or it could be the force behind clusters of terminals in any firm. The mainframe, powerhouse if not also pilothouse, storehouse, countinghouse, and switchboard for large-scale OA in the major corporation, was once the only kind of computer around. Now these big number crunchers, no longer isolated, interact increasingly with minis and micros all along their networks.

"Micros," "minis," "mainframes"—the semantics get wonderfully tangled. Sure, the terms correspond with "small," "medium-sized," and "large," but medium-sized minis in actual terminology are also known as "small business computers"; and with new superchips coming out—Motorola's 32-bit 68020, for instance, capable of executing 8 million tasks a second—mainframe power will soon reside on the desktop, hitherto the private turf of the terminal and the micro. "Micro" may stand for "microcomputer" or for "microprocessor," that postage-stamp–sized micro*chip* within the microcomputer that endows it with logic and memory. PCs, of course, are microcomputers.

In reality, no sharp cutoffs delineate the computer categories. From a micro (like the breadbox-sized Compaq transportable) to a mini (like the washer-dryer–sized Hewlett-Packard 3000) to a mainframe (like an IBM 4341 the size of several refrigerators and freezers), there is only the gradual escalation of power, capacity, and (perhaps yet for a while) physical bulk.

Even so, OA watchers make attempts to define zones of the spectrum. Popular writer and speaker James Martin classifies computers on the basis of speed. Machines that handle up to 1 million instructions per second, he says, are micros; up to 3 million, minis; and beyond that to about 10 million, mainframes.

Other writers have used price—putting micro prices in the four- to low-five-figure range, mini prices in the mid-five- to low-six-figure range, and mainframe prices in the upper-six- to seven-figure range.

For OA planners, of course, the key issue is not what you call the things but how you use them. The question goes beyond the work they'll do and the software that helps them do it, to the "design" they form as a system. How might the micros, minis, and mainframes be configured to work together? Should all machine communications be trafficked through the mainframe? Should there *be* a mainframe, or should there simply be a network of fairly powerful minis and fairly intelligent terminals *distributing* information closer to users who need it, yet making it callable at other sites if necessary?

The issue is:

Is centralized or distributed processing more useful? This touches the related issue of network design, and we'll deal with that shortly. But the question involves a hardware issue, too, and is reminiscent of a tussle in the early days of WP. The technology used to—and in some cases, still does—pitch shared logic systems against others known as "distributed logic" or, as some vendors preferred, "shared resource" systems. A common feature to all was that several terminals worked off one central computer. In shared logic, however, the terminals were fairly "dumb," meaning that nearly all the intelligence resided in the central unit. A selling point was price: the more terminals you added, the cheaper the system became—per terminal. You could draw nice cost comparisons against pricier standalones and even against the per-terminal costs of shared resource clusters. But the shared resource systems had a selling point, too: if the central processing unit (CPU) went down, the terminals could still function—not fully, but adequately. After all, the logic of the system had been *distributed;* some of it was right there behind each user's keyboard. Not so with the shared logics; if the CPU "went down," all the operators sat idly until the computer was "up" again.

Mini- and mainframe-centered systems are more sophisticated now. Not only is computer power of some strength out there among the lesser units to which the central unit is tied, but the idea of redundancy, of backing up one vital computer with another, is no longer considered an extravagance where systems must run, come what may.

Today's faster-acting power backups also make sure systems stay up in emergencies. At Federal Express headquarters, for example, where time is money, not only do redundant computers log all the delivery orders placed though this vast courier service, but also batteries of batteries—row upon row of Exides—stand by, ready to switch on the instant any utility glitch deprives the computers of the power they need to function. The batteries will last about twenty minutes, I was told during a recent tour of the Memphis facility, enough time for fuel-powered auxiliary generators to swing into action and keep the system running indefinitely.

I saw a similar setup at the headquarters of the Automobile Club of Southern California near Los Angeles. The last thing a member wants to hear when calling the club for emergency road service is "The computer is down." Computers are apt to go down during storms, just the time road emergencies go up. To offset this, management has cushioned its mainframe with ample storage batteries and emergency power generators.

Auxiliary power systems are one of those OA features seldom mentioned in OA promotions. They're not cheap, but they're vital where interruptions of service must not be allowed.

HOOKING THEM UP

Inevitably, the relationships among micros, minis, and mainframes pose issues of linkage. The idea of PC users exchanging data with a "host"—some bigger computer, be it mainframe, mini, or even smart terminal—involves interface structures of some type. It can involve software and also hardware, like special circuit boards, which help smooth kinks from the links and make the PC behave as though it were the host.

There are six basic ways to effect these linkups, and obviously some suit certain situations better than others.

- *Terminal emulation* (TE). This most widely used of the methods employs circuit boards or software to fool the host into thinking that the PC it's dealing with is actually one of its terminals. TE is fairly easy to set up; in fact, some PCs are sold with emulation capabilities built in. TE in its various forms may allow micro users to access a host's transaction data, such as accounts payable and receivable; to plug into the larger system's financial planning programs or database management systems as aids in personal computing; or to use the mainframe at a service bureau as repository for personal files. Ordinarily, files pulled from a host through TE can only be read or printed; they can't be altered or removed from host memory. This is both a security safeguard and an occasional nuisance. To actually hold and work on a file, you need some of the following.

- *File transfer software.* Enabling PC users to do more than just look at host files—to download, edit, and store them—transfer packages also work in reverse by allowing PC users to upload. Some programs support PC-host interactions that let users zero in on specific data—sales for a particular month in a particular territory, for instance—obviating the need to cull through screens full of unwanted numbers. Some let users store the often bothersome setup routines that, by the protocols of communication, must be repeated each time unlike machines wish to speak. Even so, file transfer software is no piece of cake. Many employees balk at its command strings and other complexities. Managers worry over the security implications, even though most transfer ware allows them to draw security profiles which bar unauthorized searches. (The personnel section, for example, gets access to salary data but not to product secrets.) Moreover, to take advantage of important support software like DIF (Data Interchange Format), companies may have to reprogram existing files. DIF automatically reformats files downloaded from a host for immediate use on a micro—a nice trick. Developed as a VisiCalc file format by Software Arts of Wellesley, Massachusetts, DIF is quickly becoming a de facto industry standard. So are PC add-ons like "Irma boards" which provide for both terminal emulation and file transfers. But file transfer software isn't cheap. For example, Answer/DB, a mainframe database program, and Visianswer, which runs on PCs, are popular; both are available from Informatics General, Canoga Park, California—at a current cost of $45,000 for one Answer/DB and fifty Visianswer copies.
- *Intelligent LANs.* The intelligent LANs must be distinguished from those that function merely as conduits. The smart local area networks store the parameters and perform the setup routines required by communication protocols. They handle format conversions from host to micro. Often, all a user need do is signal the network that he or she wants to download a file from the host; the LAN then clears the way. LANs are intelligent but not geniuses; they can't transfer coded character sets to machines that use different character sets. For example, they can't transmit a common code called ASCII to a computer that understands another code, such as EBCDIC.
- *Protocol converters.* A "PC" of another kind, the protocol converter translates for one machine what a foreign machine just said. The trade sometimes calls the converters "black boxes." Protocols are

communications standards—an ironic problem being their lack of standardization.* There are dozens of different kinds. Mainframes and minis use synchronous types of standards; micros use slower asynchronous ones.† Recently, a development called "Microm Networking Protocol" (MNP) has shown promise of becoming a protocol standard—a standard standard, if you will. Released by Microcom, a Norwood, Massachusetts, software house, and made available to other manufacturers, MNP has taken off, receiving endorsements from AT&T, GTE, IBM, and Apple, among others. Why this success in a field so resistant to standards? Opinions vary, from the "technical soundness" of MNP to its "right product, right place" timing. "Whatever the reason," wrote *Computer Decisions* microsystems editor Susan Foster Bryant, "MNP-based products may alleviate one of the major headaches of remote micro-to-host communications."[5]

- *Micros with built-in linkage capabilities.* Rather than retrofitting micros with boards and software to emulate host terminals, as in the first alternative above, vendors have been introducing PCs with these capabilities built in. For example, the IBM 370/XT, in actuality a Personal Computer XT with extra boards containing two 32-bit Motorola 68000 microprocessors and an Intel 8087 math chip, enables its users to run applications slowly off an IBM 370 mainframe. A kindred product, the IBM 3270 PC, another upgraded Personal Computer, works with the firm's popular 3270, a relatively smart terminal which works in turn with a mainframe or mini, enabling users to window into multiple host applications. A number of vendors regard "3270 country" as a lucrative future environment for catering to micro-mainframe traffic of this kind. Upon introducing Hero, a PC product aimed directly at 3270 users, Mohawk Data Sci-

*I have heard that the term "protocol" as applied to telecommunications derives from its usage in diplomacy. Among governments, protocol holds that communications occur at like levels of power—minor diplomats with minor diplomats, secretaries of state with foreign ministers, presidents with heads of government. In similar fashion, telecommunications protocols deal with like levels of technology. The lowest level is the physical, such as making sure that plugs fit into receptacles. Higher levels deal with codes, transmission speeds, and loftier matters of international standards policy.

†In both synchronous and asynchronous communication, codes for the alphanumeric characters in a message consist of sets of "bits"—combinations of electrical pulses and the absence of pulses, standing for the 1s and 0s of the binary language that computers understand. In synchronous transmission, the bits (eight to a character, let's assume) just string along with nothing to mark the end of one character and the beginning of the next. The receiving unit must therefore synchronize its clock and use other checking routines to *know* when to mark off one 8-bit set from its neighbor. In asynchronous communication, two extra bits, a start bit and a stop bit, surround each character, rather like the spaces between words. Timing isn't as critical here, but the extra bits slow the rate of transmission.

ences' former president Ralph O'Brien went so far as to say that OA "will evolve from the 3270 network." What makes this environment so special? As much as anything, it's the rumors, perhaps confirmed by the time you read this, that IBM plans to develop many other products for it. In one of those policy statements on future intentions, IBM has already committed to plans for integrating many of its office systems, the 3270 prominent among them. Industry watchers say a LAN of the token-passing variety (defined in the LAN section, below) could figure importantly in these plans; and that IBM's acquisition of Rolm Corp. points to later voice and data products capable of operating on both 3270s and switched telephone networks. Meanwhile, Data General offers three micros with host communication capabilities, and Digital Equipment Corporation puts forth the MicroVAX 1, a PC with terminal emulation, file transfer, and Ethernet LAN capabilities for reaching its VAX (value added exchange) line of minis. But this was not supposed to be a catalog of product specs.

- *Timesharing services.* Always thinking of ways to give the not-yet-ready-for-prime-time user a chance to test OA, outside timesharing services offer programs that tie their powerful mainframes to individual PCs. Once connected on a time-charge basis, with perhaps also a monthly fee, micro users can upload and download files to the service and generally take advantage of other mainframe software as though it were resident within their organizations.

A future issue is:

How will OA vendors address this need for power at the work site in the next PC generation? Will users be given, say, true decision support capabilities and financial systems more sophisticated than spreadsheets so they don't have to resort to the kinds of patchwork solutions described above?

Professor Raymond Panko comments:

> If some OA vendor got smart about it, they could steal the show. As of now, it's kind of like Mr. Rogers on television. There's the Neighborhood of Make-Believe and a place called Someplace Else. Office automation's been using DP as Someplace Else. And unless vendors come up with more rational solutions, managers unfortunately will probably keep on doing what they're doing now—depending on special software and special links into Someplace Else to get corporate files downloaded from mainframe to micro, and then get that into Multimate or Lotus 1-2-3 or whatever. It's patchwork.

OFFICE LAN-SCAPE

It's obvious that a micro capable of communicating with a mainframe is more valuable than a micro standing alone. And a mainframe, valuable as it may be in itself, only increases in value when micros share its power. An expensive peripheral like a laser printer becomes more effective when several departments can send it work, sharing both the costs and benefits. Underlying all these examples is an implied ability of machines to speak with other machines. It's this ability, plus optionally the means for people to speak with people, that local area networks deliver—or promise to deliver.

Although LANs facilitate communication, they're not communication systems in the public, common-carrier sense of that term, nor do they use the public services. They have an ability to *connect* with such services for longer-distance transmission, but they are by definition private, and they are by definition local.

How local? While some can stretch to lengths of forty miles, most LANs operate within spans no greater than two or three miles. Many never leave the confines of a single building; some interconnect several nearby buildings, as in an office park.

In a LAN-wired building, terminals can be moved simply by unplugging from one wall jack and plugging in at the new one. With prices dropping—from about $4000 per terminal connection when LANs first came out to under $300 for some versions today—LANs are sometimes justified merely because they provide a cost-effective means of rewiring a building. The so-called intelligent building has become the hot new property among commercial realtors. Being developed through firms like Integrated Building Systems and Services, and Communications Systems and Services, both subsidiaries of United Technologies Building Systems Co., intelligent buildings allow small tenants to enjoy all the benefits of LANs and other OA services that larger firms have. In many cases, the building management provides all the necessary technical support to keep the networks running.

LANs vary in power, intelligence, methods of transmission, speed of transmission, kinds of cabling, cost per connection, and topology or basic layout. Some can support as many as 24,000 attached devices; others can't handle a hundred. Some can connect the wares of many vendors; others are vendor-specific. Users today can choose among more than a hundred different LANs employing more than two dozen different technologies, and hardly a week goes by without new LANs being announced.

All this choice may seem a good thing, but some OA watchers

think otherwise. LAN vendors have outsmarted themselves with this profusion, says International Resource Development Inc. (IRD), "and have thrown much of their marketplace into confusion." As a result, says the Norwalk, Connecticut, research firm, the LAN market has grown more slowly than expected. "The proliferation of different LAN techniques is also exasperating the semiconductor industry," IRD goes on, "which wastes millions of dollars attempting to follow the twists and turns in LAN standardization."[6] Rumors that standard-setting AT&T and IBM will introduce newer LANs in the mid-1980s is yet another FUD factor. FUD? Why, one of OA's many acronyms: *f*ear, *u*ncertainty, *d*elay.

By the mid-1980s, beFUDdled or not, American business had installed some 16,000 LANs, 65 percent of which supported OA. The rest were in factories or dedicated DP operations. By 1990, nearly 1.2 million LAN-connected devices will be in operation, nearly five times the number in 1985, according to Venture Development Corp. (VDC) projections.

The Omni Group's survey of service and industrial firms found that 72 percent of those in the Fortune 500 class expected to have LANs by mid-decade. Among small and medium-sized organizations, 25 and 35 percent, respectively, expected to have them. If the expectations materialize, it would represent a doubling of LANs within a two-year period for the surveyed group.

The feature most users want in LANs, to cite yet another study,[7] is "editable document interchange"—the ability to create a document on, for example, a WP device and edit on something dissimilar, like a PC. A survey of 500 major firms by Brian R. Blackmarr & Associates, Dallas, found electronic mail and message systems scoring almost as high as a desired LAN feature. Then, in order, came access to external databases, high-speed communications between computers, and "gateways" from one type of LAN to another.

Another LAN benefit is the savings possible in multivendor situations through lower expenses for data lines and modems.* LANs may also reduce the need for communication controllers.† Still, the LAN's biggest value lies in its ability to share resources, including that resource so central to all OA efforts—information.

---

*Modems, or, to be formal, *mo*dulator-*dem*odulators, are black-box devices that convert a computer's digital signals into various audible code-tones for transmission over telephone lines and then convert them back to digital form, enabling one computer to receive data sent by another, by way of a regular phone call.

†Controllers—microprocessor devices, typically—oversee communications between a CPU and peripherals.

STANDARD ARGUMENTS

First of OA's prominent LAN-lords, Xerox introduced Ethernet in December 1979. By December 1982, the IEEE—better known as "I-triple-E" and seldom referred to by its full name, the Institute of Electrical and Electronics Engineers—recognized Ethernet as a LAN standard. This delighted Xerox and dismayed others who saw Ethernet as limited. "It limits *progress,*" they argued, "to standardize a technology that will be outmoded in a few years." People opposed to standards always say that. On the other hand, users always clamor *for* standards. There'll never be peace (but stay tuned).

Years earlier, around 1975, IBM had introduced SNA (Systems Network Architecture), a communications capability first seen simply as a link between large host computers and remote terminals. Thanks to further SNA development, to IBM's aggressive marketing, and to IBM's power to impose de facto standards, SNA has evolved into a strong non-LAN alternative to Ethernet and other LANs. More than just hardware and software, which it embodies, Systems Network Architecture is an overall plan determining the way data are sent over lines. Establishing relationships with other communications protocols such as the Virtual Telecommunications Access Method (VTAM), IBM software which gives other software access to SNA networks, SNA is in effect a structure of numerous protocols.

One major development advancing SNA has been synchronous data-link control (SDLC). Simply put, SDLC controls, checks, and otherwise governs communications among devices using SNA in full-duplex mode.* Being at heart a protocol-converting program, SDLC enables devices to transmit virtually any bit sequence or character string. And it does this "transparently"—meaning that the user doesn't see (and presumably cares less to know) all the code translations and other operations that support the "simple" command to transmit.

In the very year that Ethernet became an IEEE standard, 37 percent of manufacturing companies and 47 percent of banks and insurance companies surveyed by Yankee Group, a market analysis firm, said they were, or would soon become, SNA users. "Eventually, every IBM product will be developed under the SNA umbrella," said Yankee Group, "and IBM users who migrate to new products—and new re-

---

*In duplex mode, communication can run in two directions—that is, from point A to point B or from B to A. In simplex mode, by contrast, data move in only one direction. In full duplex, points A and B can both send simultaneously. In half-duplex, data can move in only one direction at a time.

leases of old products—will find themselves, knowingly or not, SNA users."[7] Speculation now quickens over a so-called token-passing LAN code-named "Alligator" which will be part of SNA, taking up its lowest two layers. Alligator will also be able to operate outside SNA, as other IBM products do.

Meanwhile, to get *some kind* of LAN to market, IBM unveiled a local area network for its PCs in 1984. Industry speculation then held that it would take yet another two or three years for Alligator to crawl out of the labs and test sites and be renamed as a real product offering.

Ethernet and other LANs like Apple's AppleBus, Compucorp's OmegaNet, North Star's Northnet, and Wang's WangNet are what the trade calls "proprietary" networks. Each has been optimized to work with that particular vendor's line of products. This one-happy-family approach gives users greater assurance of trouble-free performance and a single source to deal with should the system unhappily "crash." For their part, vendors see proprietary LANs as protecting their installed product base.

But who wants to stick with one vendor? A fact of OA life is that offices are, and ever more want to be, multivendor environments. Most proprietary LANs permit the wares of other vendors to attach through some type of interface, but you can't count on total application and format compatibility. So enter another kind of LAN: the "open" network. Developed largely by small firms in the cable TV or the LAN component business, the opens seek to accommodate all vendors' systems. They're pricey, but they're flexible in their tolerance of many equipment combinations, and they may be the only choice in unusual situations. Companies making such LANs include Corvus, Sytek, 3M, Ungermann-Bass, and perhaps soon, your local Bell operating company. By virtue of its standard technology, which many vendors use, Ethernet rates as an open network, although it is also proprietary, speaking the LANguage of Xerox's own line of products.

Proprietary or open, LANs can be (and usually are) distinguished by other means. Sometimes they're classified by speed and market size. The largest market segment comprises the high-speed links between mainframes. Next in share of market are the medium-speed types that link together various kinds of office equipment; these are thus the LANs that figure most prominently in OA planning. This could change, however, as more of the networks which connect standalone PCs vie for planners' attention. They're slowest in speed but the fastest-growing as a market segment.

LANs are often distinguished by their shapes—topologies known as "stars," "buses," and "rings"—and sometimes by their connecting cables—coaxial or twisted-pair.

Coaxial cable, or coax, comes in two basic types: baseband and broadband. Twisted-pair wiring, the kind that for decades has connected telephones to company PBXs, may yet outshine coax. It's more familiar; it's already *there* and usable in many cases; and networks based on it could be natural extensions of digital PBX (and PABX) voice and data systems. Twisted-pair can be costly. On the other hand, it has many advocates; it has been networking voice for decades; and as telephone vendors' competition heats up in the wake of the AT&T divestiture and new features flood the market, twisted-pair wiring could be the approach must users will prefer.

The issue is:

Which LAN, which topology, to choose? This is a tough one, a source of much confusion and scant consensus within the OA community. Perhaps in time most users will opt for twisted-pair wiring, but the issue is far from settled. Until it is, perhaps the following discussion can help in making the decision.

BUSES AND TOKENS

PBXs exemplify star topology. So does a host computer driving attached terminals. So does any network in which a central device acts as a switch, shunting signals from one connected device to another, all lines radiating from a hub. If the hub develops problems, however, so do all the devices attached to it.

Buses take their name from, yes, buses—mass transit that travels a linear route back and forth. In a LAN bus, devices attach along a "highway" of coaxial cable, which carries signals from any one device to any other. The path is, in a sense, open-ended, and could be lengthened to the functional distance limits of the particular LAN. No one component controls the network, so a bus can continue working even if one of the components fails, unlike the star formation.

A "ring" is a bus whose two ends have been joined to form a loop. Being closed, the ring can't always be enlarged as easily as the open-ended bus.

A fourth topology, the "tree," sometimes grows in places where LAN-scapers see an opportunity to branch auxiliary bus lines off the main route. Despite the mixed metaphor, trees can cut installation costs by connecting various points with the least amount of cable. They are useful in combining high-capacity broadband coax (the "trunk") with single-signal baseband buses (the "branches") designed to serve low-volume users.

All four topologies can use coaxial cable, which as noted, comes in two bandwidths, baseband and broadband. All four can use optical fiber cable, although most OA watchers regard those glass strands as cables of the future. Twisted-pair wiring, because of its close ties to the PBX, which is after all a central switch, almost always takes the star shape.

In practical office terms, what does all this signify?

Let's start with baseband coax. Its LANs are oriented toward the short end of the distance scale and to short, "bursty" transmissions of data. A drawback of baseband is its narrow bandwidth—50 megahertz, or 50 million cycles per second. That may sound like a lot, but it allows only one "packet" of data to course through the system at a time. The packets do move fast, typically from 2 to 15 megabits per second, but any user sending long transmissions could tie up the system for what seems like an eternity.

To keep messages from colliding should two users transmit at the same time, both baseband and broadband LANs use collision prevention schemes of one kind or another. One kind is token passing. Another is Carrier Sense Multiple Access/Collision Detection (CSMA/CD). In a CSMA/CD network, a device trying to send a message first checks to see if the line is busy. If the line is clear, the device proceeds to send packets of data. Sometimes collisions occur anyway; then, under the guidance of a monitoring computer, the packets return to their sending devices and wait to try again. When traffic is heavy, as in any traffic jam, a message takes longer to reach its destination.

In the token-passing method, devices with data packets to send must wait until a coded electrical signal called a "token" passes by. The token moves from device to device along a predetermined path, and only the device possessing the token may transmit. In other words, you can't get on the bus without a token, regardless of whether the bus is linear, as in Datapoint's token-passing LAN, or looped, as Alligator is expected to be.

Broadband networks, in contrast to baseband, offer capacity and diversity. Their cable can be divided into 100 or more "bands" or frequencies, allowing information to stream down each band independently of the others. Since more users can communicate simultaneously, broadband fits well into environments where user demands and user density are high or where communications tend to be of long duration. Baseband may promise to carry voice, graphics, and video eventually; but broadband does it now. For companies well along in OA development or which expect to move along fast, broadband may well be the way to go, despite the higher cost. Connections run between $800 and $1200 per workstation, as against baseband's ballpark prices of $300 to $500 per connection.

"While baseband vendors promise to actively work on the ability to carry voice," warns Sierra Group consultant Marty Gruhn, "the major application for these systems today is data. Still, for many users, baseband is a logical first network, and most cost-effective. Coaxial cable is in ready supply, and connection costs are rapidly declining."[8]

For OA veterans, however, a common experience seems to be an almost insatiable need for bandwidth. Remembering what was said in Chapter 1 about OA contagion once a system has attained a certain critical mass, OA planners would be well advised to err on the side of LAN capacity if they are contemplating a system of any size. OA usage seems only to grow at this scale, not shrink.

TWISTED TRADE-OFFS

The fact that twisted-pair cabling may already *be* in an office, a holdover from the days of simple telephones, gives it a strong competitive edge over coaxial cable. There's no question that the costs and mess of installing new cable, to say nothing of the lack of adequate duct space to run all that new line (see Chapter 4), are factors for planners to weigh. According to Brian Blackmarr, the cables, connectors, and other network hardware account for 34 percent of costs for a major broadband LAN—one in the $120,000 range. Labor and associated installation costs account for another 32 percent. At these rates, it's no wonder many observers think PABX-type networks, or SNAs (another *established* base), will ultimately prevail.

But be careful. Some of that existing wire may be so old that Alexander Graham Bell would recognize it. Often it has been crammed into musty ducts and wall recesses, probably in violation of building codes. Whatever the case, much of it is poorly suited to bear the loads that OA would impose. Also, there simply may not be enough of it in a building to run both voice (telephone cable's strong suit) and data if demands for both become heavy. In addition, twisted-pair is slow, cycling for data at rates typically no higher than 9600 bits per second (bps).

For some idea of what that means, the optimum throughput for Telex transmission is only 55 bps, but for color video it leaps to a staggering 92 million bps. Broadband LANs, with their hundreds of channels for voice, video, and data, can support videoconferencing. Twisted-pair LANs can, too, but only the freeze-frame variety, not full-motion videoconferencing. “Don't assume that PBX connection is always less expensive than coaxial LAN connections,” consultant Gruhn warns.[9] “With the addition of digital PBX, connection is frequently in excess of $1000 per user.”*

What about optical fiber? It's already providing public telephone service in Chicago, where a test of fiber optics began in 1977. By 1986, Illinois Bell and other midwestern phone companies in the Ameritech service area will have installed more than 125,000 miles of optical fiber. Ameritech's six sisters, spun off from the Bell System in the AT&T divestiture, keep pace in the spread of this technology. West Germany's Bundespost—the government-run postal, telephone, and telegraph service, or PTT (most European governments operate PTTs)—is testing not only telephone service but also stereo radio and full-motion video over broadband digital systems using glass fibers.

Siemans, one of the German firms involved in the network construction, praises the excellent transmission properties of optical cable. An economical “monomode” version operates with repeaters, or signal boosters, spaced every thirty-two miles, and can transmit sixteen TV programs or some 8000 phone calls simultaneously. Conventional coax, Siemans states, would require repeaters every 0.9 miles to transmit a comparable number of calls.

A technological stumbling block to wide use of optical fiber has been the matter of splicing. Couplers do exist which connect fiber to fiber and cable to device, and advanced versions are promised which could multiplex, or transmit several broadband signals simultaneously at different wavelengths. It's not uncommon for offices under construction to prewire (or is it prefiber?) optical cable for the day when this technology comes into its own in their localities.

LANs IN THE SHORT RUN

Given the vendor battles, the user confusion, and the outlook for better things in the long run, what's the outlook for LANs in the short run? In

---

*“Digital,” as applied to telephonics, describes a type of signal different from—and newer than—the analog type long associated with voice communication. In digital transmission, a signal is divided into discrete pulses which can be patterned into tonal or binary codes (conveying data) that electronic devices understand or into tonal patterns (speech) which humans understand. The analog type transmits a continuous energy wave, rising and falling and changing wavelength in patterns *analogous* to the variations in human speech. When voice is sent digitally, the broken signal segments are “stepped” so closely that the ear scarcely detects any difference from analog. See the sections on telecommunications below and in Chapter 6.

the course of writing Chapter 5, I contacted several authorities for comment.

"LAN technology is slowly but surely being intermeshed with the PBX," confirmed Francis X. Dzubeck, widely read telecommunications consultant and president of Communication Network Architects, Inc., Washington, D.C. "Voice and data are being commingled in every new PBX announcement." The IBM-Rolm linkup not only will allow IBM to introduce a PBX, Dzubeck continued, but will also allow Rolm to enter the world of OA. "AT&T has yet to be heard in the OA area"—this was early 1984—"but it will [be], and the PBX with LAN functionality will be its primary interconnect vehicle." Full LAN-PBX integration won't happen immediately and will take years to be fully realized. "Until then," Dzubeck concluded, "the standalone LAN will continue to enjoy sales and OA acceptability."

Alan Purchase of SRI International told me,

> I see a big push for LANs all the way through the OA industry. IBM is right to select token passing. Collision-detecting buses have not been that reliable, and Ethernet has never been good for voice. Stars work well for department-oriented systems. Keep your eye on AT&T here. Once you get your departments together, then you might throw in a high-speed loop.
>
> Dual voice-data systems will be here reliably in five or ten years. In ten-plus years, look for the ability to add voice commentary directly into the image on a screen. Here, watch AT&T, GTE, and IBM. If I were planning a new building, I think I'd go for IBM cabling—it might be overkill, but in general [it is] worthwhile.

From England, the well-known publisher and OA consultant Keith Wharton wrote: "OA will favour SNA plus its higher-level document interchange protocols, and Ethernet, because both are established. If OA planners have a mainframe on site, they will likely choose SNA. If they are wiring up for the first time, then [they will choose] Ethernet. It is the de facto standard toward which most of the independents are building."

Paraphrasing former Prime Minister Harold Macmillan, Wharton opined that "communications, like politics, is the art of the possible." What has not yet proven possible, he reported, is full development of standards to support a concept known as "Open Systems Integration" (OSI). "OSI is the declared aim of many European organisations to break the IBM stranglehold, but agreeing on the specifications is proving incredibly difficult."

Also proving difficult, Wharton said, is Teletex, a public message network akin to Telex but which promises to be more sophisticated, less costly, and about thirty times faster than that venerable worldwide teletypewriter network. Alas, things aren't going as planned. "The telecommunications protocols associated with Teletex—X.21, X.25, and X.27*—were put together too fast," according to Wharton; at present only one PTT, West Germany's, pushes the concept hard. "However, they recently published a tighter X.25c specification which may work."

Back on the subject of LANs, Wharton advises:

> Plan to implement either SNA or Ethernet. While neither is ideal or makes ideal use of today's technology, they are both here and are supported by a range of suppliers.
>
> I also have a personal belief that all types of operational problems are in store for anyone who tries to network and automate an office fully. In a fully networked system, there is no carpet left under which to sweep the awkward bits. I think LANs will remain specialist single-application systems for a number of years. They will be installed for well defined systems operated by dedicated and disciplined people—the dealing rooms of banks, for instance, or among realtors in matching properties and buyers.

Consultant Marty Gruhn:

> Selection of a LAN has more to do with the kinds of applications, the volume of transmissions, and the frequency of traffic than almost any other issue. Users should move away from technical specifications and claims, and focus on the environment to be served. It may be that a "hybrid" strategy works best; quite simply that different networks will be best for different areas. Don't fall into the trap of being overwhelmed by networking as a company-wide issue; view it as a local or departmental problem to be solved. Remember that, for most, LANs can be installed as natural extensions of existing, or planned, systems.

---

*X.21 and other and "X-dot" protocols are published telecommunications standards negotiated among vendors, users, and other interested parties under the auspices of CCITT, the Consultative Committee on International Telephony and Telegraphy of the International Telecommunications Union, based in Geneva. One protocol of growing importance for OA is X.25, which lets users send data over public networks rather than over leased private lines, as is typical with SNA and certain other systems. Recently announced was X.400, a collection of standards which reportedly allows most forms of electronic mail to work together over publicly or privately owned EM networks. Like most standards (at least in the United States), protocols carry no force of law; they are simply agreements. CCITT also publishes S-, T-, and V-dot standards; the letter merely designates which of several groups within CCITT did the work.

Consultant Brian Blackmarr:

> LANs clearly need to perform more "value added" services in regard to network intelligence. The LAN of the future definitely needs to move beyond the role of . . . high volume bit carrier and provide increased automatic data conversion and interpretation services during transmission. LAN network management services must offer increased security . . . and possibly some form of encryption.

As carriers of data among co-workers, as highways for information transport, as a means for sharing resources, LANs are central to OA development. Today they tie machine to machine and speed electronic mail in many of its forms among growing numbers of users. Tomorrow, harnessing the aggregate power of many attached PCs, LANs could emulate and perhaps supplant large host computers.

Whose LANs they will be, and what kind of technology will predominate, remain clouded questions. But sufficient good technology exists already to LANscape large areas well. Happy is the office gardener whose first plantings take root, spread, and upgrade the whole estate.

INTERLUDE

It's day 2 at the OA trade show. Refreshed and more knowledgeable, let us stop briefly at some displays worth noting before we get on to bigger subjects in Chapter 6, like electronic mail and telephonics. The things discussed below are not trivial matters, but in the present context are not especially issue-prone.

Portables and Transportables

Mobility being a fact of executive life, "computers to go" allow managers, writers, and other professionals to take their work with them and remain productive, in the high-tech sense of that word. To classify these products as the industry does, the portables (sometimes called "lap computers" and lately even "knee computers"—what next?) are the smaller and lighter units, usually battery-operated but with optional power cords. *Trans*portables—heavy crates fondly dubbed "luggables"—definitely require normal AC house current of 115 to 125 volts. My own luggable weighs in at 26 pounds.

Being micros, both the portables and transportables can perform with the versatility of any garden-variety, stationary PC. They'll do spreadsheets, graphics, WP—the whole repertoire. Some have built-in modems, enabling the user to communicate with public databases or files at the office, if all the protocols are observed.

To me, the biggest difference between portables and transportables lies not in their weight but in their screens. Being battery-dependent, the portables favor liquid-crystal displays (LCDs), which draw little power. LCDs should not be confused with LEDs (light-emitting diodes), the little glowing displays typically found on hand-held calculators.

Operating on normal electric current, the transportables can light up regular CRTs—the TV-like cathode-ray tubes—which are the biggest and brightest of all the displays, and my choice. I find LCDs hard to read; their black-on-buff images don't always project well through the surrounding glare, and they fade as the battery runs down.

Screens

Any device that workers stare at for much of the business day deserves careful consideration. Ergonomic features like nonglare coatings, detachable keyboards, and tilt-and-rotate mechanisms should count every bit as much as operating capabilities like windowing or full-color display.

Flat screens and brighter LCDs may be coming, but for now the bulky CRT reigns. Some CRTs are built right into the computer, and if you don't like the screen there's not much you can do except not buy the product. Other CRTs, however, are the main ingredient of separate components known as video display terminals, or VDTs, and offer wide choice.

A key ergonomic issue centers on screen colors. The battle rages as to whether white on black, black on white, green on black, or amber on black makes the best color contrast for characters on a screen. So far, the best of the tests have been inconclusive; your liking of this background or that foreground is probably more subjective than physical. With more *full*-color screens in evidence, "Which *one* color?" could soon be an obsolete question.

More lasting will be questions of screen brightness and character resolution. These physical factors bear directly on eye fatigue. Most CRTs have brightness controls similar to those on TVs, adjustable to personal liking. What can't be so easily adjusted after purchase is resolution—the sharpness of screen images.

Characters are formed on CRTs by matrix patterns, the arrangements of individual dots into recognizable A's and B's, 1s and 2s. A person's eyes work harder to discern a 5- by 7-dot character than a 9-

by 15-dot character. The greater the concentration of dots, or pixels, the higher the resolution.

With the right software and the right CRT, pixels can be "bit-mapped." That is, they can be placed on a screen one by one, and not just as prepackaged character matrix sets. Bit mapping makes possible the display of graphs, charts, diagrams, and other graphics. Attach the proper printer, and you can render both the graphics and text as hard copy.

Mice

Not truly a product but a computer accessory, the mouse represents an alternative method for instructing a computer and finding your way on the screen. Before mice appeared, function keys (Move, Delete) and the cursor keys with their directional arrows were the more usual means for handling these operations.

A mouse is a hand-held gadget which rolls around on the desktop (or on a special pad) beside a VDT. As the mouse rolls, a pointer correspondingly moves on the screen. Veteran mouse movers say mice get you to the action point on a screen a lot faster than cursor keys. Mouse critics agree, but they point out that frequent mouse-to-keyboard hand movements slow overall performance. Recently, one company introduced a means of overcoming the problem—a footpad cursor control.

A popular misconception is that mice first appeared in the early 1980s on the Xerox executive workstation, Star. Actually, the device goes back to 1962 and Stanford Research Institute where it was invented by Dr. Douglas Englebart. The mouse has made a recent and popular appearance alongside the Apple Macintosh. As we look around now, we see mice everywhere, and the industry buzzes with other new and promised ways of instructing systems, like touch screens and voice input.

Today, rudimentary voice systems can accept spoken input delivered one letter or number at a time. Industrial machines exist that accept limited spoken commands. D. Thurston Griggs of Baltimore recently obtained patent 4,435,617 for an "automatic dictation machine" designed to convert speech into typed or visual signals on a screen.

By the 1990s, OA futurists say, practical systems recognizing common vocabularies could cut keyboard work considerably. The system will probably respond to only one set of voice patterns at a time and must learn these through several programming sessions. How well they will respond to the voice if it's muffled by a cold remains an inderesding question.

Scanners

Because they cost anywhere from $7000 to $15,000—a lot less than they used to but a lot more than a $2000 PC—most scanners fit best in high-volume WP or DP operations where they "read" printed words or data and put them directly into memory without the need for keyboarding.

Scanners aren't perfect; they misread characters (sometimes flagging them when they've made a best guess), but a WP operator can call text on-screen and clean up the errors with considerably less effort than would be needed to key in the entire document. Known more formally as optical character recognition (OCR) devices, scanners read only those typefaces they're programmed to recognize. Certain high-end scanners, however, are capable of programming themselves; given a strange typeface, they'll scan and learn a sample alphabet and then proceed to read text printed in that face.

At the low end, a number of vendors have recently introduced light-duty desktop scanners. One, looking more like a tablet and T-square than the conventional OCR box, reads a line at a time as the user manually rolls the device's "eye" along a rule held below the text to be input. The machine was introduced at the astonishing price of $450.

Printers

Printers use various ways of making images: they can do their work by *striking* a ribbon against the paper, as in a typewriter; by *spraying on* the characters, as in an ink-jet device; by *heating* special paper, as in a thermal device; or by *electrostatically charging* and toning the sheet, as in a xerographic copier.

Some printers can't quite replicate everything you see on a screen, yet others are regular WYSIWYGs ("wizzy wigs"—*w*hat *y*ou *s*ee *i*s *w*hat *y*ou *g*et). The noisy line printers associated with computers and the letter-quality daisy wheel printers associated with WP can't produce graphics. And if the daisy wheel (or the printing element in any other shape) doesn't happen to have certain characters, it may not even be able to fully reproduce text. A dot matrix printer, however, whose array of tiny image-making pins corresponds to the pixels on a CRT, may be able to reproduce whatever graphics the screen displays—even in color, with some models.

Ink-jet printers and the high-end intelligent copiers are OA's most powerful performers in print. Fast, and so fully under computer control that each sheet in a run can be imaged differently, they play important roles in mass operations like billing utility customers. Ink-jet printers literally fire tiny drops of ink onto paper in a steady stream. An electrostatic field surrounding the stream constantly alters the line of fire so that the drops "draw" characters as they hit the sheet. It all happens incredibly fast; to see it performed in slow-motion microphotography is to marvel. The computer controlling the electrostatic field reads electronic files of, say, customer accounts. It can thus generate a different invoice on each new piece of paper—a far cry from conventional printing, where the first and last sheet are imaged alike.

A comparable but newer technology, the so-called dot matrix "drop-on-demand" printer, feeds ink through several channels instead of only one; variable pressure in the channels causes the channels to eject droplets selectively, forming a character matrix. Drop-on-demand printers do not lose ink in the process, the way continuous-stream ink-jet printers do, and thus do not require costly recycling systems.

The so-called intelligent copiers, more properly known as laser printers, show similar flexibility but use electrostatically directed toner instead of flying ink to form, and then fuse, images. Some of the ink-jet printers and the laser units can, with the proper attachments and software, handle ancillary jobs like automatic sorting and collating. Neither kind is cheap, although prices keep dropping. One unit, the drop-on-demand Hewlett-Packard Thinkjet, was introduced at around $500, shattering earlier four- and five-figure price levels.

Not many years ago, ink-jet and laser devices were hulking monsters almost requiring rooms for themselves and for the supplies, worktables, and other devices that went with them. Today, many still are that way, but it's possible also to find serviceable ink-jet printers that fit comfortably on top of a desk and that have price tags proportioned accordingly.

Whatever their cost, whatever their size, these types of printers are clearly where reprographics is heading in the automated office.

Copiers

Paper proliferators but indispensable, copiers represent a sunset technology. As one- or two-copy convenience machines and even as workhorses for runs of a dozen or so, they will stay around. And thanks to optical fiber technology, they, too, diminish in size and price. Recently announced plain-paper units have broken the $1000 barrier. The Japanese now dominate the market; and the erstwhile leader of the field, Xerox, no longer stakes its future on copiers. We've just had a glimpse of that future—the intelligent, computer-linked printer. Even so, that doesn't mean Xerox won't persist as an important name in copiers. Seventy-five percent of its revenues derive from these products; Big X will remain a major factor in the market, sunset industry or not.*

Micrographics

A century-old technology whose time may not have gone because, in a way, it never fully came, micrographics seems an odd-fitting piece in the scheme of OA integration. A photographic medium in an increasingly electronic world, microfilm ties up with the computer in several indirect ways, but it never connects directly over cable the way other technologies can.

Computer-aided retrieval (CAR) systems used in micrographics follow electronic search methods not to come up with electronic files, but to physically locate hard copy. (And a microform—whether a frame in a strip of film or a card-sized *fiche*—is a tiny hard copy.)

In another link with computers, computer-output microfilm (COM) systems bypass bulky paper printouts by putting such output directly onto fiche. Users can then enlarge any data they seek on a reader device and make a copy by using a reader-printer.

The strong suit of micrographics has always been its compact form. Given the high cost of office space, it wins every time against the cost of storing a comparable number of paper documents. Electronic files are compact and they're easier to transmit, too; but they are also easier to alter. With the exception of a few specialty films, microfilm cannot be altered—and this is another strong suit for the micrographics industry. Electronic files, being so temporary and prone to erasure, are not "archival." Microfilm is.

It is, and for a long time to come it will remain, the best medium for storing all the birth certificates, death certificates, marriage

*Just how big a name Xerox is in copying can be seen and heard in the prevalent misuse of this proper noun as a synonym for *any* kind of copying: "Please xerox this." Put that kind of usage into print and you'll hear from the Xerox legal department. They'll warn that "Xerox" is a trademark, not a generic term. (If they weren't vigilant, it might become a generic term. Then, any copier *could* produce "xeroxes.") What you should say, according to the lawyers, is "Xerox copy" if you're using one of their machines, "xerographic copy" as the generic term.

licenses, and property sales of Cook County, Illinois, for the year 1912. The book on that year is closed. Archive it. For active records, however, while micrographics gamely makes a case for itself, electronics is plainly the way to go.

Optical disks could eventually play a role in this area; the disks store tiny images—not digital code, but actual laser-written images—in the grooves of what look like iridescent phonograph records. As with microfilm, these images are nonerasable, and the handful of vendors who have ventured into the market stress the archival qualities of optical disk. Moreover, they claim strong cost advantages over magnetic disks. "The marginal cost of storing the image of an 8½- by 11-inch document on magnetic disk is about $1.25," says David Seigle, marketing vice president with FileNet Corporation, an optical disk pioneer. "The cost of storing it in our optical library is just 4 cents."

One new approach to editing the uneditable—to updating images stored on film—may have surfaced in workstations like the ED, a product of Tera Corporation, which manages to combine film, paper, and computer graphics in one system. ED can call up a filmed image, digitize it electronically, permit the user to edit the digitized image, and then transmit it back to new film via COM technology or to paper. Useful in CAD (computer-aided design), the product also aims at financial institutions "and other organizations with growing inventories of film-based records."

Meanwhile, old-style COM, micrographics' biggest claim to a place in the OA neighborhood, may have put its best years behind it. 3M Co., long a COM leader, recently halted production of its Series 700 line and said it's looking at "alternative technologies," as well as COM, for meeting its customers' information storage needs.

Putting the various document retrieval methods in perspective, FileNet's Seigle concedes that for needs involving multiple thousands of retrievals per hour, as in airline reservation systems, magnetic disk is best. Where several million documents must be stored but are seldom retrieved, "microfilm is appropriate." But where several million documents are in active daily use, optical disk–based systems can retrieve any of 20 million images "in seconds."

CHOICES

What sense can you make of this deluge of products? That's the wrong question. Which of the products fulfill particular needs? That's the right question, but simplistic. You *can* draw certain conclusions in this raucous bazaar, even if they're only surface observations, such as

"Equipment is getting smaller." But below the surface, you can also draw important long-range conclusions, such as "Standards are emerging." Ethernet . . . 3270 integration . . . SNA . . . cull the exhibitors' literature stuffed in the plastic carry bags and notice how many items speak of "3270 integration" or "3270 emulation," for example.

The challenge remains to move successfully from the ways of fulfilling particular needs today to the state-of-the-art solutions tomorrow. Obsolescence can't be avoided but dead ends sometimes can. A dozen years ago, an office systems planner who looked no further than the immediate need might have opted for punched cards, and he or she would have done all right for a while. OA planners today could also opt for immediate, close-fitting solutions and do all right for a while, but the ones who will experience a less shocked future are those who also keep up with the advances in optical-fiber LANs, optical disk technology, protocols, and other OA issues whose present state may not invite commitment but whose promise it would be rash to ignore.

6

More Technology Issues

Boxcars, Skews, and Life without Mother

In 1860, the Pony Express could deliver a message from Missouri to California in the incredible time of eight days. What is generally not remembered about the legendary courier service is that it lasted only eighteen months. Electronic mail killed it. The transcontinental telegraph line, completed in October, 1861, sped messages to California in minutes. So the hell-for-leather riders entered history while copper wires and telegraph poles opened the west and solidified a nation.

Now the poles begin entering history. Along the Alaska Highway and other parts of the remote west you can see them standing uselessly, shorn of their wire by scrap dealers, stripped of glass insulators by enterprising collectors. Great satellite dish antennas have moved in, shouldering out what's left of the overland lines and pulling worlds of information from the sky into little towns like Chicken and Eagle and Snag, spread sparsely across the Yukon-to-Fairbanks wilderness.

Further north but with similar aplomb, an oil company executive inspecting field operations at icy Prudhoe Bay can pick up a telephone, tick into its keypad a Texas area code, a Houston number, and a personal code, and hear a computer recite messages waiting in a "voice mailbox" back at company headquarters. Hitting more keys in response to computerized queries, the executive can then dictate replies to any messages requiring them, hold other messages for later review, and delete the rest as having been delivered—or not worth further bother.

OPTIONS IN ELECTRONIC MAIL

Voicemail is but one of several forms of electronic mail (or EM) that today beam information instantaneously, or nearly so, among automated and not-so-automated offices. Forms of EM involve communicating text editors, communicating PCs, and other terminal-to-terminal linkages for the exchange of text (and possibly graphics). EM also involves facsimile (ideal for graphics), TWX, Telex, Teletex (if available), and, lest we forget, the telegram.

In one way or another, these systems promise to alleviate telephone tag, reduce interruptions, overcome time zone differences, and *maybe* expedite communications at less cost than users have paid up to now.

EM promises (or threatens) to reroute considerable mail right past the post office. It has had the Postal Service worried stiff. After all, 80 percent of all first-class mail is business-related. A Commission on the Postal Service reported to Congress and then-President Carter that some 17 billion messages which the Postal Service ordinarily would have carried will have been diverted to electronic communication by the mid-1980s. That amounts to a 23 percent gouge into first-class volume under normal growth projections. EM, the commission ruefully said, "portends disastrous consequences" for the Postal Service.[1]

In the courageous spirit of Herodotus* ("Neither snow nor rain nor electronic mail . . ."), the Postal Service has kept on completing its appointed rounds with offerings like E-COM (Electronic Computer-Originated Mail), an EM service for high-volume mailers, and Express Mail, an overnight parcel service akin to Emery or Federal Express. The public mail establishment has also had a breather, because private EM hasn't taken off quite the way OA watchers expected. What holds private EM back is technology (that old bugaboo, standards); cost; and a great deal of human resistance (not enough people who could use EM do, or bother to pick up their messages).

None of this deters OA industry analysts, those eternal optimists,

*The famous motto on the New York post office is from Herodotus: "Neither snow nor rain nor heat nor gloom of night can stay these couriers from the swift completion of their appointed rounds."

from predicting skyrocketing rates of growth for EM products and services. Voicemail alone, says Venture Development Corp., will experience a compound growth rate of 185 percent through 1987, when industry revenues will total $2.3 billion.[2]

Such optimism isn't necessarily misplaced. Work does proceed on standards. CCITT's long-awaited and recently announced X.400 protocols promise to let many forms of EM work together. The number of EM users does increase, though not yet to critical mass proportions, where everyone easily uses the system and confidently assumes that the person to whom a message will be sent uses EM too. (You don't wonder if a business colleague uses a telephone; you simply look up the number and dial. "Looking up the number" is another EM impediment: its directory assistance services aren't always what they could be.)

While EM costs have declined, it still takes some deep arithmetic to find out whether the cost per message really is more favorable going one route over another. For example, using dumb terminals and a remote mainframe as "post office" for interpersonal messages sounds like a plausible way of avoiding postage and other delivery costs—and the cost of a mainframe when allocated among many workers isn't that much. At, say, $200 to $400 per user, it comes to pennies per message if heavily employed for EM. However, the cost for long-distance services during message creation and retrieval—especially if messages are created and retrieved under standardized formats like IPMS, further defined below—could average several dollars per message. This is why users in well-managed offices are asked to prepare and read messages off-line. But now add the cost of terminals. At, say, $600 to $2000 each, or $200 to $800 annually over an assumed three-year life, and assuming 750 messages per user per year, a terminal's cost ranges roughly between 25 cents and $1 per message. When all the costs are taken together, at least at the high end, you can see it's not exactly postage stamps.

The issue is:

What is a user's optimum choice among the several alternatives in electronic mail? Cost per message and ease of use are obvious deciding factors. But so are the kinds and frequency of the information sent by EM, the importance of electronic speed over hand delivery, the degree of mobility among users and their need to keep in touch, and the degree of user dispersal across widely separated time zones. Because EM systems vary widely, comparisons aren't easy.

Teletypewriter Networks

Key it here, receive it there—that's the essence of the teletypewriter network.

Largest of them is Telex (Teleprinter Exchange Service), a national and international Western Union offering. Its terminals employ 1950s technology but they enjoy critical mass: they exist in nearly all large firms. The low-end units have hardly any intelligence. Smarter WP devices using the right software and interfaces, however, can send and receive over the Telex network.

Older, available, and comparable to Telex is Western Union's TWX (Teletypewriter Exchange Service). Newer, not so available, and faster than Telex is Teletex. It pushes messages at around 300 characters per second as against Telex's interminable 10.

Compared with other EM costs per message, public teletypewriter services are relatively expensive. Many firms build their own intracompany Telex- or TWX-like networks, however, and here the costs are lower.

Facsimile

When pictures count more than words (and when words need movement in bulk), facsimile, or fax, comes into its own. That executive in Prudhoe Bay, needing prompt analysis of seismic probes into likely oil deposits under the North Slope, could fax the squiggly lines to Houston and await results. An engineer needing help with a broken piece of equipment could ask for dispatch of a drawing or photo showing the item intact.

Fax technology is fairly straightforward. The sending unit scans a document and converts the blacks and whites of the image into telephone signals. The receiving unit reproduces the document by converting the signals back into the blacks and whites of a duplicate image. Most units today fall into what CCITT calls "Group 2." Analog* machines, they can send a letter-sized pageful of text in three minutes. Group 1 machines take a leisurely six minutes, and few are sold any longer. Still, they represent a large installed base. The big excitement centers on Group 3; its digital units can send that pageful of text in a minute or less over standard voice-grade phone lines.†

*See footnote, page 102.

†The qualifier "pageful *of text*" is important. To save transmission time, most fax units skip rapidly over white space and send only black "information."

More than fast, Group 3 machines are smart. Two connected units can "negotiate" delivery options before beginning to send, setting up agreeable speeds and levels of quality. Like the 2s, they can be programmed to send and receive overnight when phone rates are lowest, but the 3s add sophisticated polling and delivery options of their own. A machine "polls" by routinely contacting other devices to see if they are trying to get its attention—in this case, to see if the other machines have documents they're trying to send. Many Group 3s can communicate with 1s and 2s, but what's probably the best feature of Group 3 is the quality of its output. Image quality in fax depends on the number of dots per inch, and the 3s have twice as many as their forerunners. The dots are called "pixels"—like their CRT counterparts.

Initially high, Group 3 machine costs have fallen rapidly. The units' speed, moreover, makes them strong alternatives to TWX and Telex when sizable text blocks must be sent. Philip Wexler, an in-house consultant with Du Pont, figured out that average messages contain approximately a hundred words and thus represent easy 2-minute transmissions via TWX or Telex. "But as the number or length of messages increases, facsimile, especially Group 3 machines, becomes a lower-cost alternative."[3]

With phone rates in wild flux since the AT&T divestiture, accurate cost comparisons may not last the day, but Wexler recently guess-timated the cost of sending a 1-page, 300-word document from the U.S. east coast to the west coast and from the east coast to western Europe using various EM alternatives, as follows:

	U.S. East Coast to West Coast	*U.S. East Coast to Western Europe*
Telex	$1.89	$9.60
TWX	1.51	7.68
Group 2 Fax	1.72	3.78
Group 3 Fax	.74	1.78

When Group 3 comes, can Group 4 be far behind? No; its standards are expected soon and should be out by the time you read this. The machines will work with packet switching networks,* will offer image

*"Packets" are short, fixed-length blocks of data; when transmitted, each contains extra bits of data to govern routing, error control, security, and the address to which the packet is sent. A group of linked devices which communicates by means of packets is called a "packet switching network." Each device uses software which helps identify which packets to keep and which to send on to other devices.

quality even higher than that of the 3s, and, to no one's surprise, will be faster.

"In the longer term," writes Raymond Panko, a close observer of EM developments, "you will be able to store facsimile transmissions on computers for timed delivery, multiparty delivery, [or] retrieval at subsequent times, and even display [the images] on bit-mapped computer terminals." Fax to terminal screen; terminal screen to fax delivery—it's beginning to sound like OA integration.

Communicating PCs and Text Editors

Electronic mail was never the main task envisioned for personal computers or dedicated word processors. Personal computing and word processing were the objectives. Still, the capability to communicate was inherently there; it was promoted; and, not always without difficulty, it was used. This area was partly covered in Chapter 5, in the section titled "Hooking Them Up" involving micros, minis, and mainframes, and implied in the discussion of LANs. It also has relevance to the section titled "Message Systems," below.

Strictly as an EM option, the "my-screen-to-your-screen" type of system can range from a simple pair of matching machines that need manual dial-up for sending and manual connection for receiving to a worldwide network of dissimilar machines in which all get-ready work is handled automatically. The difficulty of setting up such networks obviously ranges from low to high. The operating cost versus other EM methods ranges from low to medium.

An abiding issue is:

Despite all talk about ability to communicate, you frequently cannot communicate across vendor lines. While text editors can understand another's text signals well enough, they often get mixed up on formats. The codes one machine reads as "center" or "indent" another reads as something else—maybe gibberish. And while many PCs have intelligent modems which can automatically dial other machines, answer the phone, or store messages if a receiving PC is turned off, the fact is *there are absolutely no EM software standards* as yet for PC-to-PC message delivery. "Each software package on the market is totally incompatible with its competitors," EM watcher Panko states flatly. "PC mail is limited to cases where only a few people need to communicate and can agree on one software package to support them."[4]

Voicemail

Ways of avoiding telephone tag, of letting phone calls get through when you're not there to take them, have been around since the day some unsung secretary first took a message for an absent boss. Telephone answering services soon made a business of taking calls after the office had closed. More recently came the telephone answering machine: "After the beep, you have thirty seconds in which to leave your message. . . ." None of these come close to the versatility and potential time and money savings of voicemail systems—those here now, those coming soon.

OA authorities maintain that nearly half of all business calls do not get through to the intended party on the first attempt. Moreover, studies show that many calls don't really involve two-way dialogue, that despite the "hellos" and "how are yous," the substantive business of the call is simply to convey information *one way*. The called party could just as well have heard it later, without being interrupted.

Three economic arguments make a strong case for voicemail:

- It saves executives' time.
- It allows mobile executives to keep in touch on the road irrespective of time zones ("Mobility is death on communications," an OA planner has said).
- If that first call "works," it does not have to be placed again, doubling and perhaps tripling the toll charges. High-salaried executives are not paid to place calls and "hold the line"; they are paid to reach decisions and help advance organizational goals, and phone calls which convey information can help them do that—but the only useful part is the *information*.

Voicemail also allows executives to be efficient in other ways. Systems which permit a "voice memo," spoken once, to be distributed to the voice mailboxes of many recipients avoid all the typing and filing, pickup and delivery of paper memos going the route of interoffice mail.

Voicemail systems aren't cheap. One of the lowest-priced, accommodating up to 100 users, costs $50,000. Larger ones, serving 1000 users and more, can run in excess of half a million dollars. And while integration is a hallmark of OA, many voicemail systems stand sadly alone.

According to a Venture Development Corp. study, PABX integration—the ability to reach voice mailboxes through the company's in-house telephone network—is the feature most users would like to see voicemail provide. As it is, without such integration, the mailboxes can only be reached through a separate phone number which the user must periodically query for messages. If that number is busy, the user must redial, and this, critics say, defeats the whole purpose of voicemail. The second-most-desired feature, VDC reports, is a message desk. This feature automatically transfers messages to an operator or secretary for relay, if the intended party has not personally checked the system in some time.

And third-most-desired is a "message waiting" indicator. Standalone systems generally can't notify you that a message is waiting. Integrated systems—and they're available—can, much as hotel phones with their winking message lights have done for years.[5]

Another voicemail problem stems from the fact that you deal, after all, with a machine. To instruct the system to hear, save, delete, reply to, or forward messages involves routines to be learned, codes to be keyed. Yes, there are "help" features, and yes, users have learned to accept other multidigit dialing routines—for example, the kind that connect them to low-cost long-distance networks. But unless most workers willingly use voicemail, it will not be perceived as reliable, nor will other forms of EM to which this practice (or is it lack of practice?) pertains.

Message Systems

The most sophisticated form of EM today, the electronic message system (EMS) performs on a grand scale what communicating PCs or text editors attempt on a limited basis (see above). Known also as an IPMS, for interpersonal message service, such a system employs software that does more than send and receive. It directly aids users by offering, for example, basic WP functions which speed message writing and spelling checkers which help catch typos. The users—who tend to be managers and other professionals, not clerical workers—typically log into the system once or twice a day, rapidly scan new messages (and old ones kept for reference), act on those needing replies, and delete those no longer needed. It's not unusual, however, for principals to delegate "terminal work" to secretaries.

The easiest but most expensive way of obtaining EMS service is through a timesharing network. Given normal connect times, this option could average a dollar a message. Most large firms therefore elect to set up an in-house EMS, writing their own software as the surest way of integrating the function within their broader OA structures.

A problem with EMS is what managers call "skewed use." Some people use the system all the time, others frequently, the rest hardly ever. The avid users take advantage of the software's many advanced features. The frequent users tend to just read incoming and type outgoing messages. The hardly-evers soon forget the operating routines and become virtual nonusers.

Panko and others blame skewed use on designers who build stereotypes based on their own usage into EMS systems; they forget that not all users are the terminal tigers they are. Commands should be tailored to accommodate the differing mindsets and experience levels of users, Panko says. Moreover, good secretarial subsystems should be built into an EMS. As it is now, a secretary asked to handle terminal work for various principals must log into each one's mailbox successively—a time-consuming chore. A subsystem would permit the secretary to log in once and access all of the principals' messages.

While any secretary given that kind of authority should be a person of utmost discretion, management still has the obligation of laying down policies on the kinds of information which may, and may not, be sent via EMS. Even so, management's biggest problem with EMS—indeed with all electronic mail—may not be security as much as the prevailing disinterest.

Management has several ways of treating this. They can establish a default system, one that perhaps sends to the mailroom printer, for conventional delivery, those messages which have lain unread for some fixed time. Or the messages might first go to the electronic mailbox of a secretary and only later to the printer if none of the parties took action. And, as confidence builder for the sender, the system could signal in some way that a message had indeed been received. Ultimately, EM success may rest less on the EM system and more on policies which state firmly that the end user or secretary *will* be responsible for timely reading of, response to, and maintenance of message files.

Implied here, and certainly possible technically, are reporting capabilities which could inform the boss whenever a subordinate has not been using the EM system well: "Jones left 17 messages unread for 04 days the week of 09/16-20." Even more probing, such "snitch systems" could actually forward to the boss "blind carbons" of the electronic messages Jones was sending to others, as a way to check on Jones's work. No vendor has offered such software yet, to my knowledge, but you can be sure some programmer already has the bugs worked out (or in). Fanciful or not, notions like these can give workers the jitters—but this is a people issue to hold for Chapter 7.

The issue is:

Electronic mail use. What's holding it up? What qualities does EM still need to function more effectively?

Default systems, say critics, may be all right for a while, but they're no lasting solution to what ails electronic mail. They make EM appear to function when, in fact, the systems are sporadically and grudgingly used.

Nothing ails EM, say others; they point to firms where contingents of satisfied users employ EM not only for intracompany messaging but also for substantial nonmessage traffic. At accounting firm Touche Ross & Co., for example, while 80 percent of the traffic on the EM network does consist of electronic memos, the remainder takes the form of reports, proposals, and other "rush documents." Tymeshare Inc. reports greater use being made of its timeshared EM network, Ontyme, for substantive nonmessage information that is part of specific processes, in contrast to informal communications. It's this type of traffic, volume EM, that will spur EM's eventual wider use, says senior analyst Audrey Mandela of the Yankee Group.

What most observers would agree on is that EM still has a way to go. Standards have emerged, but not yet enough to topple OA's electronic Tower of Babel. Costs have dropped, but not yet enough to whet the interests of the wider business community. It's in that wider perspective and easier functioning that EM's success awaits.

Professor Panko has written:[6]

> Once we have systems that work properly, the issue will be whether firms will implement them. Most firms are so well adapted to mediocre communications that it is difficult for them to envision and evaluate a corporatewide electronic mail system. . . .
>
> The real impediment to these systems, and to integrated office systems in general, is that many firms only can see the need for integration in small corporate areas, such as linking personal computers with word processing software to text-editing machines. . . . [OA planners must] convince management that a comprehensive system will be cheaper than patch-by-patch integration in the long run, or make the advantages of integration tangible instead of abstract.

What Panko is saying is not that linking PCs to text editors is wrong, but that thinking only in terms of that "patch," to which later other patches may be sewn, is limiting. Design the whole garment first; then seam it a piece at a time. Otherwise we're back to systems that grow like Topsy, not exactly a stylish dresser.

A PC-to–text editor link, or any strong EM connection, could serve as the backbone to support—with protocol conversion help—a multifunctional system, assuming the price was right. "Converters that transform Telex into facsimile output and convert internal formatting codes among different brands of text-editing machines are readily available today," Panko continues, "but their cost is substantial. If they can be shared among many devices, however, their cost per message should be attractive."

LIFE WITHOUT MOTHER

On January 1, 1984, Ma Bell was no more. That day was called the day of divestiture. Ma Bell's corporate breakup satisfied many parties who wanted it so. The Justice Department wanted it so, saying the public interest would be served, saying Ma had too long violated the antitrust laws. The big non-Bell telecommunications companies wanted it so, saying that divestiture would increase competition and that technological progress would follow. Many office administrators wanted it so, saying they'd had enough of take-it-or-leave-it dealings from so powerful a monopoly, despite choices that a slightly open marketplace was offering. And I wanted it so, having editorialized against AT&T as far back as 1976 for "lobbying like mad [to] stifle that small but invigorating amount of competition" which had stirred the industry up to that time.[7]

Why then did feelings of unease come over so many of the industry's executives, customers, and observers as the great day of divestiture approached? Was it a kind of eleventh-hour remorse at seeing Ma done in? Nothing as rueful, certainly, as the shame of a mob in movies where it shuffles away after shouting "Kill him!" and then actually doing it. Nevertheless, there was a wistful acknowledgment that Bell really had run the best telephone company in the world. Such sentiments were there, but most of the disquiet stemmed from more practical concerns: simply that the early effects of divestiture weren't working out as people had expected. What had been done in the public interest wasn't delivering sufficient relief.

It delivered confusion. A mad scramble ensued among vendors trying to secure niches in a now wide-open marketplace. Seven new holding companies, formed of Ma's many local telephone companies, came into being—each so big that it immediately leaped into *Fortune*'s famed 500. Many of them leapt also into businesses rather removed from POTS (which as everyone knows is *p*lain *o*ld *t*elephone *s*ervice). Meanwhile, one formidable AT&T entity which had a year's head start—American Bell, launched January 1, 1983—ran into trouble. It got into a legal tangle over its name and soon had to reintroduce itself as AT&T Information Systems. It had started from scratch with 110,000 employees, a $4 billion annual payroll, and U.S. District Court Judge Harold Greene, the antitrust case overseer, overseeing every move. Amazingly, in its first year AT&T Information Systems launched thirty-five products; not all were winners, but they were precursors of power to come. A year later, its act together, the company introduced its own PC and seemed ready to go head to head with IBM.

Edmund B. Fitzgerald, chairman of Northern Telecom, second-largest North American telephone equipment manufacturer, and surely no mourner at Ma's demise, charged than an ironic result of the breakup "has been to expand—not diminish—the number of regulatory forces affecting the industry."

It was against this unsettling background that planners had to limn certain essential future structures of their OA systems: their *communications* structures, which not only would connect people and machines within their automated offices but also would tie their organizations to countless contact points outside.

The issue became:

Communications strategies in the OA environment. Figuring out which kinds of telephone equipment and service are best was complex enough. Overlaying the question of whether voice should run in its own communications system separate from data or be combined as one made the problem tougher. In addition, trying to look ahead five years as rates constantly change, new long-distance services constantly appear, and the FCC, to say nothing of Judge Greene, continues to hand down pronouncements, made strategy the wildest of gambles.

The communications links discussed so far in this book have been mainly local ones or, if wider-ranging, mainly intraorganizational: local area networks, Systems Network Architecture, terminal emulators, electronic mail, and similar technologies for tying together the machines and people who, in a corporate sense, work together anyway. Corporate wide area networks (WANs as opposed to LANs) and long-distance services do that, too, while also tying the corporation to the outside world.

Let us seek such patterns of OA understanding as we can in this turbulent district. We begin with everybody's friend, the telephone, and my friend, telecommunications consultant Frank K. Griesinger of Cleveland, who knows the subject well and will help to guide us through. We will discuss commercial services first and then go on to in-house telephone systems.

PLAYING "COST PER MINUTE"

The key to assessing long-distance services, Frank Griesinger advises, is cost per minute. To know whether to stay with AT&T or to go with a competitor—and if a competitor, whether to choose a so-called resale carrier or other common carrier (or OCC)—you need to do some homework. The assignment is to find cost per minute.

Check long-distance direct-dial calls on recent phone bills. Get some feeling for average call lengths and cities frequently dialed. Calculate costs per minute for those cities. Then check competitive offerings.

Major OCCs include GTE Sprint Communications, MCI Telecommunications, Western Union, and the U.S. Transmission Division of ITT. As the term "OCC" suggests, they are *other* common carriers whose networks you reach usually by dialing locally and keying a user code, then dialing the long-distance number. The resale carriers, on the other hand, buy low-cost long-distance services from other firms—such as Wide Area Telephone Service (WATS) from AT&T—and pass savings along to users who may not themselves subscribe to such services. Many resellers operate locally, like Teletec Saving Communications, which at this writing serves three Florida counties. Lexitel Corporation of Birmingham, Alabama, began with service in seven cities but has plans to go national. Combined Network offers its Allnet service in fifty cities.

Already caveats have surfaced. Not all of AT&T's competitors necessarily serve all points. And placing a call via their lines can mean dialing as many as twenty-four digits, although this will change as access agreements in the wake of the AT&T divestiture shorten the dialing routines to as few as one digit. Actually, you don't dial; these services' computers understand the tones of push-button instruments only.

All these caveats can be overcome. It's possible to fit special devices onto rotary phones so they transmit the proper signal. It's possible to install automatic dialers to quickly place frequently called multidigit numbers. And if you have to call South Succotash, which the other carriers may bypass, it's still possible the old-fashioned way: AT&T.

In its ads, AT&T makes a proud point of its service to almost anywhere. (Why do you think it keeps running that "making-angels" commercial in which two sisters—one American, the other Canadian—stay in touch by phone? To remind expatriate Canadians to call their sisters? No, to subtly advance the argument that with some of the OCCs you can't reach Canada at all.) If you talk to AT&T's managers privately, they'll be less subtle in accusing their competitors of cream-skimming: of moving in on high-volume areas and ignoring the rest, while AT&T, utility that it is, must stick by all the Succotashes—North, South, and wherever—profitable or not.

Besides cost per minute, several niceties of performance are worth comparing:

- *Accounting data.* AT&T's WATS bills don't spell out the destinations reached by its users; they list only the duration and number of calls. Competing carriers, says Griesinger, supply not only destinations and phone numbers called but also provide as many as ninety-nine accounting codes by which management can identify users, departments, and other cost-control items.
- *Clarity of conversation.* The more that a call gets handed off from one network to another—from the caller's local service, say, to an OCC and then back to a local at the receiving end—the greater the chance of signal deterioration somewhere along the line. The only way of checking quality beforehand is to ask for user references and then get permission to place a few test calls at the user's premises.
- *Data communications.* While voice-grade lines with modem adaptors can carry data, several OCCs offer services meant for data alone. Tymnet, a big name in this field, recently expanded its high-speed, 2400 bits per second service to thirty-four U.S. cities, offering it nationwide via an 800 telephone number. Tymnet also offers 110- to 1200-bps service in more than five hundred cities. Teamed with the firm's "value-added"* 3270 terminal emulation capability, the 2400-bps service not only turns PCs into surrogate 3270s but also allows users to transmit twice as much data at the same cost per hour as the 1200-bps service. Tymnet claims IBM users, accustomed to transmitting over leased lines, can get comparable performance at much lower cost with its service.
- *Multiple circuits.* The competing carriers make a big point of having multiple circuits available. Many callers can thus use the system simultaneously, in contrast to those served by a single WATS line, who must wait for the line to clear. On the other hand, careful WATS scrutiny and a bit of patience on the part of users can often be the least costly option. "If you can queue your traffic behind one or two

*"Value added" is a term applied to networks which do more than just transmit. They add value to the communication by doing something useful in its behalf—like checking for errors, reformatting it for acceptance by different receiving devices, or, as in this case, enabling the sending PC to emulate, or behave like, an IBM 3270 terminal.

WATS lines and load eighty to a hundred hours monthly on a single line," says Griesinger, "your costs should be substantially below those of the carriers."

A related consideration, often glossed over by the OCCs and resellers, involves local message unit charges. Make a long-distance call via AT&T and that's all you pay for: the long-distance call. Make the same call via the competition and, true, you'll pay a lower rate to reach the distant city, but you'll also be paying message unit charges to your area phone company for the local connection to the long-distance carrier.

Users enjoying flat-rate local service have less to worry about—for a while. Moves are on to convert these areas to timed message unit service as soon as the regulators allow. Generally, regulators allow. While such charges typically run to 8 cents or so for the first five minutes and 3 cents for each two minutes thereafter, they increase with distance. Suburb-to-city local calls can get expensive, and thus the charges to a suburban firm whose OCC connection is city-based could wipe out the savings the carrier otherwise provides.

SMART SWITCHES

Most of the big names in telecommunications today offer some version of the terminal cum phone: the usual VDT-and-keyboard arrangement plus a built-in telephone handset, attached with its curly cord. AT&T Information Systems' workstation, the System 85; Lee Data's Series 25; Northern Telecom's SL-1 Displayphone; others—they all permit simultaneous transmission of voice and data.

Comparatively few of the industry's big names, by contrast, offer switching gear that simultaneously handles both voice and data. Voice and data integration, of course, are central to future OA. So OA planners stand at yet another issue.

The issue is:

The option in preparing for large-scale voice and data integration. Alternatives are:

- Go with good but standard PBX or PABX systems now and plan to retool in a few years when a highly integrated generation of switches becomes available.

- Go with the types of integrated switches available today, which could be costly yet might save on future conversion costs *if* they can be progressively upgraded as enhancements come along.
- Do nothing.

Pre-OA generations of telephone switches, being analog devices, can transmit data only through the use of modems. No organization serious about future OA would consider them. "The data-oriented world of the future," says Griesinger, "demands not only switches of digital architecture but also switches monitored by sophisticated microprocessors which can provide users with many value-added features."

So-called second-generation switches fill that bill partway. Driven by 16-bit processors, they are voice-oriented but have limited abilities to add on or to multiplex data. Some can also multiplex signals—that is, transmit simultaneously at different wavelengths—to other pieces of OA equipment, such as communicating text editors. They can accommodate well over 5000 "ports," or connections to individual telephones and other types of gear.

Third-generation switches, appearing now in small but growing numbers, keep pushing the state of the art to higher levels of sophistication. Controlled by fast 32-bit processors and featuring sizable memories, they add such values as LAN capabilities, format and protocol conversion, and a wide variety of data speeds. The biggest handle more than 8000 voice-data ports. Many also digitize voice signals, Griesinger explains, which makes them highly efficient.

For a while, most OA-prone firms will probably allow two or even three communication systems to coexist—one for voice use, one for computer use, and a LAN for various other OA functions. Maintaining them all is expensive, physically cumbersome, and at variance with the ease with which workers could and should communicate. Bringing in a sophisticated switch (or a LAN or another alternative) that combines the distinct networks into one manageable system is also expensive—and such a system could be superseded technologically before its expected useful life runs out.

One maker of sophisticated switching equipment cautions that any firm buying its voice-data system should have at least 1000 lines, should be prepared to keep the system for at least ten years, and should be fairly certain that the number of lines and the volume of data transmission will both grow in that time, in order to make the purchase cost-effective.

THE STANDARDS DILEMMA

For many OA users and would-be users, and for many in the OA industry, the toughest, most enduring issue of all is standards and the lack thereof. Much has been said about standards here already. Wide incompatibilities exist among OA hardware, software, and communications, and while products exist to help the others work together, the products—like customized software—are often expensive, and other solutions—like interfaces, with their clutter of cables and boxes—are often inelegant.

Seven levels of (in)compatibility have been identified for the ubiquitous PC alone:

- *Media.* Can machine A's disks run in machine B?
- *Processors.* Are two machines alike if they have functionally identical microchips, yet one is an Intel 8086 and the other an Intel 8088? No, not exactly. The two PCs will work together, yet the faster speed of the 8086 may cause problems with timing-sensitive programs.
- *Operating systems.* MS-DOS, CP/M, and the others are obviously not alike, although that's becoming less of a problem (see Chapter 5).
- *Circuit boards.* Machines are "component compatible" if each can use plug-in boards designed for the other.
- *Character and keyboard sets.* Does machine A have all the same keys as B and can it display the same characters, keystroke for keystroke?
- *Video.* Does machine A have the same "memory-mapped" interface as B, with the same locations in memory allotted for various input and output instructions for display?
- *Systems.* The highest PC compatibility level, this asks: Are the routines stored in A's read-only memory (ROM) at the same locations as those in B's, and will they produce the same end results?

While users clamor for standards to rid themselves of multilevel paralysis, others, as we've seen, argue against standards as themselves paralyzing progress. Large, successful manufacturers, moreover, while not against the idea of standards (especially if the standards are their own de facto kind) often balk at industry standards which could weaken their competitive advantages. Besides, industry standards mean sharing product specifications—may even mean giving away formulas and other trade secrets—and who would do that?

Slowly, slowly, however, vendors and others in the OA community are making an effort to arrive at industry standards. Various national and international bodies exist for this purpose. They foster development not just of OA standards but of standards of many kinds. The domestic organization closest to OA has been the American National Standards Institute (ANSI). The International Standards Organization (ISO) has led in the creation of international data communications standards. For international telephone standards, most work filters through CCITT, the Consultative Committee on International Telephony and Telegraphy, an arm of ITU, the International Telecommunications Union.

The work plods. Agendas are prepared. Agendas are distributed. Papers are read. Minutes are taken. New meetings are scheduled. Minutes are written up and mailed to the participants, along with new agendas. The participants reconvene. Papers are read. Minutes are taken. . . .

I once sat in for several go-rounds of standards committee work during WP's formative years. Like most ANSI-sponsored calls to action, it took place in open meetings. Vendors, users, consultants, just plain observers—all could attend. Not unusual either was the role played by an industry association as secretariat for the effort. In this case, the Computer and Business Equipment Manufacturers Association, a Washington, D.C.–based watchdog and lobbying group, took the attendance and the minutes and scheduled the meetings.

The first item on the agenda, before getting to the really hard stuff, was to define "word processing." That alone took two and a half months. Here were the great minds of the industry and the great names like IBM and Xerox and Lanier, piddling, diddling, and splitting hairs over draft A and version B and whether there should be a comma or a semicolon somewhere. What finally came out was a WP definition that no one liked and no one hated, and in the interests of OA historians and pursuers of trivia I present it here: "Word processing is the transformation of ideas and information through the management of procedures, equipment, and personnel."

It was a definition all right, but it wasn't yet a standard. Only one ANSI committee had agreed to it; all of ANSI had yet to act. And that might take years. I think the next item on the agenda was keyboards, but I left. And I never bothered to check whether all of ANSI had ever acted.

It was against such backgrounds that OA watchers awaited agreements like CCITT's Group 4 facsimile standard and its X.400 package for electronic mail integration.

X.400, potentially a big one for OA, specifies two services with a framework called "Open Systems Architecture" (OSA), a basic EM direction fostered jointly by CCITT and ISO. Put simply, the first service, a kind of integrated post office, delivers electronic "envelopes" from user to user without inquiring into the message content within the envelope. The second service standardizes content formats, leading to multiple standards later. For example, header fields ("To:", "From:") in EMS transmissions are standardized, aiding computer searches and retrievals. Body fields will be standardized in ways that will enable users to combine Teletex and facsimile images on the same page.

The first X.400 items "[are] only a first step to a truly comprehensive standard," says Raymond Panko, "but they can at least allow vendors to begin building compatible electronic mail systems."

USER INVOLVEMENT

Believing that users have all the votes, some observers have urged OA users to get involved personally in standards work. Some say users should even be involved in product development. Dr. Edward Currie, president of Lifeboat Associates, a major software firm, believes operating systems, for example, should be exposed to application programmers and the user public at large for review and comment during the systems' early development.

"The bottom line of these considerations," states Honeywell senior VP Stephen Jerritts, "is that the information processing industry as a whole needs to establish a better agreement on how to proceed in developing U.S. standards and in clarifying how it can participate with international organizations in developing world standards."

This is particularly important, Jerritts adds, in a post-AT&T environment, with its increased potential for de facto standards. "It is also very important that we achieve a better understanding of the ground rules as we move toward the introduction of new applications, such as videotex technology—which is happening now in Europe and is clearly going to happen in the next few years in the United States."

Videotex, a capability associated more with fields other than OA, permits users to call various kinds of public information—stocks, sports, weather—onto home or office TV screens. Pioneered in Europe, videotex might allow a user to browse through electronic "yellow pages," summon the restaurant category, and, by keying the proper instructions on a telephone keypad, make a reservation and see its acceptance confirmed.

When the many vested interests of this increasingly electronic world have agreed upon formulas to coordinate the manifold information systems of internal business operations, as well as those of external entities like the New York and American Stock Exchanges, the National League and the American League, the Mobil Travel Guide, Visa, MasterCard, and American Express—true standardization for OA and HA (household automation) will at last have arrived.

By then we shall have also paid off the national debt and achieved perpetual motion.

7

People Issues

Office Unions, Health Worries, and the Work-at-Home Trend

In 1982, protesters outside the third Office Automation Conference (OAC) in San Francisco distributed leaflets containing caustic if spurious conference "agendas." A model wearing a papier-mâché computer terminal over her head as a kind of mechanical yoke became a momentary event on the evening news.

In the name of a fictional First Church of Information, Scientist, the leaflets said:

> Join your peers in pretending that somehow human life will be improved by the unceasing growth of data creation, storage and retrieval . . . and join them in working to obscure the fact that what little individual freedom there is . . . is being quickly eroded by the expansion of modern communications.
>
> Learn how to implement schemes to garb this restructuring of the office work process in the guise of "Quality of Work-Life" and "job enrichment." . . .
>
> [Learn how] thinking, feeling human beings [can] be molded to do routine tasks over and over in front of TV screens.

Who were these people? San Francisco pranksters? Serious social critics warning of an automated Brave New World? The leaflets leaned heavily on words like "proletarianization"; were these people some kind of radical extremists?

OAC attendees hardly cared. They gave the demonstrators a bemused glance, then rushed into Moscone Center to attend the sessions.

The Nasty Secretary Liberation Front (as the group officially introduced itself) may have done no more than provide one of those silly sidelights which accompany any convention. Or, despite the brash dramatics, the protesters may well have touched raw issues concerning people which office automation has either raised or intensified.

Anxieties over OA's unwholesome effects persist in the workplace. The fears may be exaggerated, even false, but management would be foolish to ignore them. Fears create their own unwholesome effects. Fears that the work is dehumanizing and that much OA equipment, especially those CRT screens, may be hazardous to health can lead to lost work time, worker resistance, new laws—and unions. When it comes to people issues, heated perceptions can sway more arguments than cold facts.

But are these only perceptions? *Are* the screens a health hazard? Does OA, as the women workers' movement alleges, increase sexual discrimination in the workplace? And are those other trends which OA fosters—more flexible working hours, the ability to work at home—really worker benefits? Are they, as some charge, management's little trick to keep workers scattered and thus less able to organize?

It is charged that OA will turn workers into robots, erode their skills, and reduce social interactions. There *is* evidence that the labor-saving qualities of word processing erode spelling abilities. "After I learned to use the computer, I got careless about spelling because I knew the system would highlight errors for me," a WP operator told me candidly. "Then when I had to do other assignments on a typewriter, I had trouble readjusting to the need to spell correctly."

And there is evidence of "de-skilling" in the art of business courtesies. Customers are put through curt routines by telephone attendants following computerized question lists. Callers are told to hold on or are transferred abruptly. Hit a button, lose your tact.

Certainly there's evidence of the fears a high-tech world can engender: not only the fears of learning to use computers and other OA tools, but fears of being controlled by them. Who governs whom? Does the computer obey the worker or does the worker react to whatever the machine displays?

And fears of the screens themselves—again, not just radiation concerns, but anxieties over demonstrable physical discomfitures like backache, muscular stress, and eyestrain.

Industry executives like Mitch Mitchell, co-founder of the software supply firm Micro D, say workers will gradually lose their fears of high-tech environments. As more and more 7-year-olds who were exposed to home computers become 20-year-olds, and as OA manufacturers increasingly "humanize" their products, these present fears will ebb, Mitchell says.

And yet when the Communications Workers of America (CWA) explored similar themes in "Future Work," a public affairs TV program, the union claimed the show pulled far greater viewer response than any previous CWA broadcast. Among other things, the show argued that virtually no one's present work skills will apply to their jobs for longer than six years. Without new training, workers will become technologically obsolete.

"Perhaps the topic hit a nerve," said CWA spokeswoman Rozanne Weissman, "since we are *all* affected by the fact that jobs and work are changing dramatically as we move further into the Information Age."

The wide range of views on OA's people issues gets variously colored, of course, by a viewer's management or labor background, his or her conservative or liberal leanings, and other perceptions. But wide the range is, as another show in the CWA series demonstrated.

"Rewiring Your World" brought together such personalities as Xerox vice president Paul Strassmann, author and futurist Alvin Toffler, women's advocate Karen Nussbaum from the 9to5 Association of Working Women, third world advocate Narinder Aggarwala of the United Nations Development Program, psychologist and sci-fi writer Kenneth Clark, and CWA president Glenn Watts.

Strassmann was enthusiastic about increased productivity; Toffler saw benefits in worker-technology interactions; Nussbaum saw future offices as modern equivalents of sweatshops; and Aggarwala feared that third world nations would be left in an economic backwater. In some agreement with Nussbaum and Aggarwala, Clark worried that minorities, women, and low-income people in general could be added to an "expendable underclass" in society. Watts said there will be more winners than losers in the Information Age, but only "if we are aware of what's going on, if we prepare for it, and if we can get a consensus about building a good future."

Future employment? Strassman, the manager, believed that productivity, boosted by technology, will create more jobs and wealth—in the service sector through computers, in the industrial sector through robotics. Nussbaum, the worker's advocate, said clerical work will become more rigidly and extensively compartmentalized and that machines will dictate the pace at which workers must perform.

Watts, the unionist but ever the conciliator, told of the response when dial telephones appeared in the 1930s and 1940s. CWA tried to save operators' jobs by opposing the new system, he said. "Fortunately, we were unsuccessful, because the resulting boom in demand for telephone service created thousands more jobs." The key, said Watts, is to find new ways to structure jobs so workers can both benefit from the technology and enjoy what they do.

The issue is:

OA's effects on people. There is no question that OA changes the *ways* people and organizations work (see Chapter 9); it may also affect people's personal lives, but this is often a matter of individual perception. There are some valid worries, but as we shall see, hard information concerning them isn't always available.

A CHANGING LABOR FORCE

Technology notwithstanding, the U.S. labor force now experiences major change by the force of its own demographics. Before plunging ahead to examine the issues posed by white-collar unions and 9to5, by work-at-homers, and by the possibly hazardous hardware, it would be well to understand the larger context in which OA events unfold.

In the labor force, two "macrochanges" stand out: it is becoming more female and it is becoming middle-aged.

In the 1970s, business had an ample supply of entry-level workers from which to draw. The 18-to-24 age segment of the population increased by 19 percent. The 25-to-34 segment, "young adults," grew even faster, increasing by 43 percent. In the 1980s, however, young adults are increasing by only 13 percent and the 18-to-24 group will actually *decline* by 14 percent.

Population in the 1980s bulges in the 35-to-44 age bracket—the bracket of experienced workers and middle management, and the bracket *most OA planners see as their fattest cost-saving target.* Demographically, this bracket will increase 42 percent by 1990 over its 1980 size.

Meanwhile, no one has repealed the law of supply and demand. With fewer entry-level workers to recruit but with no drop in the number of entry-level jobs (at least if the forecasts are right), employers will have to pay more to attract workers at this level. And this will tend to drive up wages in the already higher-paid, and heavily populated, middle-aged ranges—something companies can be expected to fight as they calculate the cost and appreciate how OA could cut it.

Add the spark of OA to the powder keg of skewed, unstable wage rates, and *bang!* With all that OA threatens (or seems to threaten) in work changes or outright job elimination, and with a growing perception among the middle-aged that they may put in long years on the job and have little to show for it, American business could have a problem on its hands, if it fails to handle these issues with care.

The sexual makeup of the labor force changes almost as fast as the age mix. The female participation rate rises; the male rate declines.

In 1960, 84 percent of working-age males were in the labor force; projecting to 1990, only 76 percent will be. In 1960, 38 percent of working-age females were in the labor force; by 1990, 58 percent will be.* It is expected that two out of every three jobs created in the next ten years will be filled by women.

Demographers tell us that many of these women will be mothers, perhaps even heads of households—a marked contrast from 1960, when most working women were single or married and childless. Personnel authorities see at least four trends resulting from this:

- Greater pressure on employers to condone nontraditional working hours, like "flextime," part-time work, and job sharing.
- More demand by head-of-household working women for short-range benefits like strong medical plans rather than long-term benefits like retirement plans.
- More worker requests for company-sponsored child-care facilities, or payment for child care as a rightful fringe benefit.
- The possibility, but now a stronger possibility, of office unionization.

THE WOMEN WORKERS' MOVEMENT

Few people articulate (and some would say exaggerate) the plight of women in the work force better than Karen Nussbaum. Wearer of many hats, Nussbaum heads the 4000-member office worker's local known as District 925 of the Service Employees International Union (SEIU), AFL-CIO. As association executive, she leads a women's organization she co-founded, known as the 9to5 Association of Working Women; it has 12,000 members. She has also served as technical adviser to "9 to 5," the TV comedy on office life, as she did for the film *9 to 5,* starring Jane Fonda, Lily Tomlin, and Dolly Parton.

Recruiting brochures for 9to5 (the association) list office automa-

*The labor force, as distinct from the work force, consists of people both working and looking for work. The work force comprises only those actually employed.

tion as a worker issue in the same context—in the same sentence, in fact—as sexual harassment. I asked Nussbaum about that in an interview I did for *Office Administration and Automation* (*OAA*).[1]

Nussbaum replied that because it is likely to restructure the entire work force, "we see automation as either a great opportunity or a great danger. We are extremely concerned about the areas in which we see danger. And that's why we see it sometimes in line with sexual harassment and other issues. . . .

"We see a trend in automation," she went on, "that may increase the severity of problems we already face as office workers—such as discrimination in hiring and promotion practices."

"Office automation may *increase* discrimination?" I asked. "What do you mean by that?"

"Well, this is a big issue with us," Nussbaum replied. "The work force right now is characterized by discrimination. Eighty percent of women are in low-paid, low-prestige jobs. Very few advance into the better, higher-paid jobs. It's a very polarized work force as far as men and women are concerned, and the kinds of jobs they hold.

"Automation of the office will bring in a whole host of completely new jobs. Now, if we were a fair society, a society that didn't practice discrimination in employment, we would find men and women equally distributed throughout these new jobs. But we're not seeing that. In fact, we're seeing a recapitulation of the same job profiles: 75 percent of the good, high-paying jobs like computer specialist held by men, 75 percent of the low-paying jobs like office-machine operator held by women, and you find minority women in the lowest of those jobs. What office automation often means is that clerical workers are paid less for doing more."

"Earlier you called automation both a danger and an opportunity," I pursued. "You have cited some of the danger as you see it. What's the opportunity?"

"The fact that automation will create that whole host of new jobs gives us the unique opportunity to dramatically change employment practices," she replied. "We could take this opportunity to bring an end to many of the discriminatory employment practices."

We went on to other topics, but I later put as a question one of the most commonly heard counterarguments to women's advocates' claims of job discrimination: the argument that women earn less than men because they don't remain in jobs as long as men. As is usual in such encounters, questions don't necessarily reflect the interviewer's point of view, but I summed up the argument for Nussbaum, who listened as though she'd heard it a hundred times before. "What's your answer?" I asked. She was ready and replied at length:

"My answer is that, yes, women do have a high turnover rate, and that's because the only way they ever realize raises in pay is by going to a new job. I can give you a specific example of that, and a more general one.

"A member of ours joined a company at the same time her sister and brother did; they all started together. The two women were hired as secretaries. The brother was hired as a mailroom clerk. The mailroom clerk was given management training and then went on to become a management member of the company. The secretaries never realized a single promotion in their entire twelve years with the company. Now, that's a specific case and we could argue about who was qualified, but, despite the fact that they wanted to be in management training, they were never given the opportunity.

"In general, there is no reward for women to stay in a company. They aren't given training. Statistics show that the longer they stay in a company, the less they earn [in comparison with women who change jobs]. Women over 45 earn less than women under 45 and there's one study that even shows that women who were in the work force, when they returned [to full-time, equivalent jobs] after being out for childbearing, earned less in dollars than when they had left. There's a disincentive to stay at your job and the only way that women ever find a pay raise is by going to another company. That's the reason for the turnover, as opposed to the turnover creating low wages."

The issue is:

Sexual discrimination. Will OA intensify it? There is no denying that, historically, the office work force has been largely sexually segregated. Even today, 99 percent of all secretaries are female. On the other hand, greater numbers of women do hold managerial and professional positions today. You could argue endlessly whether OA will advance or retard women in any way that is related to gender. Overall, it will probably do neither; pressure from women's groups and a change in social attitudes will make the greater difference. That sexual discrimination is not yet absent from automated offices, at least when it comes to pay, is evidenced by a salary study taken by *OAA* a year after the Nussbaum interview was published.

WHAT A SALARY SURVEY SHOWED

In 1984, *OAA* conducted a salary survey among its subscribers—men and women who *had* made it to management ranks. Many, in fact, were OA systems specialists. Others were administrative managers, traditional office generalists.

With due allowance for sampling error, the survey revealed a clear disparity in the pay of men and women in comparable job categories.[2] The average female OA specialist in 1984 earned $31,600, some 23 percent less than her male counterpart, who made $40,900. The gap grew wider among the generalists. The average male here earned $38,300 as compared with $28,000 for the female administrative managers—a 27 percent disparity.

(Before leaving these figures, it should be noted that the generalists, as a class, earned less than the specialists. The reverse had been true in a survey three years earlier. While the 1984 study couldn't be compared directly with the previous ones, data did show the generalists earning slightly less than they had in 1981. Again, this may have been only a quirk of two not wholly comparable surveys, or it could be a clue that the general office overseer with little or no specified involvement in systems and automation may have plateaued as a class.)

What could explain the male-female salary disparities? The survey takers searched for clues.

Were the females less educated than the males? While overall more males (49 percent) than females (35 percent) went to college, in the two lowest income brackets of the survey—meaning under $30,000—more females than males had college or graduate educations. No clear-cut indication there, the survey analysts said.

Did women have less time on the job? Here, a small bias in the males' favor. The men—average age 42—had been in their jobs 5.5 years, with their companies 9.2 years, and in their fields or industries 14.8 years. The women—average age 39—had been in their jobs 4.3 years, with their companies 7.5 years, and in their fields or industries 10.3 years. As Karen Nussbaum confirms, women do change jobs more frequently.

Did the women have less job responsibility? This is always an arguable matter, but the data that came closest to measuring it dealt with the number of people these managers had reporting to them. And here, men had double the number of people reporting to them—eighteen on average, where women had nine. Now, you could argue that if pay is lower because reponsibility is less, then it could be said that all of the traditional roadblocks to women being given greater responsibility are themselves a cause of the inequity in pay.

Are these perceptions only, or closely reasoned arguments? Cleverly crafted rationales, or long-time injustices being recognized at last?

In a practical sense, it comes to this: these are strongly *felt* issues and OA intensifies the feelings—more powder for the keg already brimming with the anxieties and hurts of an aging work force.

THE "HAZARDOUS" VDT

The issue is:

Are video display terminals hazardous? Few of OA's people issues have been as controversial, as studied, and as seized upon by lay writers for a lay public as the question of health hazards in the automated workplace—in particular, the question of radiation dangers posed by VDT screens. At this writing, a definitive answer simply cannot be given.

Question to a syndicated newspaper columnist on medicine: "Are you aware of any new evidence proving that video display terminals can cause health problems because of radiation?" Responded Dr. Timothy Johnson: "Thus far, the evidence would seem to indicate radiation from VDTs does not pose a health hazard. However, more study and continuing monitoring of the evidence is needed."

That's pretty much how it's been since the National Institute for Occupational Safety and Health (NIOSH) studies of 1981: pronouncements that while VDTs do send out minute amounts of x-ray and microwave radiofrequency radiation and are surrounded by low-level electromagnetic fields, the emissions are extremely small and are well below current federal standards for safe exposure.

And yet, a disturbing article by Kathleen McAuliffe, "The Mind Fields," dealing with what is known and not known about low-level electromagnetic fields, in the science magazine *Omni* of February 1985, describes what has become known as the "cluster problem"—clusters of pregnant workers at VDTs apparently having miscarriages and other pre- and postnatal difficulties beyond statistical norms.

The magazine told of seven miscarriages among twelve pregnant workers who operated video display terminals at the Defense Logistics Agency in Marietta, Georgia. Four VDT operators in the *Toronto Star*'s classified department gave birth to deformed children, the magazine said, while three who did not use VDTs gave birth to normal babies. And twelve out of fifty-five pregnant VDT operators at the Department of Employment in Runcorn, England, were said to have borne malformed babies.

Some of these abnormalities have been explained as stemming from other prenatal causes, and manufacturers continue to insist that there is simply no evidence to prove that VDTs are hazardous, but as the *Omni* piece points out, there is scant objective research in the field of low-level electromagnetics to prove much of anything.

Which is not to say that all is uncertain as to health difficulties in the automated workplace. NIOSH, while finding no hazards as far as radiation is concerned, had plenty to say as far as stress is concerned. The institute measured some of the highest stress rates ever recorded among clericals who used VDTs. Other medical evidence has begun linking VDTs to fatigue, depression, headaches, eyestrain, and musculoskeletal problems. An eighteen-month, six-city study by the Newspaper Guild and the Mount Sinai School of Medicine, New York, not only showed significantly more cases of deteriorated vision and low back and neck pain among VDT users than nonusers; it also revealed that "VDT users lost more time from work than did non-users." (See also the section on ergonomics, Chapter 4.)

Groups like 9to5 and some unions are not put off by assurances that VDT screens are safe. 9to5 warns also of toxins associated with office copiers and cites Dr. Suzanne Haynes's Framingham Heart Study, which found the rate of heart disease among women clericals to be significantly greater than among women in blue-collar or other white-collar jobs. "People who say there isn't really a radiation hazard are basing their claims on inconclusive data," says David LeGrand of the Communications Workers of America, in pressing for further research.

There will be further research. NIOSH, for one, has begun work among AT&T and other large employers to find suitable groups to examine. One proposed test will study 4000 female workers—half using VDTs, half not—over a span of three years.

At this writing, NIOSH also continues investigating the cluster problem. In addition to what *Omni* cited, other reports tell of cluster cases at Southern Bell and at a United Airlines office in San Francisco. Were six miscarriages out of fifteen pregnancies a coincidence at Southern Bell? Or was some external factor—perhaps the VDTs at which all of the women worked—causing harm?

For their part, computer manufacturers say they're not worried. Additional research will only further absolve VDTs from allegations of hazard, they contend. "We have no doubt what the results will be," says Charlotte LeGates, an official with the Computer and Business Equipment Manufacturers Association (CBEMA). Nonetheless, CBEMA has been chosen to head a coalition of associations banding together to counter "misinformation" in the press and to direct the groups' lobbying efforts in legislatures in which bills restricting VDT use are up for consideration.

Such bills have been introduced into several legislatures in the United States and Canada. Some would protect workers—all workers—from "excessive" VDT exposure. At least five bills include provisions to transfer pregnant women away from the terminals. In the Ontario provincial government, a pregnant woman already has the right to refuse VDT work. Issue or not, the politicians are listening. So is 9to5, which says calls to its VDT Risk Hotline, operating out of Cleveland headquarters, are steadily increasing.

Again on the other side of the issue, CBEMA, the industry's Washington lobby, petitioned the Federal Communications Commission (FCC) to ease the rules which manufacturers must follow to test computing equipment for radiation. The FCC, after studying the requests, did ease the rules and in some cases eliminated them entirely.

WHITE-COLLAR UNIONS

The fact of office unions, and the possibility of more unions, has long been part of the office scene. As a journalist, I pursued such stories as far back as 1952. For the most part then, and for many years thereafter, they turned out to be *non*stories.

Yes, there were organizing efforts, and yes, labor leaders even then were saying that the future of the union movement lay in the office. Blue-collar member strength already was ebbing, the white-collar work force was increasing, and it didn't take much deep thinking for unionists to figure out where new members had to come from.

Yet for all the talk and the occasional recruitment drives, white-collar organizers never seemed to get . . . organized. And neither did most office workers. It may have been that since so many of them knew they would not stay in their jobs long, they didn't see the point of joining a union. They may have had a perception that office work was "clean" and "professional" work, that is was superior to factory work, and that it was simply not the kind of work to lump in with organized labor. Whatever the reasons, the office has been difficult to organize, historically.

In a fifteen-year period from 1968, white-collar union membership grew less than 1 percent per year. By the mid-1980s, fewer than 10 percent of clerical workers carried union cards. So is this still a nonstory? Or are the times a-changin'?

The issue is:

Office unionization. Is the threat now real? And if it's real, what part does OA play?

Straws "blowin' in the wind" suggest that the times *are* changing. There are rising emotions against real and perceived sex discrimination, and there is a growing belief that prolonged VDT work, if not yet proving hazardous the way radiometers measure it, is definitely proving uncomfortable and stressful to employees. There are new union approaches to organizing and new perceptions among managers.

In a six-month period in 1984, SEIU, the service employees union, signed up 8000 new members, more than for all of the previous year.

District 925 of the SEIU scored big gains at the bargaining table from Equitable Life Assurance Society in Syracuse, New York; the contract preserved fifty-four office jobs for three years and excluded attendance and attitude—meaning appraisals like "works eagerly"—from formulas for setting pay. Equitable also agreed to fifteen-minute breaks each afternoon for VDT workers, reported *Business Week,* "to lessen muscle- and eye-strain."[3]

With a work force increasingly supportive of groups like District 925 and 9to5, a separate gale could develop over a doctrine called "comparable worth."

Other straws in the wind are certain OA goals themselves. One thing OA planners forthrightly set out to do—at least among production-oriented Type I workers, to recall the distinction in Chapter 2—is to speed production. Excessive speedups, especially where work can be counted and measured, have often proven the rankling cause for union organization.

Almost half (49 percent) of personnel managers surveyed by the Bureau of Law & Business, Stamford, Connecticut, said they believed the unionization of clerical workers "will be a threat" in the 1980s. Nearly one-fourth (23 percent) saw the unionization of supervisors as a real, if smaller, threat. Significantly, large and small employers feared unionization in roughly equal numbers, though only 6 percent of the large ones reported any currently unionized workers.[4]

While the Communications Workers of America, the United Auto Workers, and of course SEIU have large shares of whatever white-collar membership there is, few unions have announced their intentions to pursue office workers as aggressively as have the Teamsters.

Since 1979, this once-muscular union has seen a 700,000-member decline. Its traditional constituents, truckers, now account for a mere 10 percent of its 1.6 million enrollment. But Jackie Presser, who took over as Teamster president in 1983, knows where the future lies: in the office and its related high-tech fields.

Presser may be as tough as his predecessors, and allegations of ties to organized crime, which he denies, may dog him, but he is far-seeing enough to have studied the office and to have sensed the strength that's in it.

White-collar workers in their 30s and 40s are "most susceptible to joining a union," he told an *Industry Week* interviewer. "They've put some time in, and realize that they may not have that many productive years left. They've seen that Social Security is nothing more than a Band-Aid."

"I'll bet," Presser said at another point, "that 80 percent of white-collar workers don't have $800-a-month pensions, or 13 days off [per year]."[5]

To help attract such workers and especially female workers, Presser hired a young, bright, female Cornell graduate as the Teamsters' organizing director. Vicki Saporta, at 31, became the only woman to hold such a post in any major union. Within a year she had won ten union victories in conservative North Carolina, and had set about to reform the union's outmoded organizing structure with better staffing methods, better service, and better managerial follow-up.

An employee at a California hospital Saporta was trying to organize said of her: "She'll yell and scream and wave her arms and she'll say, 'You don't have to take this . . . anymore.' " Saporta herself says, "Once you give people some power in dealing with employers, you see a change in them. They feel power for the first time in their lives, and they think they can win."[6]

COMPARABLE WORTH

Closely tied with other "fairness" issues on the agendas of worker organizations is the concept of comparable worth. An early case pitted female prison guards against male guards —not exactly an office environment, although most of the arguments supporting the concept of comparable worth have a strong white-collar connection.

In the prison guards' case involving an Oregon county jail, the Supreme Court ruled that women workers could sue for equal pay with men even if the jobs they performed were not identical. The 5-to-4 decision didn't rule on the touchy question of whether totally different jobs of comparable difficulty had comparable worth and should thus be rewarded equally.

In the Oregon jail, matrons who guarded female prisoners received $200 less per month than male officers who guarded male prisoners. The county justified the difference on grounds that the supervision of male inmates was harder work. The Court found, however, that while the jobs were not identical, under the Civil Rights Act they were close enough to merit equal pay.

To comparable worth advocates, that was only a small beginning. They point out that secretaries, 99 percent of whom are women; nurses, 96 percent of whom are women; and other holders of traditionally female jobs often earn less than holders of other equally difficult jobs, some of which require much less education. Is it fair, they ask, that teachers earn less than house painters?

A long and bitter strike involving 1600 clerical and technical workers at Yale University in New Haven, Connecticut, centered on comparable worth. Local 34 of the Federation of University Employees complained that while administrative assistants, for example, made

$13,000 per year, university truck drivers made more than $18,000 per year. Again, the union argued that workers who perform tasks which, though different, require a comparable level of skills should be comparably paid.

That the concept strikes fear in the hearts of employers can be seen by the vehemence with which many oppose it. Clarence Pendleton, chairman of the U.S. Civil Rights Commission in the Reagan administration, spoke for many in calling comparable worth "the looniest idea since Looney Tunes came on the screen."

Marketplace laws of supply and demand, not patterns of willful discrimination, are what determine the wage levels of various jobs, comparable worth's supporters say. Pendleton's staff director, Linda Chavez, said comparable worth would create job-market chaos and actually hurt women by decreasing their financial incentives to seek the higher-paying jobs that men have traditionally held.

"It is difficult to predict the impact this issue will have on personnel trends," comments Don Keown, second vice president for personnel at Bankers Life Co., Des Moines. "It could be tremendous." Keown says employers are caught in a trap. Without a standardized job evaluation plan, they don't know if they'd meet comparable worth criteria or not. Yet if they initiate such an evaluation plan and find that female-dominated jobs with values equal to male-dominated jobs are underpaid, "it merely opens the door for litigation."

Like the health hazard issue, comparable worth has generated political steam, at least at the state and local levels. Reforms based on the concept are being considered by legislatures, and, for their own employees, some state and city governments have already put them into practice. Federal court rulings in the summer of 1985, however, found no discrimination in the cases brought by claimants under the comparable worth doctrine, who said they would appeal.

THE WORK-AT-HOME TREND

By 1990, *Newsweek* estimates, 10 million American jobholders will be doing their work at home. OA critics point out, however, that just because technology makes it possible, "telecommuting" isn't necessarily feasible or desirable.

Believers in telecommuting praise the savings of time it provides for work—time otherwise spent on travel to and from work. "When you hire a professional you're hiring him or her for forty to sixty hours—the best part of the working week," says Donald Koch, senior VP and director of research for the Federal Reserve Bank of Atlanta. Professionals at the bank have the option of working at home from one to several days a week. "Taking one and a half to two hours a day to move . . . from home to work and back isn't making optimum use of the person's abilities," says Koch.[7]

Proponents praise also the monetary and energy savings pocketed when workers do not have to shell out for that monthly commutation ticket or burn fuel on the interstate twice a day. The flexibility of working at home suits our increasingly diverse work force, they add. For example, parents can more easily continue working while also raising young children.

Such benefits enjoy wide publicity, agrees David Redmond, a regional director of consulting services for Ernst & Whinney, Boston, and a critic of work at home; what is not as readily grasped are the subtle drawbacks. "They encompass complicated questions of continuity, values, and corporate culture," he says, adding:

> American business cannot afford to forget that teamwork, commitment to quality, and creativity are best transmitted through a personal link between management and employees. If a company breaks that link by pulling a significant percentage of workers out of the office, it risks adverse affects on its products and services in the long run. . . . A company can't teach its values through a computer terminal.[8]

Women's advocate Amy Dru Stanley sees adverse effects of another kind in the work-at-home movement. In an op-ed column of *The New York Times,* she charged that employers have begun to use the geographic mobility afforded by OA technology as "union-busting tactics."

Not only has technology taken its toll of female-dominated office jobs like stenographer and keypunch operator—"undercutting whatever security and authority women have enjoyed in their traditional stronghold"—it has also given employers a new tool to cripple women's efforts to challenge sex discrimination, she wrote.

"In response to the organizing of women workers, corporations have instituted work-at-home programs and part-time work, isolating workers and creating a casual workforce without job security and benefits," Stanley went on. " 'Run-away' offices have relocated within the United States or have gone overseas in search of cheap, unorganized labor."[9]

Judith Gregory, an AFL-CIO research specialist, makes a similar point regarding relocation. Many office jobs, she says, especially in banking, insurance, and high technology, are moving to suburban areas inaccessible to blacks and other minorities "who need [the jobs] most." Many companies seek what they call a "quality clerical worker," she says, but adds: "I think 'quality clerical worker' means a white, suburban, nonunion, part-time worker."

And yet many women say they want flexible hours and the opportunity to work at home. Management can't win either way on this one.

While much reporting and no little rhetoric surround the work-at-home movement, few large organizations have embraced it officially. In a recent Boston-area survey, none of the large insurance companies—like American Mutual, Liberty Mutual, New England Mutual, and John Hancock—had work-at-home programs. Nor did high-tech firms like Polaroid and Wang. Software International (SI) did have such a policy until its acquisition by General Electric, an SI executive said, but the program is now "ancient history."

Most corporate work at home that does occur gets informal recognition at best. Well before OA, many professionals reasoned to themselves and others in words like, "Look, I've got to work at home tomorrow in order to get something *done!*" Many have freely worked at home at night and on weekends. The self-employed regularly work at home. It's nothing new. Still, management is wary of the idea of *sanctioning* work at home among employees who would have no choice but to come to the office were it not for automation.

How can a boss control moonlighting and a tendency among workers to put personal affairs first? How can company loyalty be maintained? Can workers be trusted with expensive computers? And the bottom line: will the productivity gained by freeing a worker from travel and the usual office distraction outweigh the cost of the computers, the communication links, and the other OA apparatus? To many a boss, it looks risky.

Not all employees feel sure about working at home, either. One of the few available studies on employee attitudes toward the practice, by the Diebold Group, found a sort of "grass is greener on the other side" mentality developing among both office workers and people working at home. The office workers grew envious of the others, of the freedom, the convenience, and the apparent trust they enjoyed at being allowed such privilege. The workers at home began to develop feelings of social isolation, and, in fact, they *were* deprived of much news and gossip. Also, the workers at home, despite occasional meetings *at* the office, began to worry about being unnoticed, about being "out of sight, out of mind": "Will I be passed over for the next promotion? Will I be remembered?"

The Diebold study concluded, however, that the work-at-home idea was realistic and that management would slowly move toward accepting it as an option.

Plainly the option isn't for everyone. Patricia Seybold, whose Boston-based Seybold Consulting Group grants the option to all but production and support personnel, says working at home tends to favor the loner type, the self-motivated person who probably liked doing independent studies in college. To say that working at home suits the Type II office professional better than the Type I office process worker may be drawing the line too fine, however. Certain Type I work, like keypunching, has long been farmed out to homes. Still, there's validity to the general notion that the more creative or specialized worker, whose thought processes flourish best in uninterrupted isolation, is the more likely candidate for work at home.

"The old environment valued standardization, procedures, and machines," remark the Federal Reserve's Donald Koch and department economist Delores Steinhauser in a jointly authored paper. "The new organization thrives on creativity, individuality, and flexibility." Koch sums up: "The option to work at home has been our department's gain."[10]

At the Federal Reserve Bank, research personnel are divided into eight teams, each with economists and analysts. These alone have the work-at-home options, which they may negotiate with management for fixed periods. At home, they work with PCs, transmitting data and text via modems to comparable equipment in Atlanta, where they can also tie into a local area network.

Not as successful was a work-at-home experiment involving secretaries at Continental Illinois National Bank, Chicago. Workers were expected to be at their terminals from 8:30 to 11:30 a.m. and again from 2:30 to 4:30 p.m. Productivity was measured according to the quality and quantity of finished work. Having kept careful records, management dropped the program after four years on the pragmatic grounds that it just wasn't cost-effective.

At this state of OA development, working at home—or in the "electronic cottage," as some futurists say—hasn't taken off quite the way some had expected. OA advances may yet make the idea more feasible—which again is not always to say desirable.

JOB SHARING

Comparable to work at home in that it allows employees to cope better with the exigencies of modern life, job sharing can also benefit management by reducing overtime and the need to hire temporary workers.

Job sharing is simple on paper: two or even three employees hold a job formerly considered one full-time occupation. In practice, some extra administrative and supervisory burdens may be incurred. However, training is often not as costly or time-consuming as when one full-time worker replaces another. With job sharing, if one member of a team leaves, the other, with knowledge of the job, can instruct a newcomer, obviating the need for a supervisor to take on the task alone.

Other benefits to management include greater flexibility in work scheduling; the opportunity to draw from a wider range of skills for a single job; greater worker energy in that workers don't feel that seventh- and eighth-hour letdown; and the retention of valued employees who, because of changed circumstances (the arrival of a child, say), would have to quit were it not for the job-sharing option. Moreover, workers are at liberty to schedule medical and other personal appointments on their own time—not the company's.

In most job-sharing arrangements, the team members share salaries and fringe benefits, not necessarily on a fifty-fifty basis, but in proportion to the time and experience each provides to the job. Teams can vary in makeup: they may consist of a pair (or trio) of equals; a complementary pair, each contributing a skill the other lacks; or an unequal pair, one the leader, the other a trainee.

Patricia Lee, president of Workshare Inc., a New York consulting firm, says,[11]

> Naturally, employers question the costs that may be involved in the administration of a job-sharing program, and with the additional paperwork there may be a slight increase. Concerns about inconvenience, however, are usually grounded in fears of the unknown. If the company establishes time schedules, communication tools, and shared job responsibilities in advance, and then communicates these to the relevant people, it will find most job-sharing teams slip easily into their slots.

Lee sees OA as paving the way for what she calls "this Dynamic Duo-ism," but admits that many managements still waver, uncertain as to how to institute job sharing successfully. Among the procedures she recommends are these:

- Appoint a coordinator to "put the pieces together."
- Establish goals and objectives: decide whether job sharing will apply to the whole organization or only to certain departments or particular jobs; state also which employees are eligible for the program.
- Develop timetables broadly, so that the general organization knows target dates for various steps in the program, and specifically, so that team members know when tasks must be finished.

- Review personnel policies and procedures, relevant legislation, and union contracts, to be sure the program doesn't run afoul of laws or previous commitments.
- Issue policy statements on the program; keep upper management involved; screen employees for likely job sharers; and, as always, communicate.

Since 1900, the workweek has shrunk from a sixty-hour standard to the widely accepted forty hours now. In the 1960s, fewer than 15 percent of workers put in fewer than thirty-four hours per week; today more than a third of the work force does so. Projections indicate that by the year 2000, despite current managerial trepidations about job sharing, not only will more workers be putting in fewer hours apiece, but 10 percent of them will be part of job-sharing teams.

A NEED TO TRAIN

From general overviews like CWA's telecast "Future Work" to specific employees like Vicki Churchward and Gloria, whom we met in Chapter 4 getting their first taste of OA, an inescapable theme connects all: a pressing need for training and retraining.

The issue is not:

That organizations don't recognize the need. They do; it's what executives really mean when they moan "Where can I find good people?" It's that so few firms do anything about it. A study of leading business and industrial firms found that despite increased automation, over two-thirds lacked programs to retrain workers for new jobs. Only a fourth of the firms told Deutsch, Shea & Evans, the survey takers, that they did have such programs.

Nor is the issue that training fare doesn't exist. The "learnware" industry offers books, manuals, magazines, business schools with OA courses and machine training, vendor courses and machine training, professional associations with seminars, and supplementary materials beyond count. The issue *is* that too much of it is cursory, old, complex, or not pertinent to the immediate need.

Pity the business educator, says Dorothy Sandburg, office systems administrator for Comserv Corp., Mendota Heights, Minnesota. "They work with textbooks on new technology that could really be described as history books. They try to teach terminal keyboarding techniques on outdated, often manual, typewriters. They teach students skills for jobs often paying twice the instructor's salary."[12]

Cost is an ever-present consideration with on-the-job training, as with most other things. Managements balk as they tot up what have been called the "four costs of training":

- Time costs, lost when a worker is off the job for course attendance (costliest of the four)
- Preparation costs of training materials for the instructor
- Transportation, food, and lodging costs, if employees must travel to a training site
- Facilities costs for in-house classrooms, audiovisual equipment, and furniture

Politicians at election time can be heard proposing government programs for training and retraining workers to cope with the new technology. Whether the politicians win or lose, and whatever the efficacy of government programs, the fact is that lately most such funds have been cut.

Training, whether private or public, *is* a costly proposition. And because of OA's exceptional technology and newness, much of the course material has not been well crafted. Moreover, retraining a group of middle-aged workers is not the same as teaching a class of collegians.

"The use of texts and other learning materials written especially for adults is imperative," says business educator Margaret Bahniuk, associate professor at Cleveland State University. "If this is not possible, exercises and cases should be rewritten so they are appropriate and interesting to the adult student."

Often the texts are highly specialized, not only as they might apply to adult workers but even as they might apply to the entry-level trainee. As Dorothy Sandburg complains, the texts and other fare, in an effort to be friendly and to speak the user's language, assume him or her to be an expert in the particular application about to be automated. They assume the user understands programming of financial modeling and now only needs to learn how to go about those tasks using the new OA products. Wrong: many a student needs the subject background as well as the instructional OA foreground—and this background can't be found in manuals steeped in jargon familiar only to specialists.

The need to train and retrain well persists as one of OA's knottier urgent issues. If management and the educational community fail to equip the labor force with skills adequate to the jobs a changing high-tech world will provide, not only can social tragedy ensue through technological unemployment but management could lose the chance for higher profit and growth. For all its capital resources, an organization is often nothing more than the sum of its employees and their skills.

HOW'S YOUR QWL?

All these issues—employee unrest, lack of skills, a changing labor force—caused by OA, intensified by OA, or simply coincident with OA, infuse the workplace with a metabolism of its own, a prevailing state of health . . . or dysfunction. In current management parlance, that state of corporate tone is frequently called "quality of work life" (QWL).

QWL means different things in different places; an abstract value here, a concrete program there. Canada has taken up the program approach almost as a national campaign. American business has taken it up—or left it alone—on an individual-company basis. To some, QWL is nothing more than well-intentioned atmospherics designed to make the office a feel-good place. But in other organizations it is purposeful and participatory: workers and management sharing in decisions that affect work, sharing sometimes in the making of policy.

Whether or not an organization has a quality of work life program, it has a quality of work life, good or bad. OA can affect that quality negatively or positively. It can enhance the work of management and staff by enabling both to be more productive. Or OA can increase stress, especially where it appears to threaten jobs. It can subtly "deskill" workers by making the work more mechanical.

As a phrase, "quality of work life" was coined in 1972 at a Democratization of Work Conference held at Columbia University's Arden House in Harriman, New York, to discuss two simultaneous business movements. One, born in the politics of western Europe, sought "industrial democracy"—a strong call for worker participation in decisions, even to the point of having workers serve on corporate boards. The other movement, born of U.S. efforts to humanize the workplace along lines advocated by social scientists Frederick Herzberg, Abraham Maslow, Elton Mayo, and others, sought to stem a tide of worker alienation.

That tide was rising, the theories ran, because of the way organizations were structured and jobs designed: compartmentally, "thinkers" separate from "doers." Such structures had led to isolation and poor communication. (What would those theorists say now about working at home?) The conferees had different ideas on how the problem could be solved, but they concurred on one thing: both movements were focusing on the quality of life at work.

As described by Jacqueline Davenport, associate director for training at the American Center for Quality of Work Life in Washington, D.C., QWL programs then became the rage. Experiments got under way between General Motors and the United Auto Workers, in mines and other industries, and in the entire area surrounding Jamestown, New York. The programs all had a blue-collar, shop-floor orientation, and they coincided with yet another movement. In the late 1970s, profits, product quality, and the rate of U.S. productivity growth *moved downward.* In yet a third movement, the word from Japan and Europe was different: better productivity, better quality, better management. All were attributed to such things as Theory Z, which emphasizes worker-management collaboration, worker teams, and other dramatic ideas.

Where had American QWL programs fallen short? Says Davenport: By forgetting the managers and focusing only on workers.[13]

> QWL professionals, business leaders, and union officials began to see, and the Hayes-Abernathy article "Managing Our Way to Economic Decline" in the *Harvard Business Review* in 1980 so clearly articulated, that the problem was not just that American workers had stopped being the most productive in the world, but that our approach to *managing* our organizations had to be changed.

So QWL was revamped, to be played by new rules—fewer points for shop-floor tactics, more points for management style. At Jewell Co., managers became "first assistants." Davenport quotes the CEO as saying to the first assistants: "We mentally turn our organizational chart upside down and challenge ourselves to seek ways in which we can lead . . . by helping . . . by teaching . . . by listening . . . by managing in the truest democratic sense . . . that is, *with the consent of the managed.*"[14]

And with all of this has come a fourth movement: office automation. The leading, the helping, the teaching had to be practiced, wherever they were practiced (and at first that meant in offices of major corporations), in environments that were getting their first taste of OA (and again that meant the majors). It is fortunate that the four movements we have been discussing coincided. It is one thing to keep saying that the key to OA success is people. It is quite another to have modern wherewithal, like a QWL program, to assure that success by maintaining—or attaining—a quality work life for the people involved.

Not that QWL is all modern wherewithal. Each new management fashion, as it marches by, wraps within it many of the verities that good managers have known for years. The formalities of worker-management participation, the councils in which so much of it takes place, may be new. The common senses of fostering communication, cooperation, and respect and of listening to one another's ideas are almost biblical.

A New York Stock Exchange (NYSE) report, "People and Productivity: A Challenge to Corporate America," said in 1984 that nearly 14 percent of companies with 100 or more employees were involved in some type of QWL program. Together these firms employ over half the American work force.[15]

If what the NYSE uncovered is true, then QWL is perhaps more powerful than even OA in boosting output. The report said further that companies with the programs traced productivity gains of 20 percent and more directly to these efforts.

For all the talk of worker fears and disgruntlement, most workers still retain positive feelings toward their jobs. Recent studies from groups as disparate as the Work in America Institute, the Opinion Research Corp., and the U.S. Chamber of Commerce indicate that 75 percent of U.S. workers are satisfied with their jobs. In addition, studies show that most employees feel an inner need to do the best they can and that most would work harder if they were more involved in decisions relating to their jobs.

Companies which fail to measure such input "or who choose to ignore what they measure, may as well hang it up now," says Bankers Life's Don Keown, "because employees will demand to be heard. Where their demands fall on deaf ears, they will easily sacrifice the organization for one where they will be heard."[16]

8

Security Issues

What Is Information Worth? How Good Are the Locks?

In the movie *WarGames,* a "hacker" breaches a computer of North American Air Defense and nearly starts World War III. But of course that couldn't happen, say the pundits.

A flurry of recent reports tell of hackers breaching computers at Los Alamos National Laboratory in New Mexico, Memorial Sloan-Kettering Cancer Center in New York, and other places. Unfortunately, those things *did* happen.

Somebody rummaged among 90 million credit files in a computer of TRW Information Services, largest credit-rating bureau in the United States.

Somebody broke into computers of a bank in Los Angeles, a cement company in Canada, and the Department of the Interior in Washington, D.C.

And other breaches of high-tech security have taken place which never became public knowledge. The victims clammed up, quietly took their losses, and belatedly sought high-tech locks for their vulnerable high-tech lockers.

Hackers—some of whom try to penetrate computers for the fun of it, and the crime of it—are not the only security threats to the automated systems of business and government. The hostile spy, the trafficker in business secrets, the saboteur, the typewriter thief turned PC thief, are among the other significant threats. Fires, floods, and other natural disasters also pose dangers. One of the biggest threats is management itself, in its large indifference toward, and misdirection of, the need for beefed-up security.

Beefing up means commonsense practices as much as it means better locks. At one office I'm familiar with, management bolted all its removable computer keyboards onto users' desks. This may have kept crooks from walking off with the equipment, but it drained away the flexibility and ergonomic comfort for which these keyboards were designed. Ironically, that same office stored all its diskettes in unlocked files, as though the information they contained was hardly worth the bother of locking up. And yet information is what the offices, and the keyboards, and the work are all about. Information, far more than capital goods, will be the principal asset of the Information Age.

Neal Patrick, the contrite young hacker who entered the Sloan-Kettering and Los Alamos computers, told a Congressional subcommittee how management could make a few commonsense changes in software to ward off similar breaches. Users should replace the original, factory-inserted passwords which grant access to computers (passwords like "test" or "system") with passwords of their own, he advised. Too often users leave the original words in place, making it easy for hackers to break in with a bit of trial-and-error effort. Why would users be so uninterested in security? Sometimes they are careless, but often they leave these passwords in place deliberately—they want to make it easy for maintenance people to service the equipment.

High school honor student Patrick also advised that panel of the House Committee on Science and Technology to educate people better on the ethics of computer entry. Asked at what point he questioned the ethics of his own actions, he replied, "Once the FBI knocked on the door."

Patrick said he'd hacked out of intellectual curiosity. Member of the so-called 414 gang—named for a local Wisconsin area code—he said he didn't know at the time whose computers he'd reached. "But," he told the Congress, "the fact that we could reach them shows the potential for damage."

Sloan-Kettering undoubtedly agrees. The intrusions caused administrative chaos, officials said; computer services director Dr. Radhe Mohan told *The New York Times* that just searching for damage cost the hospital "a month of worker-hours." Lost records made it impossible to collect $1500 for computer services provided to other hospitals. Mohan said the computer had been entered eighty times and shut down twice. Fortunately, both shutdowns occurred when no patients were being tested or monitored.[1]

"LYING LITTLE CROOKS"

Many hackers are like the 414 gang—brainy kids who get their kicks from beating impersonal systems at their own electronic games. Others are what one security consultant calls "lying little crooks."

The newsletter *Computer Security* says,[2]

> Le'ts understand that most hackers aren't hardened criminals; they are kids whose mentality is that of the prankster, not the felon. . . . These children have as much time and energy for computer break-ins as others do for stamp collections or athletics. The lesson we must learn from the hackers is that "it" can be done and is being done today. *The true criminals won't be far behind.*

Belden Menkus, whose consulting firm operates out of Middleville, New Jersey, says,

> They're for rent. They're no different than 13-year-old hustlers who run numbers or dope for big operators. Oh, they're better educated and they live in better neighborhoods, but don't believe all that [business] after they're caught when they sigh, "Oh, I didn't know that what we were doing was wrong." They're well coached by lawyers, believe me. . . .
>
> Sure, some are naive. They're today's version of yesterday's phone freaks, the kids who used to beat Ma Bell out of phone calls. But naive or not, the hackers are real and they pose a genuine danger.

Another hacker who went public, or at least semipublic (he calls himself "Emmanuel Goldstein" after a character in George Orwell's novel *1984*), admits breaking into the GTE computerized mail system, Telemail. This led him to documents of the Interior Department. Describing the caper on National Public Radio, he said he gained access to Telemail by dialing a local number available to computer users. The New York teenager then bridged what he called "gaps in the system's security," creating passwords that allowed him to enter the electronic mailboxes of both GTE and Interior.

"Goldstein" said he was publicizing his action to show how lax security was on this widely used system. "I've never taken a computer class. I'm not a programmer," he commented later. "Anyone with the right equipment can figure this out."[3]

How did he get the Telemail number? "Goldstein" wouldn't say. But hackers will tell you they exchange such numbers and passwords over semisecret versions of electronic bulletin boards—the kind of service which ostensibly caters to legitimate interests, like posting cars and computers for sale, or facilitating dating and mating. Subscribing users access the electronic boards via their own computers. Menkus estimates 300 commercial and noncommercial-but-cooperative boards operate currently. People's Message System in Santee, California, a bulletin board of other bulletin boards, lists 500 of various kinds nationwide.

A writer who exposed a hacker network found that electronic revenge is swift. Richard Sandza, a *Newsweek* reporter, had infiltrated a particular computer underground and described in an article the abuses he'd witnessed. Outraged, the hackers put him on "teletrial" over a Texas electronic bulletin board called "Dragonfire." Someone known as "Unknown Warrior" acted as prosecutor; "Ax Murderer" was the judge. It all sounds playful enough until the sentence was meted out. Sandza told in a subsequent article of harassing phone calls and the posting of his Visa charge card number on Pirate 80, a West Virginia board. A friendly hacker, Sandza wrote, also tipped him off that others had obtained his credit records by rifling a computer of TRW Information Services.

If compromised words and numbers can be posted like this, it would seem that law enforcement bodies could themselves tie in, both to warn the victims and to nab the culprits.

They could, and sometimes do. But there are problems. First, some of the boards are so deep underground that they're not always known to authorities; a few secret ones which have come to light bore innocent-sounding if joking names, like "AT&T Phone Center" and "Future World." Second, electronic mischief moves extremely fast. A hacker's possession of a newly compromised password for a few hours can wreak organizational havoc. Then there's the law itself: OA technology is still too new to have its misuse codified on as many books as it might be. Also, First Amendment and Fourth Amendment rights may stand in the way. Many of the relevant laws which do exist protect a person's right to see and correct information as much as another person's right to protect it.

It has been suggested by security watchers that the spookier (or more clandestine) bulletin boards sometimes serve the cause of intelligence gathering, in the surreptitious byplay of espionage. Agencies can learn a lot simply by noticing what's on a board. It might be just the right place for a sting operation. "Sometimes," said one insider, "it's better to keep the boards than to erase them."

"The hackers may be a blessing," concludes *Computer Security,* looking to the bright side. They are generating the kind of publicity which is finally alerting management to threats that security professionals have been warning about for years. "Everyone who has ever wished that 'it' would happen (but to someone else, please!) has now had that wish fulfilled."[4] Of course, on the dark side, as the newsletter points out, criminals learn these lessons, too.

The several break-ins at TRW were not pranks. In one case, the credit-reporting bureau acknowledged that someone had obtained an account code belonging to Sears, Roebuck & Co. A Sears official confirmed that the company was informed the code had been "in the wrong hands" and subsequently had been changed to prevent more misuse. Hackers told the Long Island newspaper *Newsday,* which broke this story, that some individuals were using the TRW system to determine the credit lines available on stolen credit cards. The paper also quoted an area retailer who complained that merchants, and not banks or individuals, absorb most of the loss from credit card fraud.[5]

Small *computer* retailers—frequent victims of high-tech crime—may especially welcome news that copy-proof program disks may one day hit the market. The dealers lose millions in potential sales to software pirates who regularly make illegal copies of popular software on diskettes. The new disks employ erasable optical technology, according to an International Resource Development report; they'll fit in a shirt pocket (easier to steal, maybe?); and they'll be read by laser light. Program coding will be stamped on at a plant using equipment and techniques "difficult for a thief to obtain or employ."

HOW BAD IS IT?

Losses attributable to the security breaches of computers and related OA systems run in the hundreds of millions of dollars. No one knows the exact figure: too much is papered over, too much simply can't be valued by existing standards. For example, how great is the value of stolen information?

A sleeper issue in this area may be the reluctance of major accounting firms to fully assess client damage. Security watchers say losses often aren't reported properly because accountants aren't clever enough to find them. "Their formal statements actually say only that 'the books purport to be what the books purport to be,' " one analyst told me. "The phrase 'generally accepted accounting principles' can mean anything they want it to mean." The analyst said he wouldn't be surprised to see major lawsuits develop from this failure to properly assess loss.

And while outside hackers may have garnered attention, the inside manipulator of a system often perpetrates less-publicized crime.

According to Belden Menkus, not all losses involve manipulation of account monies; many involve manipulation of inventories. "Shipments of subassemblies are diverted to fictional destinations, for instance," he says. "The stuff virtually falls off the edge of the earth. It's very tough to trace."

The issue is:

Office and information security. Given these realities, these vulnerabilities, what can management and OA planners do to shore up their office defenses?

- First, say authorities, recognize that security involves a never-ending escalation of means in the war between the good people and the bad. A tamper-proof lock is developed. Burglars soon find a way to bypass it. So detection devices are installed. The crooks find a way to outsmart *them*. (The criminal mind seems to take to technology well. Crime historians say crooks used automobiles before the police did; motorized robbers held up horse-and-buggy passengers and then made fast escape. No sooner had snowmobiles appeared than criminals used them to burglarize summer homes otherwise inaccessible in winter.)

  Users protect computers with secret passwords. Hackers, patient souls that they are, keep trying different words. And now, like the offices the hackers seek to penetrate, even this task has been automated. Hacker-helpful software exists which does the dialing, automatically testing passwords until *bingo!*—it hits one. So new defenses must be added (see the fourth point below).
- Second, recognize that office security involves more than crime deterrence. Facilities must be protected against natural as well as human-caused disasters. If an office—the information hub—is severely damaged, the whole organization could falter.

  In spite of such obvious risk, one-fourth of major corporations do not have formal backup or disaster recovery programs. A study by the Diebold Research Program showed that none of the surveyed firms—all with EDP (electronic data processing) budgets of $10 million or more—had bothered to extend the security programs they did have into remote locations. And yet in these locations Diebold found increasing numbers of PCs and minis tying into central mainframes. From them, users (and hackers) could readily obtain and process (or manipulate) information.

  As further evidence of vulnerability, the study found that more than half the firms did not include telecommunications in their backup or disaster recovery programs.

- Third, understand that security measures can't be costed out in finite returns on investment. The threats are "iffy." If would-be perpetrators realize how difficult and risky criminal acts would be and thus refrain, no one can count the criminal acts that *don't* occur. If smoke detectors alert the staff in time, no one can know how costly a fire would have been if it had gone out of control. Yes, proper monitoring devices can tally the number of thwarted attempts to access a computer or the number of threats to safety from fires and other occurrences, but the potential for loss can only be guessed at. "Good security," said a good security agent I know, "is thinking like a crook, thinking like a pessimist, and then taking the probably right steps to outsmart [the criminal] or prevent *it*. It's gut football all the way."
- Fourth, fight high technology with higher technology. Dial answerback access controls, for example, can put extra safeguards between caller and computer before letting a connection be made. They hang up on the caller, check to see if he or she is authorized, and call back to that number only if the identity checks out. If it does not, the system alerts the company. Expensive shielding devices, another alternative, can recognize calls from unauthorized sources and directly refuse the requests. Sensitive communications can be encrypted; to decipher them, the user must either possess the key for doing so—or must attempt to crack the code.

None of the above security approaches is foolproof. Many an "invulnerable" safeguard has fallen to the diligence of a crafty attacker or because of the lapse of a careless user.

For some unaccountable reason—perhaps carelessness—officials at an office facility served by sixty telephone ports saw fit to put dial answerback access controls on only fifty-seven of them. As you might expect, hackers located the unguarded lines and penetrated the computer.

The state of the arcane art of cryptology advances to the point where the "unbreakable" code is routinely broken by ever more powerful computers. Four years after running an article on a code so unbreakable that even the Central Intelligence Agency couldn't crack it, *Omni* reported: "the 'unbreakable' code lies shattered." "And," the magazine added, "the fact that researchers have cracked this secret has generated new jitters about the security of banks and other institutions using relatively unsophisticated codes to guard your money."[6]

At issue was a code using two keys and a mathematical function known to cryptologists as the "trapdoor knapsack"—an array of numbers easy to compute in one direction but almost impossible to unravel in the other. Named the Hellman-Diffie code for its inventors Martin Hellman of Stanford University and Whitfield Diffie of BNR, Inc., Palo Alto, the code started coming apart when an Israeli mathematician, Adi Shamir, developed a formula for opening the knapsack's trapdoor. Later, computer expert Leonard Adleman put Shamir's work into his Apple computer and broke one of the Hellman-Diffie keys. "For all practical purposes," *Omni* quoted Diffie, "trapdoor knapsacks are flat on their back."

Then there's the case of the escalating prime numbers. As you remember from Math 101, a prime number—for example, 5, 7, and 11—can be divided only by itself or 1. A composite number is the product of two or more primes—for example, $385 = 5 \times 7 \times 11$. Mathematically, it's fairly easy to determine whether a large number is prime, but it's difficult to break a large composite into its prime factors. This difficulty gives one form of cryptography its relatively secure edge.

In 1980, it was thought almost impossible, even with the largest computers, to factor a 50-digit product of two numbers. But mathematicians say 50-digit numbers are almost trivial now. So they went to 80 digits. These looked secure for a while, but no longer. Now they're talking about 200-digit keys, "which should remain secure for some time," opined *Omni*.

But past progress in code breaking and the relative simplicity of codes used by banks make us wonder. Says cryptographic consultant Peter Schweitzer: "The banks' response to [insufficient protection] appears to be to deny its existence rather than to put in systems that will cure it."[7]

Another response to the threat to security might be:

- Fifth, maintain interest in the problem. Putting in higher-tech safeguards is one thing. Keeping them running properly and technically auditing their strengths in light of new developments is another. Management must develop, document, and assign responsibilities for information security, the Diebold Group advises, and also specify penalties for infractions. Management must incorporate these policies into training programs for users and executives.

MANY WEAK LINKS

It is ironic that two of the most beneficial features of contemporary offices also form two of the weakest links in the security of corporate property. One feature is open layout, sometimes termed office landscape (see Chapter 4). The other is nothing less than automation itself, in particular its weak communication links.

The strengths and weaknesses of the open office lie in its very openness. Freestanding screens, files, machine stands, and desks on a wide expanse of floor permit fast change economically. They also expose the entire floor to view. Messengers, visitors, other strangers—to say nothing of employees, who are office culprits more often than companies like to admit—can see, and if given an opportunity can walk away with, typewriters, calculators, diskettes, PCs. They can walk away with sensitive *information* carelessly exposed on a VDT screen; or (with a little knowledge of how the system works) they can call it up at an unattended terminal. Moving about in a place like that is no big deal; workers in open-plan offices are accustomed to seeing people walking around.

Security-wise organizations take the commonsense precaution of setting up perimeter defenses: putting a reception desk in the path of visitors, for example, and making sure visitors are escorted in and out, to and from whomever they wish to see. Without destroying the flexibility of the open plan, companies can cordon off large areas with interior walls, giving authorized employees controlled access from one section to another. Common access-control systems include combination locks which open if you push perhaps five buttons in the right sequence, or card-in-the-slot devices which unlock doors if your card has the proper coding on its magnetized strip.

And with no more than a 180-degree turn of a workstation, companies can make sure that computers displaying confidential data are turned inward, facing away from aisles.

Again, none of these techniques is foolproof, but nothing in this area is. As security officials never tire of pointing out, whether you're protecting an office or a home, if you can somehow *delay* and *discourage* a perpetrator from completing a crime, you're moving in the right direction. Locks and other barriers delay. Receptionists, alarms, and security personnel discourage. Beyond that, you're back to gut football.

Among the strongest of physical defenses for office buildings is the integrated security system (ISS), which not only suppresses unauthorized access and detects intrusions but also detects fires and other hazards. The ISS doesn't eliminate the need for a security staff; it extends a staff's capabilities. Called "the most powerful aggregate of security technology currently available for an office building environment,"[8] the ISS in essence is a minicomputer-driven communications network which embraces an array of sensors, TV surveillance cameras, data collectors, and the like. Information is funneled to a central console where operators can monitor cameras overlooking loading docks, parking lots, lobbies, and other points, and where lights will flash and alarms will sound if unusual conditions arise.

Networks, whether local area (of which ISS is a specialized example) or wide area, grant OA much of its power to move information (see Chapter 5). They are, if not the heart, then certainly the nervous systems of OA; they are vital. They present also a sprawling opportunity for intrusion, wiretapping, hacking; they are vulnerable. Any communications that travel over wireless paths, such as via satellite or terrestrial microwave, can be picked up by outsiders. That's what makes encryption so necessary. Any satellite voice traffic that moves overseas can also be picked up—and much of it is routinely monitored by intelligence bodies like the National Security Agency (NSA).

"Anytime information moves over a link—whether it simply connects two telephones or two machines in one office, or whether the devices are thousands of miles apart—the information is potentially compromised," states Belden Menkus.

"Securing a data center no longer resolves the issue of information security," states Ted Freiser, president of a Diebold Group division. "The problem now extends beyond one room, one location, and even beyond the company." At least half the computing power of most large organizations will soon be in the hands of non-DP professionals, he says. PCs, portable and even pocket-sized terminals, increased on-line access at multiple points, and other rapid advances in technology all pose new threats to old rules.

To the five points listed earlier for shoring up corporate defenses, Freiser, Menkus, and others would urgently add:

- Sixth, take a fresh look at yesterday's security assumptions. Between one-fifth and one-third of OA systems are "critical to business," according to Diebold; many new and different exposures to informational compromise are developing; power to access and manipulate the system is moving into more employees' hands; increased computer literacy is only widening the base of potential manipulators; and user friendliness is making the mischief easier. Managements need to coordinate their security efforts more closely with corporate policies and plans, which include personnel policies, accountability policies, and certainly OA plans.

"TEMPEST" SECURITY

Perhaps it is only a footnote to assessments of security or perhaps a major issue (it depends on whom you ask); but the fact is that electronic office equipment can be "listened to" by outside devices separate from any network. This has people worried, especially the military.

Text editors, computer terminals, and other electronic keyboard devices give off radiations—a slightly different signal for each key—which, theoretically (or actually), spies could pick up and decipher.

Whatever the case, many Defense Department office machines are secured against the problem. Machines used in business presumably could be secured too, if management thought it advisable. In government, the special shielding which keeps the machines from broadcasting any secrets being typed goes by the odd name of Tempest Security.

I first heard of Tempest while pursuing a story about an early word processing system at the Pentagon. (The Army, incidentally, did some of the best pioneering research into WP ever published. Its Regulation 340-8, a public document, holds up as one of the best papers anywhere on WP cost analysis. Similarly, an excellent Air Force book, dogtagged AFP-88-41, could serve as any manager's text on office-space planning and interior design.) Without Tempest, I was told (though the fellow may have been pulling my leg), a Russian trawler in the Atlantic could zero in on a particular text editor somewhere in Washington, D.C., and know exactly what was being typed.

"No way!" said a source with whom I checked this information. "That's crazy!" But there is something to these emissions, he said, which are known technically as radio-frequency interference (RFI), and to government's need to shield them. RFI emissions can be intercepted within some reasonable distance from the source: an eavesdropper with listening equipment in a van parked near a building, for example, might be able to pick up signals from a text editor on the seventh floor. A concealed enemy in the field would have an even easier time tuning in to an unshielded WP device housed in an army tent.

U.S. government standard NASCEM 5100 defines the amount of leakage Uncle Sam will accept on Tempest-secured equipment. Not much is known publicly about these specs because secrecy is what this is all about. However, published reports have said, "It is believed that the allowable leakage is less than 100 microvolts per meter (μv/m)."[9] A TV video game, by comparison, emits more. Vendors wishing to sell equipment to the government in accordance with NASCEM 5100 must go through an elaborate procedure involving tests and reports. If all goes well, the National Security Agency puts the equipment on the preferred product list of its Special Committee on Compromising Emanations (SCOCE). The NSA also must approve in advance all literature and advertising concerning Tempest products.

Apart from its counterespionage use, Tempest Security is sometimes employed where high levels of radio-frequency interference will affect other nearby electronic equipment. This can happen if several sophisticated devices work off the same power line.

Use of Tempest products can substantially increase, and perhaps double, the original cost of the product itself, says consultant J. Michael Nye, president of Marketing Consultants International in Hagerstown, Maryland.[10]

> In addition, such products have reduced operational flexibility and portability. They also require carefully applied operational procedures to assure complete systems integrity. . . .
>
> In the real world, when classified information is only occasionally used—on a word processor, for example—applying Tempest procedures does not justify their cost. If an adversary does not know when the operator is likely to type classified information, and if [it] represents a small percentage (say 10 percent) of the total equipment use time, Tempest procedures are generally not necessary.

MORE LAWS, FEWER ETHICS

At this writing, thirty-three states have passed laws defining and prohibiting various forms of computer crime. In some states, victims can bring charges even if the defendants do no more than *enter* a system, hacking for fun. Much of what goes on could also be tried in U.S. courts on grounds of breaking federal laws against wire fraud. So another defense may be:

- Seventh, take legal action. (Of course, be prepared to show that the defendant isn't an innocent someone who simply dialed a number—your computer's number—by mistake. A citizen once inadvertently reached President Kennedy in his bedroom in just that way.)

Seen whole, however, OA's security issues make a sorry scene: thieves, embezzlers, spies, saboteurs, and spoiled-rotten kids. There is perhaps one other way to shore up security; few people mention it because it is not a "hard" defense and it is, to many minds, impractical. I will mention it: we might advocate a return to ethics. If these adversaries, or even a significant number of them, came to understand that what they were doing is wrong—wrong enough to stop—and if others learned never to begin, there'd be that much less of a problem. It's as simple (and perhaps naive) as that.

Hacker and congressional witness Neal Patrick called for stepped-up ethics education. Was this only a ploy cooked up by Patrick's attorney? A better question is, did anyone listen? Congressman Ron Wyden of Oregon did go so far as to say, "No matter how many laws we pass, we cannot prevent computer crime. I think education is just going to be the heart of this problem."

"Ethics," says Belden Menkus, "is not what you will do but, effectively, what you won't do." And maybe instruction in such thou-shalt-nots is beyond the limits of business. I asked several security sources whether ethics ever came up in their professional discussions, or was it always just bigger locks and higher tech? I was told that Donn Parker, security consultant at SRI International, often raises the ethics issue. I was told that IBM addresses it. But often as not, security pros debate the *contra*-ethics of those who, seeing nothing wrong in it, would cheat, rob, and otherwise harm business and government.

And it's a sizable group. Where is the office worker who has never taken home stationery supplies or made personal phone calls on company time? Who has never taken sick days while in perfectly good health, just because the days were there? But these misdeeds are petty compared to the million-dollar heists and security breaches taking place with computer assistance.

There *is* a contra-ethic which finds corporations oppressive—to the terrorist mind, they're power bases which can justifiably be blown away. There *is* a contra-ethic which finds employers unjust—and, to the minds of disgruntled workers, proper targets for sabotage. There is even a contra-ethic among the high-tech elite, as my probings among security people confirmed, which holds that any strategem in the access and use (read "misuse") of technology is proper if it is elegant enough.

But back to our larger group. How many of them, given OA resources, do you suppose will refrain from stealing the fruits of someone's labor by making an unauthorized copy of a copyrighted computer program? Doing so violates copyright laws, as would reproducing this book on a copier.

What's being stolen? Information. *Information?* Perhaps the single "blindest" issue raised by OA involves the value and ownership of that intangible asset, information. It is accountancy's blind spot, a management blind spot, an ethical blind spot. Companies lock down the keyboards and allow diskettes to lie loose; and they can't figure out what they've lost when they've lost business secrets. Hackers think there's no wrong in just "trashing about" in some files.

Information raises so many other issues, including public issues of freedom and rights, that we treat it as a separate world-scale topic in Chapter 10.

OA planners have enough to deal with just wrestling with the safeguarding of information. Security issues are sure to intensify, ebb, then reintensify in the constant war between victim and victimizer, between the force-counterforce technologies both use to attain their ends.

May this issue be resolved. It would be tragic if the improvements latent in OA went not to support useful enterprise but rather to make even meaner a world which once seemed so close to betterment that we trusted in modern technology to help us bring it about.

9

Management Issues, Longer-Term

New Roles, New Rules, but Still a Lot of Paper

Picture a company with fewer layers of middle management, where the executives who remain process information themselves rather than having computer technicians do it for them; where employees and the knowledge they possess are carried on the books as assets; and where automated office equipment, while still valued as tangible property, is judged not merely as an investment for financial return but for its impact on the performance of the people who use it.

It is a company using information as an active, competitive resource and not simply as a byproduct of trade, a company so aware of information's importance that it tries constantly to improve the information systems upon which its workers rely.

It is a company in which end users actively participate in the purchase of personal computers, now in their second generation.

It is a company that still consumes large amounts of paper, despite a commitment to office automation.

But because of OA, it is a company in which new and profound organizational relationships have evolved, and it is a company that reflects the longer-term effects of OA as many authorities see them.

Forecasters may quibble over matters of kind and degree and may even dispute the reasons certain effects come about, but in general they agree that the effects OA has had thus far are nothing to what they will be longer range.

Even so, many also believe that further managerial mind openings must occur before greater change can take place. Mind openings which sparked the OA revolution saw automation for the most part as mechanistic efficiency. Much OA literature and many vendor campaigns still reflect this attitude: cut costs, reduce staff, increase output. Nothing is wrong with that outlook, but in the view of many observers, the real payoffs will occur only when management accepts the bold idea that beyond mechanistic efficiency lies OA's greater benefits: worker effectiveness, competitive advantage. That is the great leap forward. And it does take courage to attempt that leap, because it involves big investments aimed no longer at back-office cost-cutting but at improving "front business" performance—investments which cannot be traced as directly to bottom-line results.

But a few enlightened companies have begun moving in that direction. Their managements—intellectually certain that by helping people perform better, their organizations compete better—understand that not every return on investment can be traced in neat rows of figures through conventional accounting. They employ instead new methods of performance accounting which *can* reflect the impacts of particular investments as they involve people. At Merck & Co., for example, a human resources department uses sophisticated accounting models to plot the kinds of investments this big pharmaceutical company must make in OA systems and OA training to ensure that its people, its human resource assets, meet various company goals—for example, the sales targets its marketing arm has projected.

Earlier chapters of this book have dealt with OA's more immediate workplace impacts. From those experiences, and from the examples of Merck and others, we get a sense of trends in OA management. That's what Chapter 9 explores. Speculation is always easy and the higher forms of "blue-skying" are almost addictive. Everyone partakes, so it's not surprising that issues arise even here.

NEW WAYS OF WORKING

OA changes the ways people work. These new ways of working in turn change organizational relationships. Whether or not these new relationships require more or fewer middle managers is open to debate. Consider this scenario:

Fred Jones in marketing has a problem. One of the company's products isn't working properly in the hands of an important customer. Jones doesn't have the solution and probably shouldn't have been presented with the problem in the first place (perhaps it should have gone to customer service). But the customer, being important, got through, and Jones has elected to deal with the problem himself. He gets on the company's electronic message system, outlines the problem, and asks, "Who can help me?" The message is broadcast among a number of people, not all known to Jones personally. Somebody in manufacturing sees the query and sends back a message: "Have you tried such and such?" It solves the problem.

Consider that this communication link never existed in the past. Marketing people may have dealt with order distribution of similar groups but seldom if ever with manufacturing. It's a new experience, and Jones will remember it; he has a new person to turn to when a similar problem arises. Thus, a new pattern develops. OA has introduced a difference in the way Jones works.

At a medical insurance service in Wisconsin, ninety part-time workers process claims from their homes. OA helps make the setup possible. The home workers, mostly married women with children, like the convenience and the hours—fewer than twenty per week. This gives them more time to be with their families. The company likes the arrangement because at under twenty hours per week, the home workers don't come under its union contract. While an office-based claims adjuster starts at $4.10 per hour, receives group health benefits, and can retire after thirty years at around $600 per month, the home-based worker starts at $3.75 per hour, receives no health benefits, and has no retirement plan. Union officials, of course, liken the setup to an electronic sweatshop. But, again, a form of OA has introduced an organizational change.

In many cases it's not possible to tell which is the prime mover—a white-collar union which management finds a way to circumvent or OA systems which simply make working at home feasible. The result in any case is a U.S. force of more than 2 million home-based workers. As we saw in Chapter 7, estimates put this force at 10 million by 1990. OA abets this trend.

FEWER LAYERS OF MANAGEMENT

The electronic message system through which Jones zapped his query to co-workers completely bypassed secretaries, messengers, and other administrative go-betweens of the traditional office. It totally bypassed organizational channels through which—going by the book—communications must flow. So again OA affected organizational relationships, making functions unnecessary, rules obsolete.

If working at home had not been feasible for those ninety part-timers with the Wisconsin insurance service, it is reasonable to assume they would have been replaced by forty-five full-time workers in the office. Four supervisors might have been necessary to oversee the work of these forty-five, if grouped in elevens or twelves. As it is, only two supervisors monitor the work of the ninety part-timers.

OA appears to have lessened the need for administrative and supervisory personnel. Its power to reach across lines, to gather information and deliver it swiftly without the aid of intervening staff, allows control to be maintained by fewer executives. This greater "span of control," as it's called, this thinning of executive ranks, may seem no different from the thinning of clerical ranks—it is what OA is supposed to do, isn't it? Well, not always. At least not directly.

The issue is:

The effect of OA on middle management. The issue is hotly debated. In Type I offices, automation does indeed "mechanize" production work. Machines outperform humans at routinized tasks and thus fewer workers are needed. In Type II offices, however, OA supports knowledge workers with information tools—tools no less swift and electronic than their Type I cousins, but installed for different reasons: not to eliminate workers, but to assist them. And yet a curious byproduct of these systems appears to be that in their powerful outreach, certain jobs become superfluous anyway. These jobs may not have been targeted for elimination; OA simply changed the conditions under which they were needed.

A recent item tells of certain purchasing and transportation department employees being offered retirement incentives at Hercules Inc. Their jobs were being eliminated "by videoconferencing and computer systems that enable the company to operate with fewer middle managers." OA consultant Ed Smith of Wilmington, Delaware, who passed this item to me, says it supports his thesis, reached after studying managerial jobs, that "to a large degree *vital job content* may be missing" in the middle ranks. "That 'content' may be more susceptible to automation than the job of the secretary," Smith says.

If the vital content of a job isn't there, can OA be said to have eliminated it? Or did OA only bring its absence to light? John Connell, director of the Office Technology Research Group, believes the latter.

> Sure you can eliminate a layer of management, but did technology do that? Of course it didn't do that. The company didn't need that layer in the first place. Technology merely opened peoples' eyes to that fact. By changing things, OA changed perceptions of what was needed to carry out the work.

> The same thing happens when a recession comes along. All of a sudden, companies find they can wipe out all kinds of staffs. How come? Because the recession changed perceptions. Good as those people may have been, management discovered it really didn't need them.

During an interview granted me at his palatial, art-filled home near Pasadena, California, Connell picked up a business magazine which featured, that week, another of its frequent advertising supplements on OA. "Look at this," he gruffed; " 'Cut costs,' 'cut staff,' more of the same pop approach, always pandering to management's obvious questions, 'Where's the money?', 'Where's the savings?' The fact is, with these systems, 'savings' aren't there. *Value* is there."

Taking a contrary position on the fate of middle management is the Diebold Group. "Many futurists speculate that access to decision support systems by senior levels of management will reduce the need for middle management," then–vice president Joseph Ferreira said at a briefing in 1983. "We do not subscribe to this view."

While strongly agreeing that OA technology will continue to improve decision-making processes, Ferreira argued that OA cannot replace "highly context-dependent" managerial judgments. "We are not as pessimistic as some regarding the 'declining' role of middle management, except"—here in line with Connell—"as it results from other more immediate forces like earnings declines and unwieldy bureaucracy."[1]

To the contrary, productivity planner Shirley Andrus, manager of corporate services at Forward Technology of Santa Clara, California, says:[2]

> The role of middle managers will be managed by higher levels. [But] if we continue our current practice of promoting "technicrats" (most technically qualified) to manage throughput, rather than promoting "managers" (individuals who are people-oriented), productivity improvement will be offset by mediocre performance and high turnover.

TECHNOLOGY'S TWO DIRECTIONS

In the beginning was Data Processing, and nothing that could be computed was computed without it. And it was good. It held seeds of great knowledge, beyond the mere counting of what was owed and what was paid, two by two and four by four—knowledge of much use to the elders of the tribes. And it seemed good. And ministering angels appeared to Data Processing and said, "Henceforth ye shall be known as Management Information Systems." And no information that could be systemized was systemized without it. So it was; but many murmured it was not as good as had been promised. All this took place in the days before Office Automation.

Then arose OA, and with it arose a new people unmindful of decrees of old laid down by MIS, for this new people began to systemize information themselves. And they said, "Information shall be for all the people, and its systems shall be for all the people; and it shall be good." And even elders of the tribes fell under these teachings, saying, "Now we can obtain knowledge ourselves, and we can command our systems, 'Grant us information,' and it shall be granted, and we can exchange this knowledge amongst ourselves and it shall be done. The priests of MIS who were once our masters shall henceforth be our servants."

Then among the priests contentions arose, and great rivalries troubled the tribes of the land; tongues were confounded; and the new people of OA, following many prophets, were yet leaderless and much confused.

But certain prophets told of ministering angels which had again appeared, declaring unto them:

"Henceforth shall this land be divided into two kingdoms. One realm will hold fast in a great center and shall be called the New MIS; the other will be scattered and shall be called the User Community. And the two will hold council from time to time, for the talents which MIS received of old shall not be taken away but shall be imbued with new spirit, and shall be used to support the User Community in its dealings with information, and knowledge, and the making of noble decisions. Amen."

- *Press release, New York, September 11, 1984.* "End-user computing is likely to be the *dominant means* of providing information support in major corporations. In fact, many believe that by 1990 information processing done by MIS professionals will constitute only about 25 percent of the total processing done in those companies." [Emphasis added.] John Diebold & Associates, quoting president Theodore Freiser.
- *Interview, San Marino, California, October 1984.* "One has to look where technology is going, and it's moving in two integrated directions. One is toward a continuing buildup of the large centralized data center; the other is out to the office workplace. And we've got to come up with organizational approaches that address each separately, yet with a technological architecture that supports both." John Connell.
- *Interview, Honolulu, October 1984.* "I think we're moving toward an integrated structure, and yet a split. Like personal computers,

where do they belong? Data processing claims them; office automation claims them. What I think you're going to see is the technology managed at one level and the applications managed at another—MIS the one, end users the other." Dr. Raymond Panko.

- *Corning Glass Co., Corning, New York.* An information center (I-center) originally set up to relieve a backlog in MIS now serves more than 1000 end users whose needs range from market planning to creating the graphics for sales literature to spreadsheet analyses to word processing. The story is told of how John Parker, one of America's more enlightened MIS executives, recognized the growing desire of Corning end users to do their own computer work. He set up an in-house PC store and in effect said to the users, "Here are your computers; take them. We'll support you, we'll give you technical help, *but it's your show.*"[3] Users agreed, later forming their own council, which meets periodically with central MIS. The council reviews and passes on all matters of information policy, including new technology.

  "But it took a very enlightened MIS director at Corning to be willing to back down on the traditional way of doing things and say okay," comments Connell.

  The Corning information center gets credit for dramatically improving decision making and productivity and for holding down overhead throughout the company. It saves a reported $1 million annually in traceable hard dollars, and management estimates an equal amount has been earned in soft benefits.[4]

THE NEW "MIS"

Other notable I-centers include those at Country Companies, Bloomington, Illinois; Liberty Mutual, Boston; Monsanto Co., St. Louis; and United Technology's Essex Group, Fort Wayne (see Chapter 4).

With a staff of six, the Country Companies I-center consults with and trains some 200 end users annually. Calls for assistance level off as users become adept at processing information on the investments and insurance policies in which the companies deal. This direct user involvement saves the organization an estimated $325,000 per year.[5]

A walk-in operation staffed by a manager, four consultants, and an aide, the Liberty Mutual center serves—as many do—not only as a training facility but also as an equipment facility. Here, special or occasional devices like a graphics plotter can be used as needed. According to center manager John Ulery, results have been excellent. It has helped users in one department save 1344 hours on a project, enabled the company fleet administrator to cut two days of computation from certain recurring reports, and chalked up "dramatic savings" in financial and actuarial areas.

Monsanto's central MIS manager Hal White reports that fifteen such centers operate throughout the corporation. His own facility serves as a kind of I-center for the other I-centers. Like many automated companies, Monsanto also operates an in-house hot line over which equipment users can get emergency help with problems.

It may be that the I-center as presently set up will be only a short-lived phenomenon—a way station in the transition from MIS servicing data projects and writing programs for others to the time when this work will be done with considerable self-sufficiency in the separate user departments needing it. Not only will departmental staffs process their own work and develop software for new projects, they will also have a greater say—perhaps a decisive say—in buying their own OA products and services.

While MIS will maintain considerable influence in its own sphere and will probably have governance over matters like systems integration and technostructure operations, its budgets tomorrow may not be simple extensions of what their growth has been in the past. In fact, as surveys confirm, MIS budgets already have failed to keep up with the sharp increases in informational work loads being experienced by most companies.

It may be that many firms held the line on spending because of the recessionary-to-only-mildly-bullish economic climate of the mid-1980s. But it may also be that MIS budgets are being clipped because more information processing work is flowing to end users—OA's inexorable organizational change. No doubt a combination of forces is at work.

A MORE INFLUENTIAL USER

The issue is:

Who *is* responsible for governing affairs in the divided, yet integrated land of information? Who should hold the purse strings? Will early experiences with OA change not only working processes but also planning and purchasing processes?

To the regret of many onlookers, the technically oriented priests of MIS still hold too many levers of power. But in light of the trends just discussed, numerous OA watchers believe this condition can't last. End users, they maintain, will exercise considerable influence in the purchasing decisions of products like second-generation PCs.

End users already have begun demanding effective interconnection between their first-generation PCs and mainframes (see Chapter 5), and many are of sufficient rank in their organizations that their demands can't forever be ignored—even though meeting them is often very difficult. MIS never had to deal with demands like that before, with outside people wanting a say in what goes on. There is consternation in the land.

"I'm troubled by this chaos and the manifold directions in which everybody's going," exclaims John Connell. "No coordination. Vendors out for the short haul, not educating for the long haul."

Connell agrees that with technology moving in two directions, there probably will always be someone at the top to oversee the exchanges going on between MIS and the user. "But the real fleshing out of the system, the programming of it and so forth, will have to come from the users. Really, the best systems architectures have always come up from users' desires, not down from technicians' designs."

The trouble with most I-centers today, the user-group director went on, is that they're still run from the DP point of view. "They'll say, 'Here, you can use my Digital computer.' But . . . the user . . . wants to know, 'How can I use *my* computer and occasionally pull information out of *your* computer?' Sure, [the user] needs the specialist. But not to control, to facilitate."

LOSS LEADERS, LOST LEADERS

John Connell, like others, reserves special scorn for vendors seen to be out only for a short-haul killing. In his keynote address to the fifth Office Automation Conference, in Los Angeles in 1984, Connell wisecracked that the only winners in the entire OA movement thus far had been the advertising agencies with their commercials and four-color inserts. In our conversation, I reminded him of that. "Yes," he sighed, "And what do all those ads say? 'Buy my machine, it's faster, it's got more software.' Price, bucks, loss leaders. You're hard pressed to find an ad that talks about these machines as investments to improve your ability to compete, and to say how and why. It's always, 'We've got more keys than they have.' Or another tack is 'Trust me. I've been around a hundred years. So trust me. Buy my machine'."

Connell recalled a time when large computer firms like Burroughs, IBM, and Sperry spent fortunes on customer education. Many people currently in the computer field got their basic training that way. "IBM has probably educated more people than any other entity in the world," he said. "Today, you call them and they don't call back." (He's right.)

"There's no leadership in the industry," he went on. "No intellectual, conceptual leadership."

I asked, "What would you do differently if you were a vendor? Would you still be so critical of quick killings?"

Connell reflected. "Yes, I really would be. Information technology management in the United States today is floundering. Floundering for a sense of mission, and trying to understand what it should be doing about all the things that are happening out there.

"And there's no loyalty! With their big investments in education years ago, computer companies did build loyalty. But a new generation of buyers—users—is coming to the fore. What vendor has given them the *understanding* that fosters loyalty? All they've given is hype about bigger and faster and cheaper. I think there still are big opportunities for vendors, other than the traditional ones, if they come up with good products and market them intelligently. That means customer education, training, and support in developing their information methodologies."

THE "PAPER PAPERS"

Paper. It almost seems too humdrum to mention. The trade show we toured in Chapter 5 hummed with new systems and media for the messages of business, new ways to eliminate that business burden, paperwork.

But look again at the *paper* literature we collected. Booklets and brochures for copiers and printers, plotters and fax systems—for *makers* of paperwork. Each year it seems exhibitors offer more plastic carry bags to tote away the printed matter they give out. Shouldn't they be distributing computer diskettes? After all, it now costs less to store information on magnetic disks than on paper; and optical disks will be even less costly.

Another long-term attribute of OA will be the continued use of paper as a prevalent information medium. With luck, OA can cut into the volumes of this costly stuff which figuratively drowns us. Recall the alarming statistic of Chapter 2: the earth can be wrapped up 20 times just in the paper *on file*. But management would be foolish to try to push the tide back too far. Paper is just too convenient to expect people to work without it.

Back in 1962, well-known consultant Arthur Barcan and his Records Management Institute figured that U.S. business maintained over 2000 pieces of paper for every employee. Government held five times more per worker. (These data continue to circulate, though conveniently undated.) Barcan's estimates multiplied out to roughly 130 trillion pieces of paper, and while he didn't say how long it took to amass that much, Xerox today estimates that the U.S. market creates 1.5 trillion pages of new business documents per year.[6]

Except for cost, paper documents have everything going for them that OA planners dream about. They're technologically elegant—you don't even have to plug them in. They're user-friendly—to refer again to information, you just flip back; there are no Reverse, Fast Forward, or other buttons to push. They're convenient—you just fold 'em up and stick 'em in your pocket. They're editable, clippable, filable, disposable. And you can read them in bed. Not so easy with an IBM PC-XT.

OA media are manifold, of course, and suiting medium to message poses special user issues. It's not simply a question of paper or something else. It's a question of appropriateness to the nature and frequency of use. For call-ups of quick-reference information, there's no need for permanence, and even the coarsest alphanumerics on a CRT will do. For graphics and for long labors over spreadsheets and other data, users need high-resolution screens if they are to work effectively. For archival permanence, microfilm and optical disks are proper media. For document permanence and reading matter generally, paper is still best. If it's only a brief notice, any legible "quick and dirty" reproduction could suffice. If it's a lengthy report, correspondence-quality printing is needed. And if you're out to impress an important client, the cleanest typography on the finest linen stationery wouldn't be overdoing it.

ACCOUNTABILITY AND CONTROL

In the automated office in the longer range, with centralized control of information resources lessened if not abolished, individual managers will be held accountable for whatever resources they use. Even such seeming minutiae as media choice may figure in performance audits, for it could make a major difference in the effect of one persons' work upon that of others.

Some MIS executives will graduate to senior corporate officerships, still responsible for managing the MIS shop but also responsible *to* users who seek their help in running their own OA gear. These will be positions to which many will aspire yet not all will fill with distinction. The curious, almost inner-conflicting duality in what is being asked—that a technician-manager also be a facilitator for users—will be too much for many a technological warrior who was deemed to have earned the promotion, no one realizing that it was for a much different branch of service.

With the advancement of MIS executives, certain juniors will step up to become operational managers of the new mainframe centers, with their OA links and user support facilities. The idea of a *center,* however, with its connotations of control, will gradually give way to a concept of *utility,* with connotations of service. Its personnel will be accessible, its response immediate and sufficiently unnoticed by the user as to be, as they say, transparent. This service group should do well.

Organizations will wrestle with problems of multilingual and multilevel literacy among users, for which early, differing experiences with computers will have been responsible. The more successful training and education fare will no longer attempt to be all things to all people but will be separately designed for at least three types of users: the "learning literate," the "reasonably literate," and the "computer literate."

Whether or not automated organizations operate with fewer levels of middle management remains an open question.

Whether or not automation cures management of its addiction to short-term gains over long-term results also remains an open question. OA watchers like John Connell confess to being "totally frustrated" on this score. OA watchers like Joseph Ferreira are more sanguine.

"When it is discovered that a key leverage point in the corporation can be improved by information technology, it will be accepted even when a greater return on investment is demonstrable in the near term with competing options," Ferreira says. "Return on investment and other such metrics will be given subordinate roles to alternative decision paths based on broader business considerations."

These will be turbulent times for both MIS and the corporation, Ferreira says; and times with "unprecedented means for improving the quality of management in our offices," as think-tank operator Charles Lecht, founder and chairman of Lecht Sciences Inc., New York, sees it. The very technology that aids office-based professionals in their work can aid managers in appraising that work, says Lecht. Task definition, task assignments, appraisal of available resources, status reports of jobs on-line, all can be done speedily through critically located, management-operated PCs.

The lag between performing a task and assessing it becomes almost negligible through recourse to these channels, Lecht continues. What it means is:[7]

> . . . more efficient management decisions, and fewer office "black holes" engendered by paper and physical distance. . . . When pertinent details can be summoned by a manager at a terminal, all aspects of constructive (rather than inhibitory) control can be enhanced, to everyone's benefit, provided the manager is as intelligent as the terminal.
>
> I realize that, to some extent, I seem to be suggesting that management techniques can best be practiced in the future if managers never emerge from their new electronic cocoons. . . . However, I would also observe that the best managment recognizes the essential role of motivation in eliciting the best from staff. . . . [It] will remain necessary (all the more so as OA proceeds) for management to wear an occasionally visible human face.
>
> In extremis, it would surely be an abuse of electronic mail to send a pink slip to a green screen.

If discerning OA's impact on organizations is difficult, grasping its impact on society and the world is more difficult still. However, in Chapter 10, we glimpse a few visions and essay a few speculations.

10

World and Social Issues

Information: Who Will Own It? Who Will Control It?

Is it too much to say that our many office machines are actually tools of freedom? They are of course tools of information, and information—uncontrolled—is what all tyrants fear. The point was never more vividly made than in Poland's military crackdown against Solidarity in the winter of 1981–1982.

Among the first bases to be controlled were communications centers. Among the first weapons of the worker groups to be confiscated were their tools of information. The order went out to offices: censorship would be imposed on all correspondence, Telexes, and other telecommunications. Links would be cut if message content "threatens the interests of state defense or security." Electronic or hard-copy dispatches would be obliterated of information "whose content may threaten the security or defense of the state."

Reports leaking out of Poland in those days told of wholesale roundups of duplicating machines and of Solidarity units furtively distributing leaflets which workers had typed one by one. "Let no typewriter stand idle," one of the leaflets urged.

In our extraordinary proliferation of information tools—our copiers, printers, computers, and more, in offices and now also in homes—Americans possess an arsenal as formidable as any for the defense of our liberties. We don't often think of office equipment that way, and fortunately we have no need to do so. It takes a crisis like Poland's to make us realize not only what we possess but how free we are to bear these arms of information and to aim our messages at whom we will.

And yet concern is often voiced that office automation and the other forms of information technology are leading us to the world of an all-knowing, tyrannical Big Brother, as in George Orwell's *1984*. Technology in the wrong hands—or, in more dire forecasts, technology by itself—will control us rather than us controlling it. Well, 1984 has passed and Big Brother, if he's coming, is somewhat late. Artificial intelligence (AI), the next stage of software development, is definitely coming, and already there's concern that we will allow AI to do our thinking for us.

Big brats, if not Big Brothers, in the form of hackers, are even now rifling the electronic files of business and government, and big crooks are right beside them (see Chapter 7). Why couldn't sinister government agencies do the same thing in the name of national security, that easy excuse for abuse?

It's an open secret that the National Security Agency regularly eavesdrops on overseas telephone traffic and pokes about in other forms of transmission "to protect U.S. communications and produce foreign intelligence information."[1] With so many business and personal messages constantly being telecommunicated, and with so much business and personal information on file in countless computers, what's to stop other, less-responsible agents from delving into these private affairs out of acute official paranoia?

"What is at stake is not so much the use of information technology as such but its use by powerful groups in society, by the large bureaucracies that already dominate much of the present societies regardless of their governmental systems," writes Klaus Lenk, professor at the University of Oldenberg, West Germany.

In an issue of *Information Resource Management* thematically entitled "Information Technology and Society,"[2] Lenk argues that a key force shaping technology is the desire of powerful groups to stay in power and consolidate their strength. "Thus the tendency of power to accrete to groups holding a commanding position in society is likely to continue."

Some OA watchers call for the United States to develop overriding policies for the creation and use of information, as other developed nations like Japan have done. Such policies could help in standardizing technology, but they would also focus national attention on the fact that technology often outraces government's ability to enforce the information laws it does have. But other people, concerned for example with safeguarding the rights of a free press, abhor the very thought of information policy.

"Once you agree to the principle of government setting information rules or goals or guidelines, however benign they might seem, *they* gotcha," a colleague told me.

In previous chapters of this book, we have examined OA's effects on work and people within organizations. We have tried to define, if not settle, various issues which OA raises before, during, and after its introduction. With this final chapter, we move beyond the office to a range of expectations and theories on how advanced information technology may affect our wider world. We again attempt to define, but surely will not settle, broad issues which involve all peoples as, together, we approach the third millenium.

SPECIAL VERNACULARS

The implications of increased office automation upon our society and our world are staggering. No one fully comprehends them, but just as OA has begun to change the ways we work, related forms of information technology are changing the ways we live and the ways we deal with our neighbors.

And just as office functions are beginning to merge in a mesh of spreading networks, these other networks, devoted to personal and public affairs, have begun to mesh with those of the office. (That's "mesh," not "mess"—although there have been messes, too.)

Special vernaculars paralleling OA's describe these other functions, and all draw from the one mother tongue of information technology. The banker speaks of EFTS, the electronic funds transfer system, and ATSs, automated teller stations, those money-dispensing machines where customer and EFTS join hands. The retailer speaks of POS terminals, point-of-sale "cash registers" which do more than hold cash and give change. They capture data on sales by product, style, hour of the day, or any other criteria important to management; and increasingly they automate this input through bar-code scanners, price-tag perforations, or other digital techniques. The publisher speaks in-house of ETS, the electronic typesetting system, and EPMS, the electronic page-makeup system. ETS and EPMS are two highly refined offspring of word processing. Publishing also offers the world EDBs—electronic databases—which are often in partnership with RCSs—remote computing services.

The TV producer speaks of CATV, community antenna television, and, in partnership with the publisher and the movie producer, conjures such offerings as HIS, home information systems, and HERS, home entertainment-request services—databases, in effect, of films and tapes available on call. Then, adding the merchant and the banker to the partnership, these partners orchestrate such info-shopping medlies as teletext and videotex (terms vary).

With them, in the age of HA ("household automation"), you could sit before a PC-TV-telephone console and call for a menu of videotex services—database, shopping, banking, and more.

SHOPPING AT HOME

Let's go shopping. Up pops a menu of merchandise for sale. How about some skis? Pictures, prices, and brief descriptions of various kinds roll by. One pair looks especially good, so we key in the item number and enter a purchase. Now it's time to pay. We tell the system to debit our bank account and credit the amount to the vendor. The system says "Thanks" and tells us the skis will arrive next Tuesday. Now that we own some skis, we should put them to use. Back to the menu for a different service—travel. To where? Resorts. What kind? Ski. Scenes of inviting places schuss past. We book a reservation at one, do the banking routine again, and get ready to pack.

Scenarios like this have been around for years. Despite the fact that they've not played well in real life, a fledgling videotex industry continues attracting confident new services, private in the United States and governmental in Europe. Videotex has made limited strides in Europe, where some of the government services operate (or plan to). And the appearance of news, sports, and stock reports—albeit in slow news-ticker format—over certain U.S. cable channels could be an electronic foot in the door.

A test of something called "QUBE" in Columbus, Ohio, provided viewers with "two-way TV" that even allowed them to vote in quickie opinion polls. The system was much publicized as heralding the future. Recently, however, the test ended with inconclusive results.

In France, what have been called the "3V" tests of videotex also appear to have ended inconclusively, on the basis of data released. The three V's were the communities of Velizy, Val de Bievre, and Versailles, and the trials lasted eighteen months. In Velizy, the computers of nearly 190 companies were networked to terminals in peoples' homes. They were the kind of terminals the French PTT—the postal, telephone, and telegraph service—hopes to install in more than 25 million homes by the early 1990s.

The average Velizy family made only two or three calls per week—

"hardly the base for an economic service," one commentator concluded.[3] However, another offering called "3MV," a free electronic community bulletin board, did take off. After a slow start, it attracted 1800 users and carried 1500 messages per week.

Perhaps videotex as an industry must be granted a slow start to gather the masses it needs. Or perhaps, as so often true in the past, capability doesn't equal feasibility. Is shopping at home too insular? Are the menu routines too slow? Is there too much to choose from?

Maybe the industry itself is too insular; for example, look at the confusing similarity of its names. So far the field has welcomed such firms as Viewtel, Viewtron, ViewMax, Videodial, VideoLog, and Videotel.

Which brings up another term, "viewdata"—not full-fledged videotex, but a marriage of television and computers for calling database information to your screen. According to International Resource Development Inc., revenues of the U.S. online database industry will hit $10 billion by 1994. How much of that will come from home TV call-ins, IRD doesn't say, although it forecasts $1 billion in revenue from electronic yellow pages by the mid-1990s.

In light of other information industry projections, these numbers seem underwhelming. Says IRD's Steven Weissman, "With all the other excitement in the air, there's a widespread sense that the on-line services industry is stagnating, but that's not true. Even if it's less glamorous than some other parts of the information industry, it's a real growth industry." Weissman warns firms against chasing a pie-in-the-sky mass market by making systems ever more user-friendly, as this could alienate current markets. "If vendors are going to flourish, they're going to have to slide their system over towards 'Everyman' without ticking their current users off. That won't be easy to do."[4]

Seth Baker, president of American Broadcasting Co.'s ABC Publishing unit, says viewdata's potential, "if I may understate the case, is tremendous." But moments after saying that at an IBM Media Industry Conference, he cautioned against current notions of future electronics at home:[5]

> There's something wrong with this image of the sedentary, affluent American hunkered down amidst all of his or her electronic gadgetry with the world at his fingertips, while the world outside is falling apart. It's hard to square the image of the American nestled in his communications cocoon with the condition of the villager in India, the peasant in China, the farmer in Mexico.
>
> What I am saying here is that the goals inherent in moving successfully into a post-industrial, information-based society will not have to do with creating the perfect communications environment for the in-

dividual American, but rather with productivity and problem-solving and improving the quality of life in the world at large.

What EFTS, EDBs, HIS, HERS, viewdata, videotex, OA, and the typewriters of Solidarity have in common are their end products: information. They are each a limited tool for finding information, creating information, keeping information, and/or moving it about. They feed a human hunger to *know* and *inform*, not just for business purposes, but for a world of purposes—education, amusement, politics, war, peace, justice, and, in the wrong hands, tyranny.

The issue is:

How are those tools to be used on a world, national, and *personal* basis?

What made the fictional Big Brother big, after all, was his technological underpinnings. Turning to the grimmest reality, we shudder at what else Hitler might have done with computers to aid his madness. How would Nazis have used today's many outlets for mass propaganda and the opportunities for electronic sabotage (to say nothing of all that microchip weaponry on the military side)?

And yet we can contrast an opposite case for information technology, as hinted at above: namely, that its very spread is liberating. It proliferates into more and more hands—and minds—and the increasing ability this gives to users to inform, and be informed by, other minds is so incredibly different from anything the world has known before that Big Brother stands little chance of controlling a people in possession of such power.

The tyrant's last hope of tyranny, in this view, lies in areas where information systems have not yet reached enough users. What to make, then, of the desire among third world nations to leap from centuries-old agricultural economies directly into the Information Age—skipping altogether the industrial age as a stage of normal development? If information technology reached enough skilled hands and understanding minds, it could propel third world populations into a twenty-first–century society of undreamed wealth and freedom. But if such systems reached only an elite, could these leaders—would these leaders—use them to exploit and enslave?

SINNERS, SAINTS, AND POWER

In the profoundest sense, information and the knowledge it brings mean power. Information technology provides the *tools* of power. It's not a question of whether this technology is good or bad. The saint can use it as well as the sinner—the *users* are the good and bad. But it may be a question of how wide the usage is. In democratic theory, power belongs to the people. And it belongs to them, as the framers of the Constitution said and as I recall from History 101, not because people are all so smart and noble but because this dispersion acts as a safeguard against the tyranny of a few, against Big Brothers, George IIIs, and the rest. So, technology to the people.

In an extraordinary book, *The World Challenge,*[6] French author Jean-Jacques Servan-Schreiber draws striking contrasts between the way the Arab world views us and the way we view the Arab world. We see them as sitting over fortunes in oil. They see us as sitting over fortunes in technology with which to create wealth that can never run out—information. What Arabs would say to the west, Servan-Schreiber contends (and I simplify) is: "You in the west need our oil." (This was painfully true at the time the book came out.) "We and the rest of the third world need your technology. Can't we strike a deal?"

A former French politician, founder of *L'Express* magazine, and intimate of the powerful, Servan-Schreiber comes across as one who deeply believes that governments, joined as partners and not at odds as now, can overcome global crises through a pooling of their respective strengths and interests. He says this is not a utopian view.

Servan-Schreiber sees a world in which the microprocessor rids humanity of strife and servile labor, not only in the disease-ridden backwaters of the third world but also in rusting America, where older industries can survive only through computerization and robotics. Echoing the call of Seth Baker, Servan-Schreiber envisions computer terminals in remote Indian villages teaching agricultural skills to the undernourished population and pulling other life-enhancing information from orbiting satellites—a scene some may find overdrawn. Servan-Schreiber quotes the view that computer power is "virtually free"—another exaggerated assumption.

And yet it makes us wonder if greater technological literacy might have prevented the Union Carbide tragedy in Bhopal, India, where poison gas leaking from a chemical plant killed more than 2000 people. Much hindsight has focused on the level of Indian technological understanding, even among workers at the plant. Two weeks after the accident, *The New York Times* quoted Rashmi Mayur, founder of a Bombay environmental research organization, as saying: "There is no continuum of intelligence [in India], as in the United States. There are only two layers: a thin veneer of highly skilled people at the top and hundreds of millions of people who don't have a basic understanding of industrialization at the bottom." Workers without an "industrial culture" may master certain steps but cannot solve crises, said Noel Brown of the United Nations Environment Program; Indian workers "have not internalized the technological culture." An inspector's report of plant operations in Bhopal seemed to underscore the point: training comprised "rote memorization [without] a basic understanding of the reasoning behind procedures."[7]

We could speculate endlessly over whether terminals in remote villages would have sufficiently enabled Indian workers to internalize enough technology to have averted the Bhopal disaster. But it probably wouldn't have hurt.

In any case, the essence of a bold plan is there, and like Alvin Toffler in *The Third Wave* and John Naisbitt in *Megatrends,* Servan-Schreiber is onto something, even though he may not have the details exactly right. Bold ideas for using information technology to aid humanity deserve a hearing from all who employ such technology now. It's the least that users of OA and allied systems can do, knowing that they are the envy of—if not yet partners to—the world.

A QUESTION OF RIGHTS

Two rights eternally conflict in considerations of information, especially the kind of personal information likely to be on file in offices—the right to privacy and the right to know. Sometimes a third right gets involved—the right to own information and enjoy the fruits of its sale.

The Founding Fathers wrangled with these questions in framing the First and Fourth Amendments to the Constitution and in establishing copyright protection, and lawyers argue still over what the Founding Fathers meant. Enter OA technology, whose speed and reach only confound these issues. OA surely was not on the framers' minds in 1787.

The Privacy Act of 1974, which prohibits the use of data for purposes other than those for which they were collected, draws sustenance from the Fourth Amendement right of the people "to be secure in their persons, houses, papers, and effects." But the act hasn't stopped government agencies from using computers to match lists of names in an effort to catch tax cheats or draft evaders. In some cases, the government bought the names from private list houses, which had obtained them legally from public files. "What's wrong with that?" ask the agencies in their own defense.

What is wrong with that? The Freedom of Information Act (FOIA), which permits citizens to see public records, with certain exceptions, upholds the "right to know" and draws sustenance from the First Amendment's guarantees of a free press. But FOIA has been under fire almost from the day President Nixon (of all people) signed it. Corporations dislike it, fearing disclosure of business secrets; law enforcement bodies dislike it, fearing disclosure of informants' identities; bureaucrats who fear a spotlight thrown upon bureau dealings dislike it, and they argue (sometimes with justification) that FOIA search requests cause too much labor and paperwork. In general, everyone who doesn't want disclosures disclosed dislikes it.

Soon this struggle between privacy and knowing may not matter. Technology, together with public sentiment, may make "knowers" of us all—just as copyright ownership made virtual "owners" of us all. Try as publishers might, they couldn't keep people from making photocopies of their copyrighted wares. Try as film and TV moguls might, they couldn't keep people from taping their creations on videocassette recorders (VCRs). Yes, the copyright reforms of 1976 cleaned things up a bit, saying reproduction by ones or twos for purposes of research and scholarship was all right and granting authors and other creators of works direct copyright ownership. And the Supreme Court settled matters a bit by okaying VCR recording for home viewing. In both instances, however, the principal information owners took losses.

I have a belief which I can't prove, but which I know others share, that the tide is running in favor of *knowing,* and if that's true we'd all better get used to less privacy. It's not just a matter of technology, although that's a large part of it. User ability to penetrate systems, as we've seen, appears to be gaining on technicians' abilities to secure systems. Computer ability to match up legally available information puts increasingly detailed profiles of people at the disposal of others, and there doesn't seem to be any workable way of preventing people from making use of what is so freely available.

Beyond technology, it's also a matter of public attitude, of how much secrecy we'll tolerate, at least in America. Even a group as powerful as President Reagan and his immediate White House staff had trouble making an order stick that was designed to keep government employees from leaking information to the press. National Security Decision Directive 84 called for prepublication review of the writings of thousands of federal officials and even subjected the employees to lie detector tests. Its heavier-handed features were eventually rolled back after much hue and cry by the media.

On Capitol Hill, efforts to weaken the Freedom of Information Act caused additional furor, but the so-called Freedom of Information *Protection* Act of 1983—some dubbed it the Destruction Act—got nowhere.

Privacy advocates demand stronger walls around the files of banks, stores, hospitals, government agencies, and all the other places where information might show what kind of people we are and what kind of habits we have—and then run home to enjoy the latest scandals disclosed on the evening news.

Freedom of information advocates say facts are facts, truth is truth: "Let the world know about child molesters, and for God's sake don't let them work in day-care centers!" (But then we hear, "Well, yes, I was picked up once on a minor drug charge, but why let that out? If they ever find out, I'll never get that job!")

ACCURASSY!

Truth is truth and it shall make us free. And facts are facts—if they *are* facts. If computer services are compiling more and more information and selling it, and if computer users are acting more and more upon what they've bought, the stuff being traded should at least be accurate.

And when future systems, embodying artificial intelligence, do more than merely process data but use it to *advise* and *decide,* the adage "Garbage in, garbage out" will seem a quaint throwback to OA's good old days. Misinformation in could mean lasting tragedy out.

As this is written, my wife has returned from shopping with the tale of a woman she'd met in a slow-moving checkout line. The woman said her husband died ten months ago. Through some error, conceivably nothing more than the keying of "Mr." as "Mrs.," "information" now shows that she, not he, is deceased. Throughout the spring and summer, this misinformation has infested computer after computer. The woman's credit has been terminated, her hospitalization coverage dropped, and her Social Security checks cut off. She writes, she phones, to set things right. A horror story.

Norma Rollins, director of the Privacy Project of the New York Civil Liberties Union, relates the story of a 40-year-old man being considered for promotion to a high-level job that required security clearance. He never got it, because an investigator reported that he had once been a member of the Communist party. Only later did the man find out that he had been considered for the job and why he was passed over. Had he known, he would have been able to set the record straight: it was his father, not he, who belonged to the party, and his father had abandoned the family when the son was five years old.[8]

Provisions of federal and some state laws allow persons to see certain records in their files to check for mistakes and correct them. But a related issue concerns not what's done with faulty records but what's done accurate ones.

Every time someone applies for insurance or checks into a hospital, he or she signs a statement authorizing insurers to see the medical records. Where else might those records go? "You have no idea what you're authorizing," says Robert Ellis Smith, publisher of *Privacy Journal*. "That information no longer stays with your doctor."[9]

At least two major networks help the insurance industry process claims information. One, Medical Information Bureau (MIB), maintains a base of coded medical data on some 11 million individuals, according to Smith. The other, National Electronic Information Corp. (NEIC), serves as a clearinghouse, converting medical data into formats insurers want while also consolidating bills for these companies.

Representatives of both MIB and NEIC deny their organizations pose threats to privacy, and they say statutes drafted by privacy advocates would not require the companies to do things differently. MIB exists, its representative added, mainly to prevent fraud by applicants, and claimants are told how they can see their records. NEIC plans eventually to issue "smart cards" to people its clients insure with data on the insured embedded in an electronic strip.

"Ideally, everything would be electronic," said an executive of the commercial network through which NEIC data flow.

Privacy advocates know how fast electronic word travels, and that's exactly what they fear.

DATA FOR SALE

While viewing outside events, we haven't forgotten inside people, those who manage automated offices where so many private data are kept. All the public issues discussed above could eventually affect what OA users may and may not do with information—legally.

Take the issue of information being regarded as a valuable corporate asset. Does this mean an asset for in-house use only? Or does it mean for outside sale—that if a company has sensitive but valuable information on customers, for example, it can ship the data to whoever pays the price? As OA plans mature, the next wise addition to the OA planning committee might be the corporate lawyer.

Publishers have long reaped extra income from the sale of subscriber lists. A yacht dealer can buy a dandy mailing list from a yachting magazine. The same thing applies with computer firms and PC publications. But these lists are for mailings—not investigations—and a mailer is overjoyed to get a 1 percent response to the tons of literature sent out.

In many states, motor vehicle departments gladly sell data on vehicle registrations. Public information, right? And revealing information. List makers and marketers know that ownership of a sports car means one thing in terms of lifestyle, ownership of a used Chevy something else. Names of station wagon owners are especially good—they're the heads of large families. Big consumers. Send 'em the catalog.

Increasingly, however, that's not why these lists are purchased. The Internal Revenue Service, in one recent test, bought a list of 2 million names for $50,000 from a firm which compiles information not only from motor vehicle bureaus but from other public files—swimming pool permits, property assessments, census tracts, that kind of thing. The IRS matched some apparently affluent Americans, as indicated by the data, against its own master list of persons who had paid taxes in previous years. Any name which hadn't shown up on a tax return was soon being placed on a stern word-processed letter asking for an explanation.

Law enforcement bodies also exchange crime records through the computerized network of the National Crime Information Center. What's wrong with that, if it helps identify criminals? Nothing, if you really mean criminals. Civil libertarians complain that the practice has already been extended to noncriminal information; for example, a file may contain the fact that someone once wrote a threatening letter to a public official. That wasn't nice, of course, but depending on how the person phrased it, it might not have been criminal either. Even so, authorities would want to keep an eye on the letter writer when a president comes to town, so they need that information. But that's not the point, rights watchers say. The point is that if information on people in crime files has gone this far, it's time to draw the line so it doesn't go further. The cop who picks you up for speeding and runs your ID through a terminal may tell you things about yourself that even you didn't know.

ARTIFICIAL INTELLIGENCE

The next great stage of information systems development, futurists agree, will involve extraordinary software that replicates human intelligence.

Possibly preceded by a warm-up phase called "artificial expertise"

(AE) or "expert systems," artificial intelligence may not so much liberate humans from the drudgery of thinking as it will liberate computers from the drudgery of behaving like computers. AI promises to endow computers with humanlike "understanding" and "thought processes." Human thinking could atrophy nonetheless, some fear.

Humans, for the first time, will be able to speak to computers in human languages. No more COBOL* routines such as "ON ENDFILE(EMPLOYEE_FILE)GOTOWRAP_UP. . . ." No more formal query language such as "Print 1984-AUG-ACT-SALES, 1984-AUG-EST-SALES. . . ." We'll use freeform English: "Compare the actual and estimated sales for August." The computer will understand.

AI as an idea has been around for thirty years, but as a new software generation it is just being put to work. AI systems play chess, analyze assay data to help prospectors find oil and minerals, and help diagnose infectious diseases.

At Stanford University's hospital in California, a program called ONCOSIN (so much for plain English) helps to prescribe treatments for cancer patients. Another called PUFF helps treat pulmonary diseases.

At the University of Texas in Austin, AI work directed by Dr. Jonathan Slocum of the Linguistics Research Center has yielded programs which translate German technical articles into English. The computer translations are often more accurate than those done by humans, a UT representative says. (However, the story is told of another effort to translate English to Russian. The computer was fed a line from Matthew: "The spirit is willing but the flesh is weak." In Russian the computer came back: "The vodka is strong but the meat is rotten.")

In the office, AI systems are beginning to advise managers and supervisors on how to handle difficult employees and business situations. Insurance companies are testing systems that help them configure policies. And like today's OA systems, AI programs pull up information from many available files, but with greater understanding of what the user wants. With a program called "Intellect," for example, an office manager might ask, "How much did we pay in telephone charges to New York last month?" Intellect would first want to ask, "New York City or New York State?" The query would be that "ordinary."

As currently promoted, AI systems *aid* and *advise*. They don't replace the knowledge worker. They supplement decision making.

---

*COBOL (Common Business-Oriented Language), one of the earliest programming languages and now offered in several versions, remains in widespread use.

They augment expertise. Yet futurists worry that later AI systems may totally and "efficiently" decide important matters unaided. They would be well programmed, of course, but they would not be overseen by any human (read "expensive") intellect, until perhaps too late.

The problem again is not that the systems would "reason" incorrectly but that they would act on wrong information. Systems automatically approving or rejecting people for insurance coverage might analyze the information they receive against company criteria exactly as they were programmed to do. But they could fail to perceive some outlandish inconsistencies in items of information which a human would readily question.

Based on garbage in, computer decisions could conceivably lead to wrongful credit denials, wrong prescriptions of medicine, and in the extreme nightmare, where AI systems would monitor entire factories, further deadly Bhopals. In early science fiction, you could always pull the plug on computers run amok. Dave Bowman did that to HAL in the movie *2001: A Space Odyssey*. But if an increasingly technological society became so dependent on "thinking machines" for running its basic systems that humans themselves lost these skills, pulling the plug would be unthinkable. It would throw society back to human decision processes for which expertise no longer existed.

A major problem with artificial expertise even now is finding enough expertise to program. Masters of various fields could well become tomorrow's stars if their career-long knowledge can be captured on program disks. The legal skills of a Melvin Belli, the economic smarts of a Milton Friedman, the management acumen of a Lee Iacocca, even the trade secrets of your local auto mechanic are wellsprings of knowledge that AI (or AE) seeks to tap.

While many attributes of AI, like natural-language retrieval, are demonstrable presently, many OA watchers believe widespread commercialization of AI applications is still five to ten years away.

INFORMATION OVERKILL

A concern as big as safety or privacy in the Information Age may be one so subtle—unless we recognize it—as to render many businesses counterproductive. We could find ourselves struggling against rising tides of information, more than enough to drown us, when at times all we require are a few drops of data to speed a particular task.

"We will have made the cutting and pasting together of all ideas into new formats easy beyond belief and we will have opened the libraries of the world to infinite replications," John Diebold declares. "It is not too soon to start rethinking what to do with it all. How will we be able to sort out the useful from the gibberish?"[10]

Why should a manager be given a 4-inch-thick report, asks writer J. E. Champion in *Impact: Office Automation,*[11] when all he or she needs is a half-page of totals? Every company tries to use information to gain a competitive edge by making managers more productive, Champion notes, but the companies that obtain the greatest advantage are those making sure the information is easy to obtain and to understand. Overabundance renders information exhaustively counterproductive, the very opposite of what OA seeks to accomplish.

Yet few pay heed to this issue. In the councils of information processing, all minds—the industry's, the media's, the user community's—focus on *processing* and only rarely on the stuff being processed, *information.*

According to a Lehman Brothers Kuhn Loeb study, American business cranks out 600 million pages of computer printout, 235 million photocopies, and 76 million letters per day. And of course such a vast body of work must be well managed and well processed; this is OA's first premise.

The issue is:

That information on this scale can't be controlled by better processing and automation alone. It must also be controlled through better evaluation of its worth *as* information—to the organization and to each individual who receives it.

Judged this way, much information might never need processing at all, or at any rate it might not need such widespread distribution.

Yet who is to judge the intrinsic value of information? Who in the organization shall decide which information is right for this person or that person to have and which isn't worth keeping at all. I do not refer here to private or confidential information which properly should go only to those authorized to see it. I refer to all the open and available information which flies so freely about; much of it we don't need, some small amounts of it we need badly, and great amounts of it simply arrive in bulk.

It is auspicious that a few OA professionals are beginning to tackle the issue. One, Hank Koehn, former director of the Futures Research Division at Security Pacific Bank, Los Angeles, says the challenge lies in finding new ways to "filter, analyze, and organize" the information surfeit. How? Koehn speaks of teams of "information gatekeepers" within organizations and a future industry of "knowledge brokers" offering help from outside.

INFORMATION GATEKEEPERS

The job of any gatekeeper, of course, is to let some traffic pass while preventing the rest from getting through. Applied to information, gatekeeping is an editing job. I find that as an editor, I've been a gatekeeper all my working life. So is anyone who produces informational goods as a business. Publishers, broadcasters, the media gatekeep all the time. They have to. They'd be out of business if they tried to disseminate all the information they could disseminate. And if they did, their audiences wouldn't have time to digest it.

Media producers try hard to understand their audiences' information interests, and they try even harder to present that information interestingly. In doing this, they hold back perfectly valid information which may be of use to some other audience but which holds little value for *their* audience. Moreover, they rearrange what they do disseminate so that it comes across clearly and fast.

This highly journalistic, highly judgmental process may be close to what organizations will have to adopt as OA presses upon them the need for more internal gatekeeping. The parallels between journalism as practiced for the public media and as its principles might apply privately suggest several things:

- An excellent source of corporate gatekeepers might be found within the field of journalism itself, perhaps among ex-editors (no calls, please), perhaps among journalism school graduates who can't, or elect not to, find jobs with the public media.
- Knowledge, it's true, is power, and since gatekeepers control knowledge, or at least information, they would hold power. This sounds more sinister than actual practice will likely show it to be. The basic motivator in journalism, after all, is to share information, not to hold it back. In professional hands, the power to withhold is wielded mainly against the irrelevant, the redundant, and the useless, and it's wielded so that information worth knowing gets through directly. Moreover, editing judgments don't take place in a vacuum. They're made under management guidelines, and any gatekeeper who ignores them will soon be out of a job.
- It could be argued that once information is stored electronically, it doesn't matter how large a database is; each user can call up what he or she wants. Perhaps, but without built-in profiles of user interest, and without later judgments by someone who decides how new information matches up with the profiles, we're back to the old user problem of winnowing through bushels of chaff to obtain a few grains of knowledge. And what about the indiscriminate communication of

chaff from voicemail and electronic mail junkies—the habitual sending of unneeded messages to scores of disinterested co-workers?

- Finally, corporate gatekeeping needs greater definition. It may yet call for the skills not only of an editor, but also abstractor, librarian, and cop. A curious mixture; but so is office automation, and yet, for the most part, it works.

AGAIN THE REVOLUTION

Most of Chapter 10—indeed much of this book—has been about information. As was said at the very beginning, big changes are taking place in offices and the cause is not just new technology. The changes involve recognition that offices are information centers—a profound discovery—and that technology can effectively help manage the use and movement of this increasingly valuable asset. OA will change the ways we work and the places in which we work, as other revolutions in information use, helped by technology much like OA's, will change our homes and our world.

If we manage these experiences well and hold human values foremost, we may yet advance globally to levels of greater, higher knowledge. And ultimately perhaps to wisdom.

Afterword

This book raised many questions, and that was its purpose. Many fears, many doubts, many claims surround office automation—some real, some exaggerated, some false. If this book helps OA planners and users to define their problems and to better understand the issues they are likely to face in their work and in their workplaces, if it enables them to trade off options more knowingly, and if it helps them to implement OA successfully, it will have done its job.

Answers? Of these we've had no lack from the many stalwart citizens of the OA world quoted throughout the work. But the final *right* answers for any OA issue must come from within the organization and the office to which the answers apply.

Only that assembly of specialists and generalists (MIS managers, administrative managers, personnel executives, financial executives, users, and others) who together understand the organizational terrain, the departmental customs, the problems, the opportunities, and the relationships among them—only they can properly answer for *themselves* the kinds of questions this book has posed.

I presume you're part of that assembly. Good luck.

References

CHAPTER 1

1. "The Office Automation Challenge: American Business Responds," survey by the Omni Group Ltd., New York, 1984.
2. The Diebold Group, New York: news release, June 1983.
3. The newsletter: *Word Processing Report,* retitled *Information & Word Processing Report* in 1981, retitled *Office Automation Report* in 1985, published twice monthly by Geyer-McAllister, New York. The association: International Word Processing Association (IWP), (no "A" is used in the acronym), renamed International Information/Word Processing Association in 1981, renamed Association of Information Systems Professionals in 1983; headquarters in Willow Grove, Pa. The magazine: *Word Processing World,* renamed *Word Processing Systems* in 1979, renamed *Word Processing & Information Systems* in 1981, combined with *Administrative Management* magazine in 1983 to form *Office Administration and Automation,* published monthly by Geyer-McAllister, and, since 1985, by Dalton Communications, Inc., New York, again as *Administrative Management*! Change is the OA constant.
4. *Word Processing World* market study, 1976, prepared for internal use; copy in the author's possession. The installed-base figure included models of the then-new electronic typewriter, a machine less powerful than a fully endowed text editor but with certain laborsaving, WP-like features not

found on the standard electric typewriter; hence the term "automatic typing device." Since more of the machines—text editors as well as electronic typewriters—were being used outside WP centers than within them, the presumption is that these machines were operating as single-station units used mostly for repetitive document production. This is a clue that by the mid-1970s the WP center was giving way to other systems arrangements. That this was indeed happening has since been documented; see "The Big Change in WP User Sites," *Office Administration and Automation,* August 1983, p. 24.

5. Representative studies of the WP industry and its growth include those of the Word Processing Institute, New York, cited in *Word Processing and the American Office* newsletter, Jan. 1, 1975, OMS Corp., New York; "Future Strategies in Word Processing," a paper presented May 9, 1979, by LeEllen Spelman, Martin Simpson Research Associates, New York; and in numerous reports issued by Datapro Research Corp., Delran, N.J.; Dataquest Inc., San Jose, Ca.; and the Diebold Group, New York.
6. "Computer Shock Hits the Office," Aug. 8, 1983, p. 46, and "Personal Computers: And the Winner Is IBM," Oct. 3, 1983, p. 76, both in *Business Week.*
7. "Surviving the Surfeit of Software," *Office Administration and Automation,* September 1983.
8. Herman, John: "What Every Executive Should Know about Office Automation," *Modern Business Reports,* 1984.
9. "Office Work," manuscript by Dr. Raymond R. Panko, College of Business Administration, University of Hawaii at Manoa. See also reference 7, Chapter 2.
10. "Forward, March!", *Computer Decisions,* Hayden, Hasbrouck Heights, N.J., June 15, 1984, p. 10.

CHAPTER 2

1. *Business Week,* Aug. 8, 1983, p. 49.
2. "Battle of the LANs," *Office Administration and Automation,* March 1984, p. 26.
3. "Getting a Line on Communications," *Words,* Association of Information Systems Professionals, Willow Grove, Pa. June-July 1982.
4. "The Gold Mine in Satellite Services," *Business Week,* April 6, 1981, p. 89.
5. This litany of office data can be found in many of the special sections or "advertorial supplements" (paid advertisements made to look like regular articles) on OA in magazines like *Fortune, Time,* and *Business Week* throughout the late 1970s and the 1980s. Typical was "Information Processing and the Office of Tomorrow," prepared for advertisers by International Data Corp., Waltham, Mass., which appeared in *Fortune* in October 1977. A 64-page consulting-firm brochure incorporating similar data is

"The Emerging Real World of Office Automation," undated, Arthur D. Little, Inc., Cambridge, Mass.

6. "Those Famed Productivity Figures May Not Be Too Productive," *Administrative Management,* October 1980, p. 23.
7. Submitted to *Office Technology and People,* Elsevier Scientific Publishing Co., Amsterdam.
8. "Occupational Projections and Training Data, 1980 Edition," Bureau of Labor Statistics, U.S. Department of Labor Bulletin 2052, September 1980.
9. "Saving Druggists in a Paper Storm," *Business Week,* June 2, 1980, cited by Raymond Panko in "Office Work."
10. Panko, op. cit.
11. Panko, Raymond R., and Ralph A. Sprague: "Toward a Framework for Office Support," *Proceedings of the ACM-SIGOA Conference on Office Automation,* Philadelphia, 1982.
12. Sprague, Ralph A.: "A Framework for the Development of Decision Support Systems," *Management Information Systems Quarterly,* December 1980; cited in "Office Work."
13. John Connell, address to the Office Automation Conference, Los Angeles, 1984.
14. Panko, "Office Work," *see* footnote 9, Chapter 1.
15. "Office Today," *The New York Times,* Oct. 2, 1983.
16. Quoted in Kleinschrod, Walter A.: *Management's Guide to Word Processing*, 1981, the Dartnell Corp., Chicago.
17. Holmes, William: "We Saved 191 Hours and $2489.28," *Word Processing & Information Systems,* April 1982, p. 12.
18. " 'Automation' Thirty Years Later—A Conversation with John Diebold," *Office Administration and Automation,* October 1982, p. 24. Diebold's *Automation* was republished without change by American Management Associations, New York, in 1982.

CHAPTER 3

1. Kleinschrod, Walter A.: *Office Automation Strategies: The Planing Process,* Part IV of the Olsten Monograph Series, "Managing the Office: 1990 and Beyond," Administrative Management Society Foundation, Willow Grove, Pa., 1985.
2. Orton, Karen: "Strategies Exhibited for Office Automation," *Office Automation Update,* TRI Newsletter Associates Ltd., Boca Raton, Fla., July 1983.
3. Ibid.
4. Ibid.
5. Quoted in Alter, Stewart: "One Step at a Time," *Computer Decisions,* June 15, 1984, p. 14.

6. Ibid.
7. " 'Here's Our Game Plan'—Position Statements of the OA Majors," *Office Administration and Automation,* July 1983, p. 24.
8. Alter, op. cit.
9. Martin, Alexia: "Commit or Hold Off? The Short- vs. Long-Term Tug of War," *Administrative Management,* September 1982, p. 24.
10. The quotations of Connell, Purchase, and Oyer originally appeared in Trembly, Ara C.: "The Successful Implementer's Many Sides," *Computer Decisions,* June 15, 1984, p. 38; used with permission.
11. A comprehensive listing of user organizations can be found in "A Manager's Guide to OA User Groups," *Office Administration and Automation,* March 1984. A listing also appears in the magazine's Reference Guide section, December 1984.

CHAPTER 4

1. *Information Industry Insights,* Issue 6, Booz, Allen & Hamilton, Inc., New York.
2. "Taking the Anxiety out of Office Automation," *Business Week,* Sept. 19, 1983, p. 96D.
3. *CP/M Operating System Manual,* 1982, Digital Research, Pacific Grove, Calif.
4. Craig Brod's article "How to Deal with 'Technostress' " (*Office Administration and Automation,* August 1984, p. 28) adapts ideas from his book *Technostress: The Human Cost of the Computer Revolution,* Addison-Wesley, Reading, Mass., 1984. The stress-reducing steps quoted here appeared in the *OAA* article.
5. This segment on OA's impact on the physical office is adapted from "Coping with Computers in the Open-Plan," *Office Administration and Automation,* September 1984.
6. "Design Issues for Office Automation Systems," report by the Diebold Group, Inc., New York, May 1983. While the report was confidential to Diebold clients, a copy was obtained by the author.
7. "Buying a Micro: What the Salesman Hasn't Told You," *Office Administration and Automation,* April 1984, p. 24.

CHAPTER 5

1. Extrapolated from matrix, "A Systematic Look at Office Information Structure," *Modern Office Procedures,* copyright Penton/IPC, Cleveland, June 1980, p. 48.

2. Sofsearch International: press releases, Sept. 14 and Nov. 10, 1983.
3. "Buzzword Basics," *Sales Strategies Newsletter,* the Sierra Group, Tempe, Ariz., August-September 1983.
4. Ibid.
5. Bryant, Susan Foster: "Micro-to-Mainframe Links," *Computer Decisions,* July 1984.
6. "LAN Choice Baffling Users, Impoverishing Semiconductor Makers," press release, International Resource Development Inc., Norwalk, Conn., Feb. 13, 1984.
7. "Report Finds SNA Alive and Well," press release, The Yankee Group, Cambridge, Mass., Feb. 19, 1981.
8. "Battle of the LANs," *Office Administration and Automation,* March 1984, p. 28.
9. Ibid., p. 30.
10. Ibid., p. 92.
11. Blackmarr, Brian R.: "Networking: Surveying the Lay of the LAN," *Modern Office Technology,* copyright Penton/IPC, July 1984, p. 65.

CHAPTER 6

1. Report of the Commission on the Postal Service to the President and Congress, Apr. 18, 1977.
2. "PABX Integration: Key to Success in Voice Mail System Sales," press release, Venture Development Corp., Jan. 18, 1984.
3. Wexler, Philip: "Fax & Figures," *Modern Office Technology,* copyright Penton/IPC, Cleveland, July 1984, p. 14.
4. Panko, Raymond R.: "Electronic Mail: The Alternatives," *Office Administration and Automation,* June 1984, p. 37.
5. Panko, "Options in Electronic Mail," *Office Administration and Automation,* November 1983, p. 50.
6. Ibid.
7. Editorial, *Administrative Management,* October 1976, p. 21.

CHAPTER 7

1. " 'Automation May Increase Discrimination,' An Interview With Karen Nussbaum," *Office Administration and Automation,* April 1983, p. 32.
2. "OAA's 1984 Salary Survey: To Earn More, Specialize," *Office Administration and Automation,* August 1984.

3. *Business Week,* Dec. 3, 1984, p. 38.
4. Bureau of Law & Business Inc., P.O. Box 1274, 177 Greenwich Ave., Stamford, Conn. 06904.
5. "Presser: Staunch Reagan Supporter," *Industry Week,* copyright Penton/IPC, Cleveland, July 11, 1983, p. 37.
6. See "Meet the Teamsters' New 'Miss Dynamite,' " *Business Week,* October 3, 1983, p. 107.
7. Quoted in "How Administrators View the 'Work-at-Home' Trend," by William M. Cowan, *Office Administration and Automation,* November 1983, p. 30.
8. Redmond, David: "Guest Opinion," *Office Administration and Automation,* June 1984, p. 108.
9. Stanley, Amy Dru: "High-Tech Will Hurt Women," *The New York Times,* Sept. 19, 1983.
10. Ibid.
11. Patricia Lee, "Job Sharing—A Concept Whose Time Has Come," *Office Administration and Automation,* April 1984, p. 29.
12. Sandburg, Dorothy: "Beware of Specialized Training," *Office Administration and Automation,* May 1983, p. 87. See also "How Instructors Can Alleviate Stress," Dr. Margaret Bahniuk, same issue, p. 89.
13. Davenport, Jacqueline: "Whatever Happened to QWL?" *Office Administration and Automation,* May 1983, p. 28.
14. Ibid., p. 28.
15. Ibid., p. 28.
16. Keown, Don G.: "Personnel Trends in the '80s," *Office Administration and Automation,* December 1984, p. 26.

CHAPTER 8

1. "Trial and Error by Intruders Led to Entry into Computers," *The New York Times,* Aug. 23, 1983.
2. *Computer Security,* Computer Security Institute, Northborough, Mass., September-October 1983.
3. "Hackers Holding More of the Keys," *Newsday,* Long Island, N.Y., Apr. 23, 1984, p. 4.
4. *Computer Security,* op. cit.
5. "Computer Security Is Breached at Nation's Top Credit Bureau," *Newsday,* June 20, 1984, p. 3.
6. Ognibene, Peter J., "Secret Ciphers Solved," *Omni,* November 1984, p. 38.
7. Ibid.

8. Menkus, Belden: "Toward a More Secure Office Building," *Office Administration and Automation,* September 1983, p. 33.
9. "A Manager's Guide to 'Tempest' Security," *Administrative Management,* March 1982, p. 36.
10. Ibid.

CHAPTER 9

1. "The Coming Transformation in Management Use of Information Technology," news release including text of briefing by Joseph Ferreira, the Diebold Group Inc., New York, Oct. 6, 1983.
2. "OA Issues: The Gurus Debate," *Office Administration and Automation,* December 1983, p. 24.
3. Connell, John: interview with the author, October 1984.
4. Cowan, William R.: "The 'I Center'—An Office Resource Comes of Age," *Office Administration and Automation,* February 1984, p. 30.
5. Ibid.
6. "Surviving the Paper Tide," brochure, Xerox Corp., Rochester, N.Y., undated.
7. *Office Administration and Automation,* December 1983, op. cit. (slightly adapted).

CHAPTER 10

1. *The United States Government Manual 1982/83,* Office of the Federal Registrar, National Archives and Records Service, Washington, D.C.
2. Lenk, Klaus: "Is Information Technology Neutral?", *Information Resource Management,* published under Ericsson Information Systems sponsorship, London, 1983.
3. Malik, Rex: "Computers in the Home," *Information Resource Management,* London.
4. "Online Database Industry Revenues to Hit $10 Billion Level by 1994," press release, International Resource Development Inc., Norwalk, Conn., Feb. 8, 1984.
5. Keynote address, IBM Media Industry Conference, Hilton Head, S.C., Feb. 13, 1980.
6. Servan-Schreiber, Jean-Jacques: *The World Challenge,* Simon & Schuster, New York, 1981.
7. *The New York Times,* Dec. 16, 1984, p. 18.

8. Jacobson, Aileen: "Watching the Workplace," *Newsday,* July 24, 1984, p. II/3.
9. Ibid., p. II/6.
10. "Information Processing: The Fourth Decade," remarks by John Diebold on the thirtieth anniversary of the Diebold Group, Inc., Sept. 11, 1984.
11. Champion, J. E.: *Impact: Office Automation,* Administrative Management Society, Willow Grove, Penn., August 1983.

Index

ABOUT THE AUTHOR

Walter A. Kleinschrod, former editor of *Office Administration and Automation* magazine, is recognized as the first journalist to alert the business community to the far-ranging possibilities of word processing—the base upon which many advanced information systems are built. Kleinschrod has written hundreds of articles and editorials on office automation, and has received several Industrial Marketing and American Business Press awards for outstanding journalism.